Discover Maine

Welcome to the AMC

Welcome to the Appalachian Mountain Club! Founded in 1876, we are America's oldest conservation and recreation organization. We promote the protection, enjoyment, and wise use of the mountains, rivers, and trails of the Appalachian region. The AMC has twelve chapters from Maine to Washington, D.C., comprised of tens of thousands of outdoor enthusiasts like you.

By purchasing this book you have contributed to our efforts to protect the Appalachian region. Proceeds from the sales of AMC Books and Maps support our regional land conservation efforts; trail-building and maintenance; air- and water-quality research; search and rescue; and environmental education programs for school-age children, at-risk youth, and outdoor enthusiasts.

The AMC encourages everyone to enjoy and appreciate the natural world because we believe that successful conservation depends on such experiences. So join us in the outdoors! We offer hiking, paddling, biking, skiing, and mountaineering activities throughout the Appalachian region for outdoor adventurers of every age and ability. Our lodging destinations, such as our state-of-the-art Highland Center, are Model Environmental Education Facilities, demonstrating our stewardship ethic and providing a place for you to relax off-trail and learn more about local ecosystems and habitats, regional environmental issues, and mountain history and culture.

For more information about AMC membership, destinations, and conservation and education programs, turn to the back of this book or visit the AMC website at www.outdoors.org.

Discover Maine

AMC's Outdoor Traveler's Guide to the Pine Tree State

TY WIVELL

Appalachian Mountain Club Books
Boston, Massachusetts

Cover Design: Terry Rohrbach, Base Art Co., www.baseartco.com
Book Design: Eric Edstam
Cartography: Ken Dumas
Cover Photographs: © Ty Wivell; except Hikers on White Cap Mountain, © Jerry and
Marcy Monkman
All interior photographs by the author unless otherwise noted.

Published by the Appalachian Mountain Club. Distributed by the Globe Pequot Press,
Inc., Guilford, CT.

Library of Congress Cataloging-in-Publication Data

Wivell, Ty.
    Discover Maine : AMC outdoor traveler's guide to the Pine Tree
State, hiking, paddling, biking, and more! / Ty Wivell.—1st ed.
        p. cm.
    Includes bibliographical references and index.
    ISBN-13: 978-1-929173-70-9 (alk. paper)
1. Outdoor recreation—Maine—Guidebooks. 2. Maine—Guidebooks. I. Appalachian
Mountain Club. II. Title.

GV191.42.M2W58 2006
917.41'0444—dc22

                                                                    2005035020

The paper used in this publication meets the minimum requirements of the American
National Standard for Information Sciences—Permanence of Paper for Printed Library
Materials, ANSI Z39.48–1984.∞

**Due to changes in conditions, use of the information
in this book is at the sole risk of the user.**

 Printed on recycled paper (30% post-consumer content and FSC-certified)
using soy-content inks. Printed in the United States of America.

10 9 8 7 6 5 4 3 2 1   06 07 08 09 10

Acknowledgments

DISCOVERING MAINE would have been an impossible journey without the boundless generosity of friends, family, and colleagues who supported my efforts, endured my absences, and shared the trail along the way. I owe a very special thanks to Jerry and Marcy Monkman, whose friendship and example have always been a source of inspiration. Thank you to Beth Krusi, former editor at AMC Books, who supported me at the outset, and to the AMC's Sarah Jane Shangraw, Belinda Thresher, and Eric Edstam for their infinite patience and generous contributions. I am so grateful to my colleagues at Stoner-Andrews—Rick Stoner, Scott Andrews, Scott Byrne, and Scott Finlayson—who have always encouraged and supported my outside interests (a special thanks to 'Fin,' whose love for Maine was both helpful and inspiring); thanks to Tracy Byrnes for her companionship and sense of adventure; thank you to Willem Verweij for his positive attitude in the face of calamity; my heartfelt thanks to Sue Cooley for always believing in me; my warmest regards to Parker Schuerman for his thoughtful friendship and reverence for the natural world; and my deepest gratitude to Andrea Rutherford, who shared some of the joy, and much of the burden, of this project with grace and love.

I would also like to thank the many individuals and organizations who showed me the way with charity and enthusiasm, and who are steadfastly devoted to Maine's lasting preservation, including the Maine Chapter of the AMC, the Maine Outdoor Adventure Club, the Southern Maine Sea Kayaking Network, the Maine Audubon Society, the Maine Chapter of the Nature Conservancy, MATC "Ridgerunner" Jeff Goldknopf, Bob LeRoy at the AMC's Little Lyford Ponds Camp, Heather Haskell at Baxter State Park, Kate Taylor at the New Hampshire Loon Preservation Committee, Drew Wyman at the Maine Island Trail Association, Jennifer Lamphere at the Northern Forest Canoe Trail, Inc., and Nan Cumming at Portland Trails.

Above all, I would like to thank my family for always being there with unconditional love and support.

Locator Map

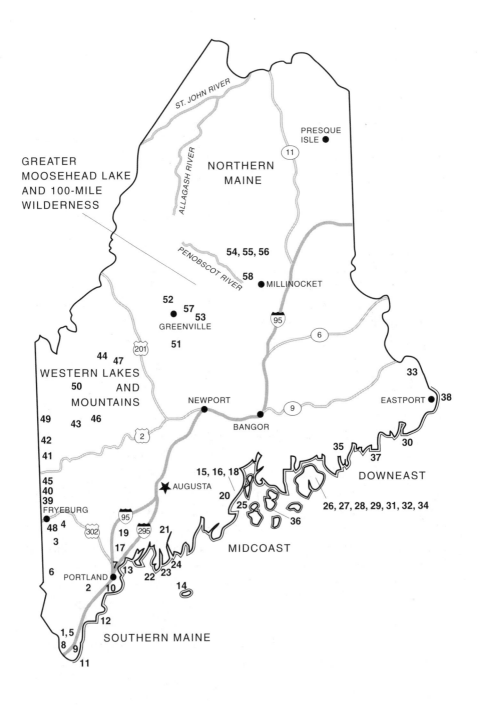

ST. JOHN RIVER

ALLAGASH RIVER

PRESQUE
ISLE ●

11

NORTHERN
MAINE

GREATER
MOOSEHEAD LAKE
AND 100-MILE
WILDERNESS

PENOBSCOT RIVER

54, 55, 56

58 ● MILLINOCKET

95

52
57
53 ● GREENVILLE
51

6

201

44 47

WESTERN LAKES
50   AND
MOUNTAINS

33

NEWPORT
●

EASTPORT ● 38

49

43 46

9

● BANGOR

30

2

35
37

15, 16, 18

45
40
39
FRYEBURG ●

★ AUGUSTA

DOWNEAST

41

42

20

25
36

26, 27, 28, 29, 31, 32, 34

48 4

3

19

95

21
295

302

17

7
13
6

2
PORTLAND ●

22 23

24

MIDCOAST

10

14

12

1, 5
8   9

11

SOUTHERN MAINE

Contents

Preface

ONE OF MY FIRST EXCURSIONS TO MAINE was a spirited but inept exploration of beautiful Cobscook Bay. At the time, my passion for adventure was decidedly outflanked by my limited outdoors skills, and Cobscook's "boiling" tides nearly swallowed my canoe. Though most of the memories of that trip have faded, I have never forgotten my narrow escape from the bay's insistent grip, or my new found appreciation of nature's indifference toward my aspirations for discovery.

Since then, I have discovered a good deal more of Maine, from wild descents of its magnificent rivers, to a winter traverse of Katahdin's Knife Edge. From Kittery to Caribou, I've explored the state's peaceful ponds, rugged peaks, and elaborate shoreline, and considerably improved my skills along the way. But, these many years later, I am still humbled by its wildness and grandeur.

With the same humility, I have ceded any hope of capturing all of Maine within the pages of this book. It is much too big to fit between the covers and, anyway, how does one begin to describe an encounter with a bull moose on a remote stretch of river, or the haunting wail of a loon under a star filled sky? Instead, I have sought to point to destinations where such experiences might be had, where the essence of Maine might be found.

No doubt, some will say I have left out important locations and, of course, they will be right. Perhaps, the best places in Maine, or anywhere else for that matter, are those less known, or as yet undiscovered. But hiking, biking, and paddling are merely the means to cultivating an intimate relationship with wild places, whether they're found in the heart of the 100-Mile Wilderness, or within a postage stamp-sized preserve in the midst of Portland.

In the end, I hope the trips described in this book will simply lead you to your own discoveries of Maine and foster an appreciation of its beautiful and boundless landscapes along the way. Happy travels!

How to Use This Book

THE TRIPS DESCRIBED IN THIS BOOK have been divided into regions similar to those delineated by the state of Maine (i.e. Southern, Midcoast, Western Lakes and Mountains, etc.). Each region is prefaced with an overview of the area as well as featured trips. Within each region, trips are divided into hiking, biking, and paddling, respectively. The **At-a-Glance Trip Planner** immediately following this section provides an overview of all 58 trips including location, trip distance and time, difficulty rating, and special features (i.e. opportunities to view wildlife, scenic vistas, options for camping, etc.).

Each trip begins with a **Difficulty** rating (easy, moderate, difficult) defined by distance, terrain, and/or exposure to the elements. The trip's **Distance** is also provided, and though accurate, is subject to variations of terrain, overall elevation gain, exposure, etc. The **Estimated Time** is given to help you plan your trip, and assumes the traveler is hiking, biking, or paddling at an average pace. Estimated times also take into account time to enjoy a rest stop at a scenic vista, a lunch break, etc. Both the difficulty ratings and estimated times are a general approximation, and intended as a useful guide, but may vary according to an individual's experience.

Location and map information, including USGS topographic maps and a page reference to DeLorme's *Maine Atlas and Gazetteer*, are provided for each trip to supplement the AMC map drawn for the specific trip route. Users are *strongly* advised to carry the appropriate maps and a compass, and/or a handheld GPS unit when undertaking any outdoor adventure.

Directions are provided with consideration given to major thorough-fares (I-95, US 1, etc.) or the closest city, town, or village. In some in-stances, I have included former exit numbers on the Maine Turnpike, because they have recently been changed to reflect miles, and may not correspond with older maps.

Trail Notes are often included to draw attention to particular features that travelers should be aware of before undertaking a particular trip. The notes are provided to help you prepare for the trip, and may include simple information such as map and kiosk locations, important details regarding tide dependency, river crossings, etc., or a strong *caution* re-garding a trip's difficulty, or potential hazards.

Trip Descriptions have been designed to include a brief overview of the trip's overall features and highlights, followed by a straightforward account of the trip itself (i.e. "at 1.2 miles, turn left and follow the trail through a grove of hardwoods . . ."). This has been done so that users can quickly key in on specific details about a given trip without having to fumble unnecessarily through interesting though less-relevant informa-tion regarding wildlife, natural, or cultural history, etc.

A **Nature and History Notes** section often follows the trip description to discuss interesting facts and features of a trip and the surrounding area. This may include information regarding wildlife in the region, cultural, historical, or geological information, as well as interesting anecdotes.

Other Options may also be included, and are provided to outline alternative routes including shorter trips, extended loops, less difficult ascents/descents, etc. This section may also feature other nearby activities and/or attractive destinations you may want to visit while in the area.

The **More Information** section is usually included to provide you with additional resources regarding that destination or the surround-ing region as well as phone numbers and websites to order maps, make reservations, obtain a fire permit, or contact an appropriate organiza-tion, department, bureau, park authority, etc. for additional details and pertinent information.

At-A-Glance Trip Planner

Sport	#	Trip	Page	Location	Difficulty	Distance	Est. Time	Fee
		SOUTHERN REGION						
🥾	1	Mount Agamenticus	4	York	Easy	1.5-mi loop	1 hr	
🥾	2	Saco Heath Preserve	7	Saco	Easy	2.0 mi round-trip	1.5 hrs	
🥾	3	Burnt Meadow Mountain	12	Brownfield	Moderate	2.4 mi round-trip	2.5–3 hrs	
🥾	4	Pleasant Mountain	15	Denmark/ Bridgton	Moderate	3.6 mi round-trip	3 hrs	
🚲	5	Mount Agamenticus	18	York	Moderate to difficult	3.5-mi loop	2 hrs	
🚲	6	Back Country Excursions— Parsonsfield	22	Parsonsfield	Easy to moderate	7.0-mi loop	2 hrs	●
🚲	7	Portland Trails —Presumpscot River Preserve	25	Portland	Easy to moderate	5.0 mi round-trip	2 hrs	
🛶	8	Salmon Falls River	29	South Berwick	Easy	6.0 mi round-trip	2–3 hrs	
🛶	9	York River	32	York	Easy to moderate	8.0–9.0 mi round-trip	3–4 hrs	

Good for Kids	Scenic Vista	Water-fall	Wildlife Likely	Remote or Less Traveled	Do it in a day from Portland	Camping	Trip Highlights
•	•				•		A pleasant hike through a diverse coastal forest to superb views from the mountain's summit
•			•		•		A leisurely walk through a beautiful and unique peatland environment
•	•				•		An enjoyable hike and scramble to an open summit with panoramic views
•	•				•		An outstanding ridge hike with excellent views to the southern Lakes Region and beyond
	•		•		•		A challenging ride at Southern Maine's most popular mountain biking destination
•				•	•	•	An outstanding beginner/intermediate ride on terrain dedicated to mountain biking
		•			•		A fun, challenging ride along the beautiful Presumpscot River
•		•	•		•		A quiet countryside paddle with excursions to an historic mansion and a beautiful state park
					•		An inland paddle on a picturesque river steeped in New England history

Sport	#	Trip	Page	Location	Difficulty	Distance	Est. Time	Fee
	10	Scarborough Marsh	38	Scarborough	Easy	3.0–4.0 mi round-trip	2 hrs	
	11	Gerrish and Cutts Islands	41	Kittery	Moderate	8.5-mi loop	3 hrs	
	12	Cape Porpoise Archipelago	44	Kennebunkport /Cape Porpoise	Moderate	10.0 mi round-trip	4–5 hrs	
	13	Portland Harbor/Casco Bay	48	Portland	Easy	2.5 mi round-trip	2–3 hrs	●
MIDCOAST								
	14	Monhegan Island	54	Monhegan	Easy to moderate	3.0-mi loop	2–3 hrs	
	15	Maiden Cliff Loop	57	Camden	Moderate	2.0-mi loop	2 hrs	
	16	Bald Rock Mountain	61	Camden	Easy to moderate	3.6 mi round-trip	3 hrs	
	17	Bradbury Mountain State Park	65	Pownal	Easy to difficult	6.5-mi loop	2–3 hrs	
	18	Camden Hills State Park	68	Camden/ Lincolnville	Moderate to difficult	10.5 mi round-trip	3 hrs	●
	19	Runaround Pond	71	Durham	Easy	4.0–7.0 mi round-trip	3–4 hrs	
	20	Megunticook Lake/Fernald's Neck Preserve	74	Camden	Easy	3.0–7.0 mi round-trip	3–4 hrs	
	21	Merrymeeting Bay/Swan Island	77	Richmond	Easy to moderate	4.0 mi round-trip or 10.0-mi loop	3–5 hrs	

Good for Kids	Scenic Vista	Water-fall	Wildlife Likely	Remote or Less Traveled	Do it in a day from Portland	Camping	Trip Highlights
•			•		•		A meandering paddle through Maine's largest salt marsh
			•		•		A spectacular introduction to kayaking the Maine coast
			•	•		•	An exceptional coastal paddle and island tour
	•						An enjoyable introduction to the multitude of paddling opportunities in Casco Bay
•	•		•	•			From enchanted forests to rugged sea cliffs, spectacular hiking on one of Maine's most beautiful islands
•	•				•	•	Magnificent views from a stunning precipice above Megunticook Lake
•	•				•	•	An excellent summit hike to open ledges with magnificent views overlooking Penobscot Bay
	•				•	•	Fun, challenging riding, minutes from downtown Freeport, with excellent trails and beautiful summit views
					•	•	A great ride through the heart of the park on a challenging multi-use trail
•			•		•		Quiet paddling on a beautiful, serpentine pond, teeming with wildlife, near Freeport
•			•		•	•	Picturesque paddling beneath the Camden Hills with a side trip to a beautiful nature preserve
•			•	•	•	•	Excellent paddling at the head of Merrymeeting Bay with an excursion to beautiful Swan Island

Good for Kids	Scenic Vista	Water-fall	Wildlife Likely	Remote or Less Traveled	Do it in a day from Portland	Camping	Trip Highlights
	•				•		A short paddle to a beautiful island and the former summer home of Arctic explorer, Admiral Robert Peary
•			•		•	•	Exploring the beautiful waterways around the AMC's Knubble Bay Camp
			•	•	•		Superb kayaking in an island-studded bay with a visit to an Audubon sanctuary
	•				•	•	Classic shoreline paddling between two of Maine's most picturesque harbors
•	•					•	A short but irresistible climb to the summits of Jordan Pond's distinctive mountains
	•					•	A challenging climb up iron rungs to spectacular views and a visit to a quiet and beautiful mountain pond
	•		•			•	A strenuous hike to two of Acadia's highest peaks, with long periods of hiking on open ledges with spectacular views
	•					•	A relatively long hike over open ledges to the summit of Mount Desert Island's highest mountain; there are great views during most of this hike
	•		•	•		•	A remote hike along a wild and windswept coastal headland, with spectacular seaward views from steep, jagged cliffs
•						•	A moderate ride next to the dramatic scenery of Jordan and Bubble ponds

Good for Kids	Scenic Vista	Water-fall	Wildlife Likely	Remote or Less Traveled	Do it in a day from Portland	Camping	Trip Highlights
	•	•				•	This ride has it all: three waterfalls, mountain and ocean views, and seven major bridge crossings
			•	•		•	An enjoyable ride through woods, meadows, wetlands, and streams in a wild and remote national wildlife refuge
•						•	A moderate paddle on a scenic lake with mountain views and wild shorelines
•	•		•	•		•	A pleasant paddle on a deep, clear-water pond with sandy beaches and access to panoramic views atop nearby peaks
			•			•	An island-to-island tour of Maine's premiere kayaking destination
			•	•			An enjoyable paddle along the rugged shoreline of Maine's southernmost landmass with an excursion to a spectacular Nature Conservancy Preserve
			•	•		•	An exceptional paddle through the "boiling tides" of one of the state's most remote, wild, and beautiful bays
•	•	•		•	•	•	A loop hike across Blueberry Mountain's impressive ledges with a side trip to a beautiful flume and pool
•	•				•	•	An enjoyable jaunt to an excellent perch with commanding views across the Wild River valley

Sport	#	Trip	Page	Location	Difficulty	Distance	Est. Time	Fee
👣	41	Table Rock	166	Grafton Notch State Park	Moderate to difficult	2.5-mi loop	1.5–2 hrs	
👣	42	Mahoosuc Notch	172	North Newry	Difficult	6.5 mi round-trip	5–6 hrs	
👣	43	Tumbledown Mountain Loop	175	Township 6/ Weld Region	Difficult	5.4-mi loop	4 hrs	
👣	44	Bigelow Preserve	179	East of Stratton	Difficult	12.0-mi loop	8 hrs	
🚲	45	Wild River Loop	183	Hastings— Evans Notch	Moderate to difficult	10.0 mi round-trip or loop	2–4 hrs	
🚲	46	Mount Blue State Park	186	Weld	Moderate to difficult	9.0-mi loop	3 hrs	
🚲	47	Carrabassett River Rail-Trail	189	Carrabassett	Easy to moderate	12.0 mi round-trip 19.0-mi loop	2–4 hrs	
🛶	48	Brownfield Bog	193	East Brownfield	Easy	Not Rated	2 hrs	
🛶	49	Umbagog Lake	196	Magalloway PLT (ME), Errol and Cambridge (NH)	Moderate	6.0–16.0 mi round-trip	5 hrs/ multi-day	
🛶	50	Kennebago River— Rangeley Lakes Region	202	Oquossoc	Easy	7.0 mi round-trip	3–4 hrs	

Good for Kids	Scenic Vista	Water-fall	Wildlife Likely	Remote or Less Traveled	Do it in a day from Portland	Camping	Trip Highlights
	•				•	•	A short but demanding hike to a wonderful granite-ledge overlook with terrific views of Grafton Notch
				•		•	A difficult, rewarding traverse of the "hardest mile on the Appalachian Trail"
	•				•	•	A thrilling ascent to one of Maine's prettiest mountain settings, with rugged cliffs, spectacular views, and a picturesque alpine tarn
	•		•			•	A fantastic ridge hike along the Appalachian Trail within one of Maine's most prominent and beautiful wilderness preserves
			•	•		•	Pick your pleasure on this scenic tour along the Wild River, with options for an easy out-and-back cruise, or an adventurous and challenging single-track ride
	•				•	•	Secluded riding on diverse multi-use trails within one of Maine's largest state parks
•	•	•		•		•	A beautiful ride along the Carrabassett River on an easygoing rail-trail, with an option for a longer backcountry excursion
•			•	•	•		A relaxing paddle on a beautiful, quiet bog within the Saco River watershed
•			•	•		•	Wonderful backcountry paddling on a magnificent lake set within a wild and scenic refuge
•			•				A quietwater paddle on a serpentine river in the heart of moose country

Sport	#	Trip	Page	Location	Difficulty	Distance	Est. Time	Fee
		GREATER MOOSEHEAD AND 100-MILE WILDERNESS (INCLUDING BAXTER STATE PARK)						
	51	Borestone Mountain Sanctuary	208	Eliottsville Plantation	Easy to moderate	4.0 mi round-trip	3 hrs	●
	52	Mount Kineo	212	Moosehead Lake near Rockwood	Moderate	4.0 mi round-trip	3 hrs	
	53	Gulf Hagas	219	Bowdoin College Grant East	Moderate to difficult	8.0-mi loop	6 hrs	●
	54	South Turner Mountain/ Sandy Stream Pond	224	Baxter State Park	Moderate	5.5 mi	4 hrs	●
	55	Katahdin— The Knife Edge Loop	230	Baxter State Park	Difficult	10.0-mi loop	10 hrs	●
	56	Baxter State Park Perimeter Road	236	Baxter State Park	Moderate to difficult	41.0 mi	Day- or multi- day trips	●
	57	Long Pond	240	Bowdoin College Grant —east of Greenville	Easy	varies due to route on lake	varies due to route on lake	●
	58	Debsconeag Lakes Wilderness	245	T2 R10 WELS/ northwest of Millinocket	Moderate	6.0–18.0 mi round- trip	5 hrs/ multi- day	

Good for Kids	Scenic Vista	Water-fall	Wildlife Likely	Remote or Less Traveled	Do it in a day from Portland	Camping	Trip Highlights
•	•		•	•			An enjoyable hike through old growth forest to an Audubon Nature Center followed by a steep scramble to an open summit with impressive views
•	•			•		•	A paddle and hiking adventure to a precipitous peninsula overlooking the state's largest lake
	•	•		•		•	An exceptional rim hike along Maine's "Grand Canyon" with side trips to its numerous waterfalls, cascades, chutes, and pools
•	•		•			•	A great introductory hike to Baxter State Park combined with a visit to a beautiful pond frequented by moose
	•					•	A demanding loop hike across Maine's most famous mountain, including a traverse of the renowned Knife Edge ridge
			•	•		•	Exploring the pristine wilderness of Maine's flagship state park on two wheels
•			•	•		•	The lake's east–west axis, islands, and narrow width provide not only wind protection but also a lengthy shoreline to explore
•			•	•		•	A paddle through a chain of lakes in a pristine wilderness watershed at the foot of Mount Katahdin

Introduction to Outdoor Adventures in Maine

BY FACTS AND NUMBERS ALONE, Maine is an interesting and impressive state. It is both the largest and northernmost state in New England, as well as the easternmost landmass in the contiguous United States. It encompasses over 35,000 square miles, more than all other New England states combined. Nearly 90% of the Pine Tree State is forested and, with the notable exception of the fertile fields sprawling across the Aroostook Plateau and the beautiful fields of low bush blueberries downeast, the remainder is largely covered in water. In fact, there are 6,000 lakes, ponds, rivers, and streams in Maine, including Moosehead Lake, the largest body of water within one state east of the Mississippi River.

As the crow flies, Maine's spectacular coast is less than 200 miles from Kittery to Quoddy Head. Yet, tracing its deep inlets, craggy coves, and beautiful bays, the shoreline extends for 3,500 miles. There are 68 lighthouses, and more than 3 million multihued lobster buoys bobbing offshore. Coastal islands number in the thousands, with several rising hundreds of feet above sea level. At 1,530 feet tall, Cadillac Mountain on Mount Desert Island is the highest point along the Atlantic seaboard north of Rio de Janeiro. Downeast in Cobscook Bay, the "Old Sow" is the world's largest tide pool.

Maine is also home to the largest population of black bears in the lower 48 states, and roughly 29,000 moose. Yet in terms of human presence, it is the East's most sparsely populated state. In the northwest "territory" of Aroostook County (which, incidentally, is the largest county east of the Mississippi River, and larger than Connecticut and Rhode Island combined) there are only an estimated 27 persons living within an area of nearly 2,700 square miles. In other words, there is but a single soul for every hundred square miles, a remarkable fact when you consider that Acadia National Park, which encompasses less than 50,000 acres, withstands nearly 3 million visitors annually, or that as many as 2 million people a year flock to the famous outlets in Freeport.

But statistics alone barely begin to capture the essence of this rugged, charming, and diverse state, and in many ways it transcends description. For sheer beauty, Maine is as beguiling as any state in the nation, and at least as fascinating in complexity and character. The wry humor and unassuming nature of its people are as renowned as the sharp, precipitous edge of its highest peak. Born of weathered earth, the saltiest of seas, and a remote, often impenetrable wilderness, "Mainers" are as spirited and unpretentious as the landscape is alluring and unforgiving. Humorist Will Rogers once remarked, "Did you ever see a place that looked like it was built to enjoy? Well, this whole state of Maine looks that way." Of course, he also purportedly quipped, "No rain, no pain, no Maine!" No doubt Mainers would agree with both sentiments, and enjoy an appreciative chuckle over the latter.

In short, from sea to summit, Maine was made for exploration, and this book is an invitation to discover its essence for yourself. Each trip represents a cairn on a captivating pathway that has beckoned adventurous travelers since Henry David Thoreau first arrived here in search of "wildness" more than 150 years ago. Like so many others, he returned again and again to explore its natural wonders, discover the character of its people, and confront its imposing wilderness with abundant curiosity and appropriate respect. I hope you will do the same.

History

Geographically, Maine was sculpted and scoured into rugged perfection by the sheer and relentless force of water. During the last ice age, glaciers cut what had been a relatively straight coastline into the myriad of bays, inlets, coves, and peninsulas seen today. The state's southern landscape is also sometimes called the "drowned coast," because the rising sea level and receding ice sheet turned valleys into bays, and mountaintops into islands.

Maine can generally be divided into three distinct natural regions, including the Coastal Lowland, the Eastern New England Upland, and the White Mountain Section. The Coastal Lowland extends from 10 to 50 miles inland, and features sandy beaches in the south and pocket beaches abutting rugged, picturesque cliffs farther north. There are also numerous tidal creeks and salt marshes. Most of the terrain is gently rolling hills, but there are also a few rugged mountains. In fact, this region is home to the three highest peaks along the eastern American seaboard.

The Eastern New England Upland is the largest natural region in the state, covering northern, eastern, and central Maine. It is a rolling plateau, with elevations from sea level to about 2,000 feet. The Upland is strewn with hundreds of rivers and lakes. It also has fertile soil, especially along the Aroostook Plateau in far northern Maine where the state's sizable potato crop is grown and harvested.

The White Mountain region is an extension of New Hampshire's White Mountains, and covers a good portion of western and central Maine, including Mount Katahdin, the state's highest peak. This is the most rugged, and thickly forested region of Maine with nine mountains rising above 4,000 feet, and nearly a hundred peaks over 3,000 feet high. Most of Maine's rivers rise here, and there are several major watersheds feeding numerous lakes, ponds, and streams.

The region's earliest known inhabitants are sometimes referred to as the "Red Paint" people because of the red clay with which they lined the graves of their dead. Some of their burial grounds are estimated to be more than 5,000 years old. The two earliest Indian nations were the Micmacs and Abenakis (or Wabanakis). Although dozens of tribes once inhabited the region, only two remain today, the Passamaquoddies and the Penobscots. However, the culture and influence of Maine's indigenous people remains a strong feature of the state, and is reflected in many of its place-names.

The first colonial settlement was established by the Plymouth Company at Popham in 1607, the same year of the settlement at Jamestown, Virginia. However, the Popham colony didn't survive the harsh winters, so Jamestown is regarded as America's first permanent settlement. Much of the region subsequently became part of the Massachusetts Bay Colony, and it wasn't until 1820 that Maine became the twenty-third state along with Missouri. That event has become known as the Missouri Compromise because by admitting both states into the union, it kept the balance between free and slave states. Portland was Maine's first capital, but it was moved to the more centrally located town of Augusta in 1832.

Maine's economy has always been tied to the sea and its vast timber reserves, and today fishing and forestry remain vital resources. The region became known for shipbuilding long before statehood, and the industry has continued to flourish into the age of iron and steel. The *Virginia* is said to have been the first ship built and launched in the western hemisphere (1607), while the *Swordfish* was the nation's first atomic submarine. Maine also produces more canoes than any other state in the union! Maine's yearly lobster catch is larger than any other state, and it harvests the most blueberries in the nation. The state is also well known for its potatoes, leather manufacturing, textiles, and pulp and paper products. Recreation has always been a major resource, and tourism is one of Maine's largest industries.

Today, Maine is home to nearly 1.3 million people, and receives an estimated 40 million visitors per year.

Climate

True to its reputation, Maine has weather for all seasons and then some. The famous quip about New England weather ("If you don't like the weather, wait five minutes.") was surely meant to describe Maine. Maine has just about every type of weather from exquisite, sun-filled, summer afternoons, to bone-chilling ice storms. Here, you'll find wind, rain, snow, and sun, and several types of each! A good rule is to be prepared for its unpredictability. That said, you should generally expect a moderate northern climate with cool, rainy springs, warm, sometimes humid summers, crisp falls, and long, cold winters. Summer temperatures are usually in the upper 70s or low 80s, with a few days that get above 90 degrees. Interior Maine experiences a greater range of temperatures in the summer, with some nights in northern areas at or near freezing. The coast benefits from onshore breezes, but rain and fog are common too. Winters in Maine are cold but not frigid. January temperatures range from 11 to 31 degrees Fahrenheit along the coast, and 1 to 19 degrees Fahrenheit inland.

Bugs

Contrary to popular belief, the black fly is not the Maine state bird. Unfortunately, the rumors about the state's copious insect population are decidedly true, and can quickly turn a pleasant outing into a desperate and miserable experience. No-see-ums, black flies, deer flies, green heads, mosquitoes, ticks, and other pesky critters naturally thrive in such a water-rich environment, and are an essential part of the environment. Eradication efforts date back more than a century when salt marshes were ditched and drained in a futile attempt to reduce the breeding habitat of mosquitoes. The practice only served to damage a vital ecosystem, which has yet to fully recover.

So, barring a Mainer's stoicism, or the serene equanimity of a Zen Buddhist, your best alternatives are to duck out or cover up. If possible, avoid the peak seasons (June and July are especially bad, though this varies from bug to bug, and region to region, and it sometimes seems that Maine has a bug for every season). This strategy has the added value of avoiding the peak travel season too. Better still, come when you please, but bolster your opportunity for an enjoyable experience by wearing clothing appropriate to the environment (light colored, full coverage, but breathable). Recent improvements to outdoor sportswear have been proven to significantly repel biting bugs, and may eventually eliminate the need for effective but toxic skin applicants.

Getting There

In Maine, the old saying goes, "You can't get *theah* from *heah*." And, while that advice is duly applicable along many of Maine's winding back roads and remote reaches, by and large the state is wonderfully accessible by car, bus, boat, plane, or train. I-95 and the Maine Turnpike provide easy access to the most popular destinations, and most secondary roads are well maintained and often scenic. Similarly, US 1 is the gateway to Maine's spectacular coast, and while it is fairly criticized for traffic jams on busy summer weekends, it is generally well maintained and easy to negotiate. Portland International Jetport (207-774-7301) is the major hub for out-of-state travelers, and services most major airlines. Bus services include Greyhound, Concord Trailways, and Vermont Transit Lines. The Amtrak Downeaster services passengers to and from Boston and Portland daily, with stops in Wells, Saco, and Old Orchard Beach. For more information about transportation services in Maine, including ferry services, visit the Maine Office of Tourism website at www.visitmaine.gov.

Lodging

Maine is a major tourist destination and offers travelers of every budget an exceptional array of accommodations ranging from rustic sporting camps to luxurious inns. For a complete listing of lodging resources, see Appendix D.

Universal Access

Several of the trips in this book have universal access facilities for the disabled including Acadia National Park, Baxter State Park, Moosehorn National Wildlife Refuge, Grafton State Park, and many others. For a complete resource to accessible recreational destinations in Maine, including arts and other leisure activities, visit www.maine.gov/portal/visiting/accessrec. For a complete listing of accessibility in Maine's state parks, visit www.maine.gov/doc/parks/accessibility/access_guide.html.

Emergencies

Report emergencies to police and fire departments or ambulance response centers by calling 911.
* Maine State Police: 207-624-7200
* Northern New England Poison Control Center: 800-222-1222

Hunting Season

Hunting is a popular activity in Maine, and some of the destinations in this book, including state parks, the White Mountain National Forest, Public Reserve Lands, Wildlife Management Areas, and National Wildlife Refuges are open to hunting during specific seasons. Please use caution if you intend to travel to one of these destinations during the hunting season. For more information about specific hunting seasons, and hunting rules and regulations in Maine, visit the Maine Department of Inland Fisheries and Wildlife website at www.state.me.us/ifw/.

Trip Planning & Outdoor Safety

Hiking

No other state in New England offers as many diverse hiking opportunities as Maine. Here you can enjoy leisurely walks through quiet, mist-filled fog forests, cliff-bound excursions on wild, windswept islands, or challenging ridge hikes atop precipitous mountain peaks. Maine is home to Acadia National Park, 281 miles of the Appalachian National Scenic Trail, more than 30 state parks, nearly half a million acres of Public Reserve Lands, a portion of the White Mountain National Forest, nine national wildlife refuges, and, of course, mile-high Mount Katahdin, the state's highest peak and the centerpiece of beautiful Baxter State Park. While by no means comprehensive, the hiking excursions described in this guidebook represent some of the best hikes in Maine and are intended to provide the reader with a broad cross section of opportunities from easy, hour-long woods walks to thoroughly demanding, all-day outings.

Trip Rating

Difficulty ratings of easy, moderate, or difficult are based on a combination of factors such as distance, terrain, elevation gain, exposure, and trail conditions. In Maine, a short, mile-long ascent can be relentlessly steep, while a relatively flat mile can be strewn with a jumbled heap of boulders. In some cases, that same mile can be steep, jagged, and severely exposed! Thus, trip ratings are determined least by distance than by the type of terrain encountered. A trip with an easy rating will generally take two to three hours or less, and will not include any treacherous terrain.

A trip labeled moderate is generally a longer trip (over three hours), or will involve a fair amount of elevation gain. A difficult trip will be even longer (though, as described above, not always), and includes sections of very challenging terrain. A few trips have a combined rating, i.e. "easy to moderate," "moderate to difficult," etc. These ratings are given to highlight sections within the route that may be more difficult, or to describe a change in the rating if a loop option or extended hiking opportunity is featured.

When a hike is described as a round-trip, it follows a trail to a turn-around point and returns to the trailhead along the same route. A loop trip begins and ends at the same point, but doesn't cover the same ground twice. In some cases, a trip may include portions of a round-trip, but also include an extension, or loop option.

Estimated Time

The hiking times provided at the beginning of each trip are estimates of total trip length and are intended to help you plan your outing. They assume a moderate hiking pace, brief water breaks, and stops at scenic vistas or featured destinations. Hiking times may vary depending on the physical fitness of hikers in your group, whether you prefer to stop frequently to observe your surroundings, how much gear you carry, trail and weather conditions, and other factors. Always assume your trip may last longer than the estimated time given, and prepare accordingly.

Safety and Etiquette

- Choose a trip that suits the abilities of all hikers in your group.
- Plan ahead and make sure you have time to complete your hike before dark. If you are planning a sunset hike, be sure all hikers in your group are carrying headlamps in their packs so you can return to the trailhead safely (headlamps should be carried at all times in any case).
- Know the weather forecast. Cold temperatures, rain, and snow can lead to hypothermia if you're not dressed in appropriate layers—those closest to your skin should wick away water, and your outer layer should be waterproof. In heat, wear lightweight wicking clothing and drink plenty of water. Lightning is a serious danger to hikers—take shelter quickly if you hear thunder approaching, and reschedule your hike if lightning is definitely predicted.

- Bring the essentials with you, even on a short hike. These include:
  - ✓ Water. At least 1 quart per person for shorter trips, and 2 quarts per person for longer trips.
  - ✓ Food. Have healthy snacks on hand for short trips, and more substantial energy bars or meals for longer trips.
  - ✓ Maps and compass and/or GPS unit. Study maps before departing, and know how to use a compass or GPS.
  - ✓ Extra clothing. Foul-weather gear, additional warm layers, and dry socks are essential.
  - ✓ Headlamp or flashlight.
  - ✓ Sunscreen and lip protection.
  - ✓ First-aid kit. Know what is in it and how to use it.
  - ✓ Multi-tool or knife.
  - ✓ Waterproof matches or lighter in case of emergency.
  - ✓ Sunglasses.
  - ✓ Insect repellent.
  - ✓ Binoculars for viewing wildlife (optional).
  - ✓ Camera (optional).

- Wear appropriate, comfortable footwear and clothing. Shoes should provide good support and traction. For easier hikes, trail running or day-hiking shoes are fine; for longer, or more rugged trips, choose hiking boots (preferably waterproof) with better ankle support. In some instances, an extra pair of light shoes or sandals is recommended for river crossings. Socks should be wool or synthetic so they can dry quickly. Avoid cotton, especially right next to your skin; it traps water and sweat and makes for uncomfortable hiking. Carry a waterproof outer layer of clothing, even if the forecast calls for sunshine. Weather in Maine can be very unpredictable.

- Be aware of your surroundings. Most of the trails described in this book are well marked, and every attempt has been made to describe them in accurate detail, but it is possible to take a wrong turn in the woods. Refer often to the maps in this guide; pick up additional maps at the trailhead if they are available, and check for postings about new information (trails may have changed); carry a compass or GPS unit, and carry a U.S. Geological Survey topographic map to keep track of where you are.

- Do not disturb other hikers. Be friendly and say hello, but refrain from yelling, talking on your cell phone (except in case of emergency), and disturbing the peaceful setting.
- If you get ahead of your group, stop and wait at the next trail junction to avoid confusion or having any part of your group become separated.
- Minimize your impact on the land: Respect signs marking trail closures. If a trail is wet or muddy, stay in the middle of it; do not widen the footpath by going around any mud or obstacles. Try to step on rocks or logs, but not on plants or tree roots.

Biking

Biking opportunities in Maine comprise everything from peaceful rides along carriage roads in Acadia National Park to stomach-churning descents on twisty, rock-bound single-track trails. Here you can ride trails within remote expanses of wilderness, on converted rail-trails next to a cascading river, and in a woodland preserve in the midst of the state's largest city. There are rides for every ability level, excursions to state and national parks, wildlife refuges and preserves, and within the national forest. The rides listed in this guide represent only a fraction of biking opportunities in Maine. In addition to mountain biking, there are many opportunities for backcountry road rides, island excursions, as well as lengthy multi-day tours. Maine is the northern terminus of the East Coast Greenway, a network of on- and off-road trails extending from Key West, Florida to Calais, Maine (www.greenway.org). In southern Maine, there is a wonderful network of trails and roadways known as the Eastern Trail (www.easterntrail.org), which extends from Kittery to Casco Bay. For more information about these and other riding options, refer to some of the organizations listed in Appendix E.

Trip Ratings
Each trip has two ratings: one for **Aerobic Difficulty**, and another for **Technical Difficulty**. Aerobic difficulty (easy, moderate, or difficult) is rated based on the length of the trip and strenuousness of its hills. A short, flat trip is easiest; a long trip with extensive climbs is considered difficult. Technical difficulty ratings (also easy, moderate, or difficult) reflect the type of terrain and the skill required to negotiate it. Wide-paved and dirt roads count as easy; while a steep, rock-strewn single-track trail is considered difficult. Some trips combine easy, moderate, and difficult

segments, and those trips are assigned more than one rating. When a trip is described as round-trip it follows a trail to a turnaround point and returns to the trailhead along the same route. A loop trip begins and ends at the same point, but doesn't cover the same ground twice. (In some cases, a loop trip involves more than one loop, but always begins and ends at the same point.) A one-way, or point-to-point trip begins at one point and ends at another; and usually requires a shuttle.

Estimated Time

The times listed for each trip are estimates that assume a moderate pace and decent conditions. Times will vary depending on the ability and fitness level of riders in your group as well as weather and trail conditions. Please leave plenty of time to complete your trip safely before darkness falls.

Biking Etiquette

Generally, Maine is considered mountain-biker friendly. Please do your part to earn the respect of land managers and conservation organizations around the state by observing posted rules and regulations, and by doing your part to support trail building and conservation.

- Stay on public biking trails. If bikes are prohibited on certain trails, please respect this—restrictions usually exist for good reason. Trails may be fragile, wet, or undergoing repair. Avoid riding through any private property.
- Share the trail. Be respectful of fellow trail users. Don't startle hikers and horses. Let them know you're approaching, allow them to pass at narrow junctures, and never let your bike get out of control.
- Take care of the trail. Don't ride on trails that are too wet and muddy— and if a favorite trail is closed in winter or early spring, skip it. Stay on the trail, because venturing off-trail may damage delicate flora and fauna. Consider joining a trail maintenance event to learn more about what goes into keeping trails in great condition (contact the New England Mountain Bike Association, or the Bicycle Coalition of Maine for more information).
- Be prepared. Know how to take care of your equipment, and always carry spare tubes and the tools necessary to repair a tire or fix a mechanical problem. Bring plenty of water, as well as a map and compass or GPS unit. Always ride with a helmet.

Safety and Comfort

Outdoor activities have inherent risks. Check the weather before you head out, and avoid biking during lightning storms. Dress appropriately, with layers that wick moisture away from your skin and waterproof outer layers in inclement conditions. Wear shorts that won't chafe your skin during your ride. Do not try to ride on trails that are too challenging for your ability level, and don't bring a group on a trail unless every rider can comfortably handle it. If you do encounter unexpectedly difficult terrain, don't be afraid to get off your bike.

Paddling

Few, if any, states in the nation can boast the wealth of boating opportunities available in Maine. With 6,000 ponds and lakes, 3,500 miles of rugged and picturesque coastline, thrilling whitewater rivers, and wild, remote wilderness waterways, the Pine Tree State is justifiably a paddler's paradise. From quiet water excursions on placid ponds, to island-to-island tours among archipelagos, Maine has a lifetime's worth of paddling destinations to discover and enjoy. The trips in this book range from easy outings on serene ponds to extended outings on remote lakes to demanding paddles on the open ocean.

Trip Rating

Difficulty ratings of easy, moderate, or difficult are based on a combination of factors such as distance, exposure to wind and waves, current and tide. A trip with an easy rating is generally confined to a quietwater pond and will comprise a two- to three-hour excursion. A trip labeled moderate is generally a longer trip, and will likely involve exposure to wind and/or current. A difficult trip will be even longer (though, not always), and include sections of very challenging paddling on the open ocean or exposed shoreline, or where tide and current demand experience and advanced boating skills.

When a trip is described as a round-trip, it follows a route to a turnaround point and returns to the launch site along the same route. A loop trip begins and ends at the same point, but doesn't cover the same path twice. In some cases, a trip may include portions of a round-trip, but also include a loop option, or other alternative. A point-to-point trip usually requires leaving a vehicle at either end of the route and shuttling back and forth.

Estimated Time

The paddling times provided for each trip are estimates of total trip length and are intended to help you plan your outing. They assume a moderate pace with rest breaks, and include excursions to featured destinations. Paddling times may vary depending on the physical fitness of the paddlers in your group, time out for excursions, how much gear you carry, weather conditions, and other factors. Always assume your trip may last longer than the estimated time given, and prepare accordingly.

Quiet Water

In this book, quietwater outings range from short excursions on small, shallow ponds to remote rivers teeming with wildlife, and chains of lakes that may require portaging. Any water-sport activity comes with inherent risks—and on windy days, even quiet water can become challenging, especially on larger bodies of water. Here are a few tips that will help you enjoy a safe and memorable experience on Maine's abundant ponds, lakes, streams, and rivers:

- As in any water sport, paddlers should always wear a certified and properly fitting personal flotation device (PFD) before setting out.
- Know how to use and control your boat. If you or someone in your group is an inexperienced paddler, make sure there is someone experienced along. Know how to get in and out of your boat safely, and spend some time paddling close to shore until you are comfortable with your equipment.
- Don't paddle farther than you're ready to go. Most physical activities rely on the legs; with paddling, your arms and shoulders can get sore and tired. Pay attention to your body, and give yourself time to build paddling-specific upper-body strength.
- Don't attempt to paddle stretches of river that are too difficult for you, or that make you uncomfortable. Take out instead. Avoid trips on rivers where water levels are dangerously high or near flood stage.
- Never paddle alone—be with at least one and preferably two other boats.
- Plan your route. Most rivers are tough to navigate upstream, so if you are planning a point-to-point trip, have transportation waiting for you at the end.
- Always watch for boat traffic, and get out of the way of oncoming powerboats—don't assume that the driver sees you. Also, be careful

of the wakes created by powerboats. The best strategy in big wakes is to turn the bow of your boat into the wave.

- Check wind conditions—breezes of 10 miles per hour can create chop in quiet water and make a paddling trip much more difficult. Account for the wind as you plan your course, remembering that staying close to the shoreline keeps you more protected. Consider choosing smaller ponds to paddle on windy days.
- Check the weather forecast, and do not go out in a boat in a thunderstorm (or if there is a threat of a thunderstorm). You are very exposed out on the water, and if you are far from shore, it's tough to reach shelter quickly. Don't get caught in a dangerous situation!
- Dress appropriately. Wear layers that wick water away from your skin, and a waterproof outer layer when necessary. Waterproof gloves are nice to have when paddling in early spring or late fall. The best shoes are waterproof, with non-slip soles—sandals, neoprene booties, or well-draining water shoes designed specifically for the activity. Remember that the water temperature is usually much colder than the air temperature. In spring, cold water can quickly lead to hypothermia and shock if you should tip and fall in. Make sure everyone in your group knows that if anyone gets soaked, he or she should get into warm, dry clothes right away.
- Recognize and avoid the following hazards:
  - Strainers. These are fallen trees and other objects that water can flow through, but you and your boat cannot. Being caught against a strainer in the oncoming current is extremely dangerous, so pay attention and give a wide berth to any potential hazards.
  - Dams. Most dams are impassable; take out well above a dam to avoid it.
- Pack a dry bag (a completely waterproof bag) to carry your supplies and stow in your boat. Items to have in this bag—which you don't have to lug on your back—include:
  - ✓ Water. At least 1 quart per person for shorter trips, and 2 quarts per person for longer trips.
  - ✓ Food. Have healthy snacks on hand for short trips, and more substantial energy bars or meals for longer trips.
  - ✓ Maps and a compass, and/or GPS unit. Study your map before you take the trip, and know how to use a compass or GPS.
  - ✓ Appropriate clothing. Bring a change of clothing as well.

✓ Headlamp or flashlight, especially for sunset paddles.

✓ Waterproof sunscreen and lip protection.

✓ Full-coverage hat with chinstrap.

✓ Multi-tool or knife.

✓ Sunglasses (polarized glasses are best to reduce glare). And a cord to retain them!

✓ Insect repellent.

✓ Waterproof matches or lighter in case of emergency.

✓ First-aid kit. Know what is in it and how to use it.

✓ Fleece or solar blanket.

✓ Binoculars (waterproof, if possible) to view wildlife (optional).

✓ Camera (optional). Be sure to carry it in a protective case to avoid exposure to water.

Sea Kayaking

There is simply no better place to enjoy sea kayaking than Maine's fabulous coast. From secluded inlets to wild islands, the state's intricate shoreline is arguably its most alluring natural feature. Here you can explore beautiful bays, quiet coves, an array of wildlife habitats, hundreds of windswept, picturesque islands, and, at the end of a day's paddle, the best lobster in the world! With so many options, choosing the trips for this book was difficult to say the least. But the selection represents a broad range of trips that will allow you to experience some of Maine's most beautiful destinations from easy harbor paddles to challenging excursions where tides average more than 20 feet. To fully enjoy your kayaking experiences in Maine, please consider the following safety information with care:

• Inexperienced paddlers are strongly encouraged to hire a certified guide, or join a reputable paddling club (listings and directories for both may be found in Appendix C and E) to help you learn necessary skills and/or enjoy an outing with an expert paddler with knowledge of the region.

• The ocean is one of nature's most powerful forces, and is often unpredictable. Never take a trip more challenging than your skill level allows, especially an open-water trip. You should be very comfortable with basic paddling strokes, know how to use a compass and nautical chart, and practice self-rescue and the use of a paddle float.

• Check the marine weather forecast and tides (a good source for weather and tide information is www.maineharbors.com) before heading out.

The weather in Maine can change quickly, with winds producing dangerous waves and rough surf without warning. Fog is a common issue in Maine, and foggy days are not safe for kayaking, especially in areas of frequent boat traffic. Tides and current are a major consideration when paddling in Maine. Take the time to learn about tides and tidal influences.

- Dress appropriately. Wear layers that wick water away from your skin, and a waterproof outer layer when necessary. Waterproof gloves are nice to have when paddling in spring or fall. The best shoes are waterproof, with non-slip soles, sandals, neoprene booties, or well-draining water shoes designed specifically for kayaking. Remember that the water temperature is much colder than the air temperature. Cold water can quickly lead to hypothermia and shock if you should tip over and fall in. Make sure everyone in your group knows that if anyone gets soaked, he or she should get into warm, dry clothes as soon as possible.
- Always wear a certified, properly fitted personal flotation device (PFD).
- Never paddle alone—a group of three or more is best.
- If you will be paddling in any kind of surf, use a spray skirt.
- Recommended safety equipment includes a sponge for light bailing, a paddle float and bilge pump, a spare paddle, a weather radio, a tow system, duct tape, and a foghorn.
- Pack your gear in dry bags (a completely waterproof bag), and/or a deck bag to carry your supplies and stow in your boat. Items to have in your bag(s) include:
  - ✓ Water. At least 1 quart per person for shorter trips, and 2 quarts per person for longer trips.
  - ✓ Food. Have healthy snacks on hand for short trips, and more substantial energy bars or meals for longer trips.
  - ✓ Maps and a compass, and/or a GPS unit. Study your map before you take the trip, learn how to read nautical charts, and know how to use a compass or GPS.
  - ✓ Headlamp or flashlight, especially for sunset paddles.
  - ✓ Waterproof sunscreen and lip protection.
  - ✓ Full-coverage hat with chinstrap.
  - ✓ Multi-tool or knife.
  - ✓ Sunglasses (polarized are best to reduce glare from the water). And a cord to retain them!

✓ Insect repellent.

✓ Waterproof matches or lighter, in case of emergency.

✓ First-aid kit. Know what is in it and how to use it.

✓ Fleece or solar blanket.

✓ Binoculars (waterproof, if possible) for viewing wildlife from a distance (optional).

✓ Camera (optional) carried in a protective waterproof case.

Boating Etiquette

To avoid having a negative impact on the environment and local residents, follow these low-impact paddling techniques:

- Respect private property and never land your boat near a house or on land marked "No Trespassing."

- Give wildlife a wide berth. Kayaks, in particular, easily stress seals. Never approach seals in a kayak, particularly if they have hauled themselves out onto rocks, where they feel especially vulnerable. Try to stay at least 0.5 mile from basking seals. You should also enjoy eagle and osprey nests from a distance, trying to stay at least 0.25 mile away from an active nest. If any animal changes its behavior as you approach, you are too close.

- Practice no impact techniques both on and off the water. Pack out all of your trash, including toilet paper and solid human waste. Urinating below the high-tide line is the most effective way to ensure quick dispersal of urine. However, do not urinate in a tide pool, as this can have negative consequences on the delicate life there. Also, try to stay below the high-tide line at all times to minimize your impact on fragile island habitats.

- Respect the local residents, particularly those who depend on the ocean to make a living. Always let them have the right of way and try to stay out of their path. Do not go near lobster traps, and be as quick as possible while using local boat ramps.

For a thorough treatment of sea kayaking safety considerations, trip planning, and low-impact paddling techniques, consult the AMC's *Sea Kayaking the New England Coast* by Tamsin Venn. For considerations specific to Acadia National Park, consult the AMC's *Discover Acadia National Park* by Jerry and Marcy Monkman.

1

Southern Region

FROM KITTERY TO CASCO BAY, Southern Maine offers excellent, accessible outdoor recreation opportunities. The state's most populous region is also one of its most diverse, with miles of beautiful coastline, abundant lakes, historic inland waterways, and interesting mountains to explore. Southern Maine is also home to the Rachel Carson National Wildlife Refuge and an interesting array of nature preserves including the Kennebunk Plains, Saco Heath (Trip 2), and Scarborough Marsh (Trip 10). There are excellent hiking and biking opportunities on and around Mount Agamenticus (Trips 1 and 5), and a surprising variety of urban excursions within Portland, the state's largest city (Trips 7 and 13). Featured trips include a circumnavigation of Gerrish and Cutts Islands (Trip 11), a coastal paddle from Kennebunkport to the Cape Porpoise Archipelago (Trip 12), and a hike to the summit of Pleasant Mountain, the region's highest peak (Trip 4).

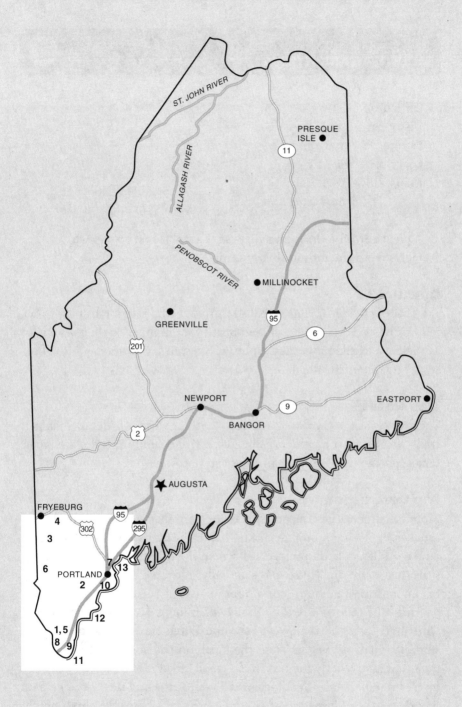

TRIP 1
MOUNT AGAMENTICUS

Difficulty: Easy
Distance: 1.5-mile loop
Estimated Time: 1 hour
Location: York
Maps: USGS York Harbor
DeLorme *Maine Atlas*, map 1

A pleasant hike through a diverse coastal forest to superb views from the mountain's summit.

Directions
Take I-95 to Exit 7 (formerly Exit 4) in York. From the north side of I-95, follow Chases Pond Road east and north for 6.5 miles to the parking lot at the base of the mountain. Note: At 3.8 miles, Chases Pond Road becomes Agamenticus Road.

Trail Notes
There is a kiosk at the base parking lot with brochures, a detailed map of trails, and an introduction to the area. On the summit, there are picnic tables, portable toilets, and an observation tower.

Trip Description
Mount Agamenticus is a perfect hike for a family outing or anyone interested in exploring a unique coastal habitat. The panoramic views from atop the 692-foot summit are well worth the minimal effort required to scale the mountain. This trip is especially enjoyable in summer or during fall migration when hundreds of raptors may be seen passing overhead.

This hike follows the Ring Trail, which loops around the mountain, with short spurs on the Sweet Fern and Witch Hazel trails to reach the summit. The trail begins from the kiosk on the southwest side of the mountain and briefly follows an old woods road into a mixed deciduous forest interspersed with stands of tall white pine and fir trees. The path quickly reaches a junction at 0.1 mile. Stay left here and climb northwest, reaching the summit road at 0.2 mile. Cross over the road and walk

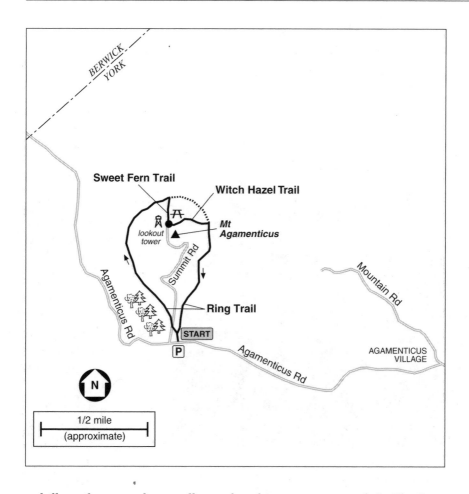

uphill until you reach a small gravel parking area on your left. The Ring
Trail continues from here, entering the woods behind the parking area.
The trail ascends moderately as it swings around the northwest side of
the mountain. At 0.4 mile, the Blueberry Bluff Trail enters on the right.
Continue on, passing the Wintergreen and Horse Trails respectively. At
0.7 mile, the Sweet Fern Trail enters on the right. Follow this short, steep
spur as it climbs to the open summit. On a clear day, you'll enjoy 360-de-
gree views to the bustling seacoast and the distant peaks of New Hampshire's White Mountains. The large, grassy knoll on the summit is perfect
for a picnic or a summer afternoon nap. To complete the hike, locate the
Witch Hazel Trail southeast of the Summit Lodge. Descend Witch Hazel
0.2 mile to the Ring Trail. Turn right on the Ring Trail and follow the
path, descending over somewhat rocky terrain to the trailhead.

Nature and History Notes

Despite its modest elevation, Mount Agamenticus has become a beacon for conservation initiatives in Maine. Many dedicated individuals and organizations are working to balance the mountain's ecological diversity with recreational opportunities and human enterprise. To date, more than 10,000 acres have been set aside to preserve what is the largest intact coastal forest between Acadia National Park and the New Jersey Pine Barrens.

Although there is ample evidence of human activity here including a summit road, lodge, fire tower, and defunct ski lift, Agamenticus supports a rich array of flora and fauna. Southern hardwoods, including the

Hawk watchers gathered at the summit of Mount Agamenticus during fall migration.

shagbark hickory and chestnut oak, reach their northern limit here. The surrounding wetlands and vernal pools support wood frogs, blue-spotted salamanders, and the rare and threatened spotted and Blanding's turtles. Hemlocks and black gum trees dot an Atlantic white cedar swamp on the mountain's eastern flank. Agamenticus is also home to many birds and mammals including black bear, bobcat, great horned owl, wild turkey, and snowshoe hare.

Other Options

Many other recreational opportunities are available to enjoy on or near Mount Agamenticus, including miles of challenging mountain biking trails (see Trip 5). In winter, this is a wonderful place to backcountry ski or snowshoe. Nearby, White Pine Programs, an organization dedicated to nature-based learning, uses the mountain to teach wilderness skills and tracking to adults and youth year-round. For more information, call 207-361-1191 or visit www.whitepineprograms.org.

TRIP 2
SACO HEATH PRESERVE

Difficulty: Easy
Distance: 2.0 miles round-trip
Estimated Time: 1.5 hours
Location: Saco
Maps: USGS Old Orchard Beach
    DeLorme *Maine Atlas*, map 3

A leisurely walk through a beautiful and unique peatland environment.

Directions

From the Maine Turnpike (I-95), take Exit 36 (formerly Exit 5), then turn left onto Industrial Park Road. Turn right onto Route 112 (Buxton Road), and follow it north and west for 2.0 miles. The parking lot and trailhead are on the right. Look for a Nature Conservancy sign posted by the roadside.

Trail Notes

This trip is suitable for the entire family. The trail crosses level ground, mostly on "floating" boardwalks over peat bogs. Please appreciate this rare and fragile ecosystem by always staying on marked paths. Neither pets nor bicycles are permitted within the preserve.

Trip Description

Saco Heath is one of Maine's most unique and fascinating natural eco-systems. The 1,300-acre preserve, bounded by suburban development and within earshot of interstate traffic, has the feel of an exotic, tranquil island. It is the southern-most example of a "coalesced domed bog" in North America, and the only known location in the world where Atlantic white cedar grows on this type of peatland. The preserve also harbors a wide range of flora and fauna including the state's only population of Hessel's hairstreak butterfly.

This trip takes you into the heart of the bog environment via trail and boardwalk maintained by The Nature Conservancy, which has owned and protected the heath since 1986. Brochures explaining the ecology of the preserve are available at the trailhead information kiosk.

The yellow-blazed path begins in woodlands of white pine, hemlock, and maple. The trail soon reaches a short boardwalk and then a second, much longer boardwalk that winds through the forest before reaching the edge of the heath at 0.5 mile. From here, the upland transitions dramatically onto the open heath. The boardwalk crosses over the bog, floating on a 15-foot-deep layer of peat mat and up to 20 feet of water. Within the heath, there is an abundant variety of plants including sheep laurel, leather-leaf, Labrador tea, iris, and rhodora, as well as insect-eating sundew and pitcher plants. The Atlantic white cedar grows on the highest portions of the bog along with a smattering of pitch pine, tamarack, and black spruce.

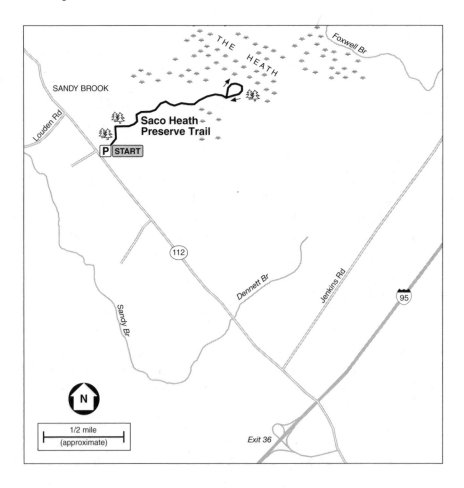

At 0.9 mile, the trail turns to a dirt path that loops around an interesting stand of tall pines before returning to the boardwalk for the hike back to the trailhead.

Nature and History Notes

Saco Heath was once a pair of adjacent ponds. The acidic water in the ponds slowed decay of dead plant material, particularly sphagnum moss, also known as peat. With each year's plant growth, more and more peat was added to the ponds until they eventually grew together. Because the peat materials can absorb many times their own weight in moisture, the peat mat eventually swelled above the existing water table, forming the "raised-coalesced," or "domed," bog seen today.

Atlantic white cedar can withstand extreme growing conditions. Because of its resistance to decay and straight bole, the tree was harvested for use as piers, fence posts,

The "floating" boardwalk at Saco Heath Preserve.

telephone poles, and boats. It was also bored out for use as water lines in many early American cities. During the Revolutionary War, the wood was used to produce charcoal for gunpowder. The larvae of Hessel's hairstreak butterflies feed exclusively on Atlantic white cedar leaves.

The preserve provides exceptional habitat for wildlife including fisher, moose, bobcat, deer, and wild turkey. It is also an excellent place to spot a wide variety of birds.

The Pine Tree State

With more than 17 million acres of forestland covering nearly 90% of the state, Maine justifiably calls itself the "Pine Tree State." Indeed, the Eastern white pine (*pinus strobus*) is so prominent in Maine's landscape, history, and economy, not only is it the official state tree, but its pinecone and tassel are also the official state flower. In fact, the cone and tassel were voted the state's floral emblem 50 years before the tree received its official designation.

For the 1893 World's Fair in Chicago, states were asked to choose floral emblems for a "National Garland of Flowers." Maine asked its residents to choose between two genuine flowers, the goldenrod and the apple blossom, in addition to the pinecone and tassel. The latter won out, garnering 10,000 of the 17,000 votes cast. It was later adopted as the official state flower on February 1, 1895. Thus, Maine became the only state in the nation with an official floral emblem that does not actually flower.

Botanically, pinecones do not produce true flowers. Rather, the reproductive structures of pinecones are known as *strobili*. The male strobili open and shed pollen in April through June, with fertilization occurring 13 months after pollination. The fragrant cones grow up to 8 inches long and take two years to mature before opening to discharge their winged seeds. The seeds are dispersed primarily by wind, and can travel up to 200 feet within a stand and more than 700 feet in open areas. Animals also disperse seeds. The tassels are needles that grow in bundles of five, with each needle reaching up to 5 inches in length.

The white pine is the largest conifer in the northeastern United States. It grows rapidly, often reaching a height of 60 feet and a diameter of 8 to 10 inches in just 40 years. White pines often live for more than 200 years and may exceed 400 years of age. Before the arrival of colonists, old growth trees 150 feet tall and 40 inches in diameter were common.

The abundance and value of Eastern white pine played an important part in the development of Maine's economy and remains a vital economic resource for the state today. Maine's lumbering industry dates back to the early 1600s. The nation's first sawmill was built here

Old growth pines at the Hermitage, a National Natural Landmark near Gulf Hagas.

in 1623, powered by water harnessed from the Salmon Falls River. The white pine soon became an essential resource for the burgeoning ship-building industry, valued for its straightness, height, and lightness of weight.

Shortages of ship masts in Europe led to England's Broad Arrow Policy in 1691, whereby tall pine trees measuring more than 2 feet in diameter and within 3 miles of water were branded with the "King's Arrow"—a mark that reserved the trees for the Royal British Navy. The practice, which effectively removed the best trees from use within local economies, would eventually stir the colonists to rebellion, and was an important factor leading to the American Revolution. In fact, the Eastern white pine was the emblem emblazoned on the first colonial flag.

Today, Maine continues to be a leading producer of lumber products, and is home to the largest paper mills in the country.

TRIP 3
BURNT MEADOW MOUNTAIN

Difficulty: Moderate
Distance: 2.4 miles round-trip
Estimated Time: 2.5–3 hours
Location: Brownfield
Maps: USGS Brownfield
DeLorme *Maine Atlas*, map 4

An enjoyable hike and scramble to an open summit with panoramic views.

Directions
From the junction of Routes 160, 113, and 5 in East Brownfield, take Route 160 south to Brownfield. At the Brownfield Community Church, turn south on Route 160. At 2.0 miles, pass Burnt Meadow Pond on your left. Continue south another 0.4 mile to a small turnout and parking area on your right.

Trail Notes
There is no available water on this trail. The hike is appropriate for children who have done some previous hiking or who will enjoy the challenge of its short, steep pitches and scrambles. However, strong consideration should be given to little legs that mean well, but may tire easily.

Trip Description
This short but challenging hike ascends the eastern spur of Burnt Meadow Mountain to its exposed north peak. The trail climbs steadily with a few steep, rocky pitches along the way before topping out at 1,575 feet. The vertical rise from trailhead to summit is 1,100 feet.

The trail begins to the right of the parking area and is marked with blue blazes. Follow the path through a series of short S-turns before reaching the first of several granite outcrops with increasingly open views to the surrounding landscape. At 0.4 mile, the trail crosses over a bluff with fine views to the south before dropping into a shallow col.

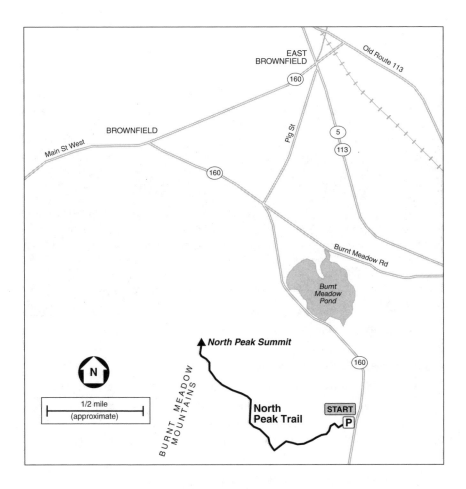

The trail then turns sharply to the north/northwest and winds through a stand of mixed hardwoods before emerging to another open ledge with still better views to the south.

Continuing, occasional views can be seen north/northwest to the summit. Pass several large boulders (glacial erratics) and continue climbing on mostly open ledges. The trail now turns northwest ascending to the base of the summit's final pitch. This is a fun but steep scramble over exposed, fractured granite ledges. Use caution, especially on the descent.

The trail now emerges onto the flat, grassy summit of the north peak with excellent views in nearly all directions.

To return, follow your ascent path, being extra careful when descending the exposed ledges over loose rock.

Hikers descending from the north summit of Burnt Meadow Mountain.

Nature and History Notes

The incredible views from Burnt Meadow Mountain's bare summit are a result of the devastating fires that swept through the region in 1947. In October of that year, fire not only engulfed the mountain, but also destroyed 85 percent of the town of Brownfield, completely wiping out its industry.

In the mid-1960s, the mountain became the focal point for economic recovery when an effort was made to establish a recreation area along its northern flank. Three slopes were cleared for a ski area and the mountain was opened for business in 1970. However, little snow fell and the plan succumbed to financial difficulties by the winter of 1972.

Today, Burnt Meadow Mountain is quietly recovering in the shadows of loftier, more popular mountains. A young forest of mostly mixed hardwoods (ash, birch, beech, oak) has taken root amidst slabs of exposed granite, low bush blueberries, Staghorn sumac, and weathered pines. A wide variety of lichens thrive here and are especially interesting on the north peak. On a clear day, there are excellent views east to the Saco River and Maine's southern lakes region, and west to New Hampshire's Presidential Range.

TRIP 4
PLEASANT MOUNTAIN

Difficulty: Moderate
Distance: 3.6 miles round-trip
Estimated Time: 3 hours
Location: Denmark/Bridgton
Maps: USGS Pleasant Mountain
 DeLorme *Maine Atlas*, map 4

**An outstanding ridge hike with excellent views to the southern
Lakes Region and beyond.**

Directions

From Bridgton, travel west on US 302 for 5.0 miles, crossing the bridge
over Moose Pond. Just beyond the pond, turn left onto Mountain Road.
This is also the access road to Shawnee Peak Ski Area, encompassing the
northern slopes of Pleasant Mountain. Travel south on Mountain Road
for 3.3 miles to the Ledges Trail parking area and trailhead.

Trip Description

Pleasant Mountain is the highest peak in Southern Maine, rising dramatically over Moose Pond and the surrounding countryside to 2,006
vertical feet and stretching nearly 4.0 miles north to south. The long,
open summit affords outstanding ridge hiking and excellent views. In
season, blueberries thrive along the ridge, providing a sweet reward for
the moderate effort required to climb the mountain.

The Ledges Trail described here ascends the eastern side of the mountain, tracing the remnants of an old fire road before proceeding on open
ledges to the main summit and fire tower. The vertical rise is 1,500 feet.
There are blue paint blazes along the entire trail. From the trailhead, hike
west/northwest following the broad path through patches of wild ber-
ries. The trail soon narrows and climbs gradually through thick stands of
young hardwoods, crossing two small streambeds (unreliable) at 0.5 mile.
The trail now rises steeply for 0.3 mile to the first open ledge with excellent views south and southeast over Moose Pond. Continue hiking along
the ledges, passing another outlook before climbing a steeper section of

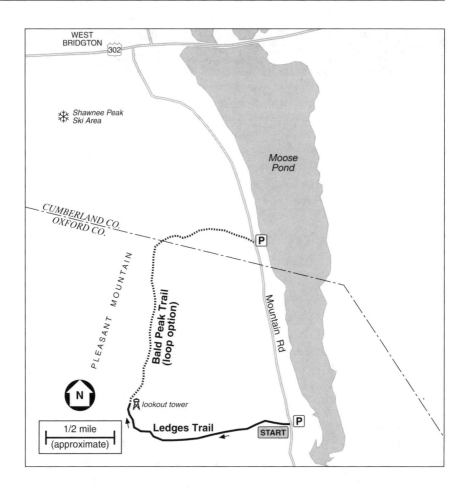

trail surrounded by lowbush blueberries. The trail then reaches a third open ledge outlook with views to the west. At 1.6 miles, the MacKay Pasture Trail (a.k.a. Southwest Ridge Trail) enters from the left. Continue climbing through oak scrub and blueberry bushes to the main summit and tower. From the height of land, there are spectacular views north and west to the Presidential Range in New Hampshire and over the Saco River valley.

To descend, retrace your steps following a southeasterly bearing into the woods from the fire tower.

Nature and History Notes

Over the years, Pleasant Mountain has been subject to significant change, both natural and manufactured. Around 1860, fire burned over

Southeastern view from the Ledges Trail.

the mountain, stunting the forest and exposing the granite ledges seen today. In 1873, the first of two hotels was built on the main summit. The second structure, The Pleasant Mountain House, operated until 1903 and was torn down in 1908. Subsequently, the summit was referred to as House Peak. The defunct, 48-foot fire tower that looms over the peak today was built in 1920 and was manned until 1992 when the state switched to aerial fire surveillance.

The mountain is also home to Maine's longest continuously run ski area. On January 23, 1938, over 500 intrepid skiers turned out to celebrate the official opening of the "Way-She-Go" trail cut on the mountain's north slope (it's now called the Jack Spratt run). The run was accessed by an 1,100-foot rope tow and was the first serviced ski trail in the state. Other Pleasant Mountain and Maine "firsts" soon followed: In 1953, the first T-bar was installed and, in 1955, the first chairlift. During the ski boom in the 1960s, more than 2,000 skiers were enjoying the mountain each winter weekend. Today, Shawnee Peak sees about 120,000 skier visits per year and is the third largest ski area in Maine.

Nature struck again in January 1998 when a severe ice storm blanketed Northern New England. The storm toppled several trees on the mountain, damaging several trails, including the Ledges Trail. Evidence of the storm is still visible today, especially on portions of the Bald Peak Trail north of the Ledges Trail.

Other Options

You can also connect the Ledges Trail with the Bald Peak Trail to its north to form an enjoyable loop hike. Begin at the trailhead for the Bald Peak Trail on Mountain Road, 1.8 miles south from US 302. Follow the trail to the top of Big Bald Peak and then follow the eastern ridge to the main summit before descending the Ledges Trail. Then, walk the 1.5 miles back to your car at the Bald Peak trailhead. The total distance for this hike is 5.7 miles.

TRIP 5
MOUNT AGAMENTICUS

Aerobic Difficulty: Moderate to difficult
Technical Difficulty: Moderate to difficult
Distance: 3.5-mile loop
Estimated Time: 2 hours
Location: York
Maps: USGS York Harbor
　　　　DeLorme *Maine Atlas*, map 1

A challenging ride at Southern Maine's most popular mountain-biking destination.

Directions

Take I-95 to Exit 7 (formerly Exit 4) in York. From the north side of I-95, follow Chases Pond Road east and north for 6.5 miles to the parking lot at the base of the mountain. Note: At 3.8 miles, Chases Pond Road becomes Agamenticus Road.

Trail Notes

The vast and varied terrain on and around Mount Agamenticus makes for great riding, and seemingly endless opportunities to explore new routes. However, with so many trails to choose from, both marked and

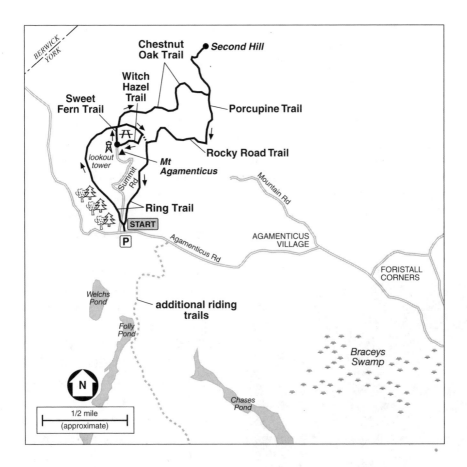

unmarked, it can be relatively easy to get lost. If you venture into un-
charted terrain here, be sure to pack a map and compass.

This trip is a variation of the "Big A Bike Loop" as described at the
kiosk at the base of the mountain. Be sure to review the route and pick
up a trail map at the kiosk before departing.

Trip Description

For good reason, Mount Agamenticus has become a prime destination
for mountain bikers. The mountain and surrounding terrain boasts some
of the most varied and technical riding in all of Maine. Despite its relatively modest distance, this trip will challenge your lungs, legs, riding
skills, and nerves. The route covers some of the same ground described
in the Trip 1 hike, but adds challenging climbs and descents to and from
Second Hill.

From the parking lot at the base of the mountain, begin riding north via the Ring Trail. At the junction at 0.1 mile, stay left and follow the Ring Trail across the summit road, re-entering the trail on the west side of the road behind a gravel parking lot. From here, the trail climbs steadily over rocky terrain, passing the Blueberry Bluff Trail at 0.4 mile. Continue climbing around the west side of the mountain, passing the Wintergreen Trail (left) and Horse Trail (right). The trail continues around the north side of the mountain, levels off and arrives at the Sweet Fern Trail at 0.7 mile. Continue past Sweet Fern and follow the Ring Trail past the Chestnut Oak Trail (take note, you'll be returning to this trailhead later) as it climbs around the east side of the summit, to the Witch Hazel Trail Junction. Turn right on Witch Hazel Trail and gather steam for the short, switchback ascent to the top of the mountain.

Take a breather and enjoy the spectacular views from the summit, then locate the Sweet Fern trailhead at the edge of the grassy knoll north of the lodge. The descent from Sweet Fern back to the Ring Trail is slick, straight, and steep with some loose rock for added difficulty (if the trail is wet, consider retracing your route from the Witch Hazel Trail and Ring Trail to the Chestnut Oak Trail).

Safely down Sweet Fern Trail, turn right on the Ring Trail and ride to the Chestnut Oak Trail junction. From here, the path descends 0.2 mile of technical single-track punctuated with steep sections, sharp turns, roots, rocks, and ruts before meeting the Porcupine Trail. Turn left onto Porcupine and begin the gradual but challenging ascent to Second Hill.

The Ring Trail on Mount Agamenticus.

From the summit of Second Hill, turn around and brace yourself for a half-mile of bumpy, technical riding down Porcupine Trail, past Chestnut Oak Trail to the Rocky Road ATV trailhead. The 0.2-mile climb up Rocky Road back to the Ring Trail is by far the most difficult part of the trip. The path relentlessly ascends the eastern flank of the mountain over exposed roots, rocks, and loose dirt.

After you've tackled Rocky Road, turn left on the Ring Trail and begin the final descent along the eastern side of the mountain back to the parking lot. This last section is 0.5 miles long, rough and rocky, but otherwise straightforward.

Nature and History Notes

Near the summit parking lot atop Mount Agamenticus, there is a commemorative plaque dedicated to St. Aspinquid next to a large pile of rocks. The plaque reads: "Died 1682, Aged 94. Aspinquid was an Indian medicine man who was believed by all the tribes of Indians and lived in this vicinity. He was converted to the Christian faith and was thereafter known as St. Aspinquid. When he died, Indians came from hundreds of miles away to pay tribute to his memory and it is alleged that 6,723 wild animals were sacrificed here to celebrate his funeral on the mountain. He was buried here on Mt. Agamenticus, and as was the Indian custom, his grave was covered with stones."

The story of Aspinquid is both fascinating and . . . fictitious. The legend apparently derives from John Albee's nineteenth-century poem about the death of the famed seventeenth-century Indian leader Passaconaway who ruled much of the area now known as New Hampshire.

Other Options

The vast terrain west and south of the mountain is also a popular destination for mountain bikers. To explore this network of trails, ride south 0.2 mile from the parking lot at the base of the mountain and turn right at the York Water District gate. There is a small kiosk with a basic map of the area just inside the gate.

More Information

For trail maps, contacts, and other information, visit the website of the Mount Agamenticus chapter of the New England Mountain Biking Association (NEMBA) at www.mtanemba.org.

TRIP 6
BACK COUNTRY EXCURSIONS—PARSONSFIELD

Aerobic Difficulty: Easy to moderate
Technical Difficulty: Easy to moderate
Distance: 7.0-mile loop
Estimated Time: 2 hours
Location: Parsonsfield
Maps: USGS West Newfield
      Back Country Excursions trail map
      DeLorme *Maine Atlas*, map 4

An outstanding beginner/intermediate ride on terrain dedicated to mountain biking.

Directions

From Route 25 west of Porter, take Route 160 south. Follow Route 160 south, passing the Parsonsfield Seminary (at 2.9 miles) to Merrill Hill Road at 3.7 miles, just beyond the Parsonsfield Union Church. Go right, and follow Merrill Hill Road 2.1 miles until you reach Middle Road. From Middle Road, take the first, immediate left onto Woodward Road. Follow Woodward Road 0.2 mile to the Back Country Excursions entrance on the left.

Trail Notes

There are more than 50 miles of interconnected trails in this area. However, most are unmarked, and the network of trails is complex and difficult to follow without a guide the first time out. For a nominal fee, Back Country Excursions (BCE) will provide you with a map and introduce you to the trail system on a 1–2 hour guided tour. BCE also offers excellent meals, a wood-heated hot tub, and operates a rustic lodge, yurt, and no-frills camping area for extended stays or to attend one of their many special event programs.

Trip Description

If you love mountain biking, a trip to Back Country Excursions is a must do. Since 1991, the folks at BCE have devoted themselves to the fat-tire

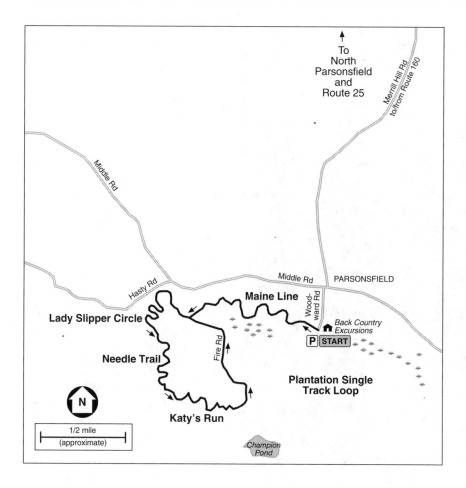

crowd, creating miles of fun and challenging trails specifically catered to off-road riders. From laid-back loops to gnarly, stomach-churning single-tracks, there are rides here for every age and skill level. Intrepid riders will enjoy BCE's "Rock 'N Log Palace," an amazing terrain park featuring a variety of apparatus, including a twisting roller coaster log ramp, where you can improve skills or test the limits of your technical abilities.

The terrain lies at the foothills of the White Mountains in the midst of a 10,000-acre semi-wilderness preserve crisscrossed by fire roads and the trail network cut and maintained by the Back Country staff. The Plantation Single Track Loop described here is one of BCE's newest trails and a great ride for a first outing. The 7-mile loop is actually comprised of three single-track trails and a long section of double-track all connected by fire roads.

Fun, challenging riding at BCE's Rock 'N Log Palace.

The loop begins on the Maine Line Single Track trail from the west side of Woodward Road, adjacent to BCE. The trail meanders west through a forest of tall pines, crossing a series of log bridges, before reaching a four-way intersection of fire roads at 1.0 mile. Turn right and follow the road north for 0.1 mile to reach the Lady Slipper Circle trailhead (unmarked) on your left. This section of the loop is known as the "plantation area," an outstanding segment of rolling single-track beneath a beautiful stand of tall red pine trees with exciting loop-de-loops crisscrossing a shallow ravine.

At 1.5 miles, the trail crosses a fire road and joins the single-track Needle Trail (unmarked). The Needle Trail runs south and west over smooth, level terrain with broad, relaxed turns through a thick growth of tall ferns, mixed hardwoods and white pine trees before reaching a fork at 2.5 miles. Bear left (south) here and join a mile-long section of the Needle Trail known as Katy's Run. The trail winds through open pine forest over rolling terrain before reaching a fire road at 3.5 miles. Turn left (north) here, following a 2.5-mile section of double-track over undulating terrain interspersed with a few short climbs.

At approximately 6.0 miles, the trail returns to the four-way intersection of fire roads. Turn right here and retrace your path on the Maine Line Single Track, reaching BCE at 7.0 miles. ·

Nature and History Notes

Back Country Excursions is the first and longest running mountain-bike touring company in the eastern United States. Owner Cliff Krolick is an avid mountain biker and patient teacher of the sport. The extensive trail network at BCE has been carefully handcrafted to provide great rides while also minimizing environmental impact. A portion of BCE's annual proceeds is donated to local environmental causes.

More Information

For more information about trails, special events, or accommodations, call 207-625-8189, or visit the Back Country Excursions website at www.bikebackcountry.com.

TRIP 7
PORTLAND TRAILS—
PRESUMPSCOT RIVER PRESERVE

Aerobic Difficulty: Easy to moderate
Technical Difficulty: Easy to moderate
Distance: 5.0 miles round-trip
Estimated Time: 2 hours
Location: Portland
Maps: USGS Portland West
Portland Trails Map and Trail Guide
DeLorme *Maine Atlas*, maps 5 and 72

A fun, challenging ride along the beautiful Presumpscot River.

Directions

From I-295 in Portland, take Route 26 north (Exit 9N) for 2.1 miles to the junction of Routes 26/100. Turn right onto Allen Avenue (no sign). Follow Allen Avenue for 0.7 mile to Summit Street. Turn left onto Summit Street. The Oat Nut Park trailhead is on the right at 0.4 mile. To reach the Overset Road trailhead, continue down Summit Street for another 0.1 mile to Curtis Road, turn right onto Curtis Road and travel 0.4 mile to Overset Road. Turn right onto Overset and park at the end of the road in the small parking lot marked with a Portland Trails sign.

Trail Notes

There are two access points to the Presumpscot River Preserve. This trip starts from the small parking area on Overset Road. The ride from the Oat Nuts Park trailhead adds 0.6 mile (1.2 miles round-trip) to the trip; however, there is limited parking available on Summit Street.

From either trailhead, this trip begins from well-developed, residential neighborhoods. Please be respectful of speed limits and home-owner's privacy. The trail within the preserve is mostly single-track. Please be especially attentive and respectful to visitors on foot.

Trip Description

The Presumpscot River Preserve provides a serene diversion from the bustle of city life in Portland. The preserve is the newest addition to Port-

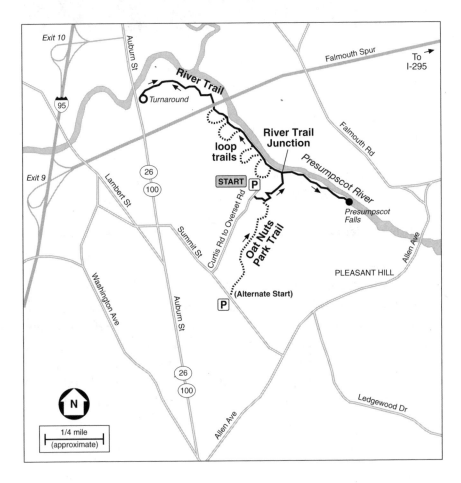

land Trails, an exceptional network of multi-use recreational pathways accessing nature preserves and sanctuaries, the Portland waterfront, and islands in Casco Bay. This trail traces the footsteps of Abenaki tribes who migrated to the river each spring to enjoy its abundant fishing.

From the Overset Road parking area, follow the Preserve Trail to the right of the Portland Trails sign. The path makes a brief, sharp descent from the trailhead, reaching a wooden bridge and junction at 0.1 mile. Stay left here, cross a second bridge, and continue descending the deep ravine leading to the river. The abrupt transition from suburban neighborhood to tranquil forest is remarkable.

At 0.3 mile, the Oat Nuts Park Trail folds into the Preserve Trail near the bank of the river. At the river's edge, a trail sign directs visitors upstream or downstream

The Presumpscot River Preserve offers quiet woods riding and fun single-track only minutes from downtown Portland.

along the River Trail. The path upstream is 1.1 miles long, offering great riding with opportunities to explore a series of loop trails into wooded, upland areas. Downstream, the trail follows the riverbank for 0.4 mile to beautiful Presumpscot Falls. I suggest riding both pathways, starting with the longer ride and then visiting the falls.

From the sign, turn left and follow the trail along the bank of the river. The riding here is excellent with challenging twists and turns through dense forest, punctuated by short, steep climbs and descents, bridges and boardwalks. Soon, the trail reaches the first of the loops that climb and descend the slope of the ravine. These short side trails are fun and worth exploration, adding length and a modest aerobic element to the ride.

On the main path, just past the first loop entrance, the trail makes a sharp left turn just before a wooden bridge. Look to your right here and note the rope swing attached to a large tree jutting over the river. This is a great spot to cool off after your ride! At 0.5 mile, the trail passes underneath I-95 and continues along the river, zigzagging through dense undergrowth before reaching Routes 26/100. Turn around here and make your way back to the sign at the trail junction.

From the junction, continue downriver for 0.4 mile to reach Presumpscot Falls. In places, the trail to the falls is more difficult and challenging than the upstream route, but worth the effort. Here, the character of the river changes dramatically from placid water to boiling rapids as it is squeezed through a small box canyon. There are several places to pull off near the river's edge to enjoy the scene.

Beyond the falls, the trail peters out and turns to private property, so turn around here and return to the trail junction, then shift gears to make the 0.3-mile climb out of the ravine and back to the trailhead and parking area.

Nature and History Notes

Portland Trails is a non-profit urban land trust founded in 1991 with the mission of creating a 30-mile network of multi-use trails and greenways within Greater Portland. The Presumpscot River Preserve is an inspiring example of the organization's efforts. In 2001, Portland Trails and the City of Portland Landbank Commission joined forces to save the area from development by creating a public nature preserve. In 2002, the state's Land for Maine's Future program together with more than 250 private donors, businesses, and foundations supported the land acquisition and trail building project. In 2005, Portland Trails reached its 30-mile trail network goal. There are now more than two-dozen multi-use pathways and greenbelts in and around the city.

Other Options

The Portland Trails network is a great way to explore the city. Other popular rides include the Back Cove Trail, a 3.5-mile loop with great views of the city skyline and the South Portland Greenbelt, a 5-mile rail-trail that runs from Barberry Creek to Bug Light Park.

More Information
To acquire a map of trails or learn more about Portland Trails, call 207-775-2411 or visit the Portland Trails website at www.trails.org.

TRIP 8
SALMON FALLS RIVER

Difficulty: Easy
Distance: 6.0 miles round-trip
Estimated Time: 2–3 hours
Location: South Berwick
Maps: USGS Dover East
DeLorme *Maine Atlas*, map 1

A quiet countryside paddle with excursions to an historic mansion and a beautiful state park.

Directions
From Kittery, take ME 236 (Exit 2, I-95) northwest for 6.0 miles. Turn left onto ME 101 and follow for 1.1 miles to the river. The parking area and launch site are located to the left on the east side of the river. There are no bathroom facilities here, but there are facilities at Vaughan Woods Memorial State Park.

Trail Notes
To avoid working against the current, this trip is best taken with the rising tide to the falls and a falling tide back to the put-in. To access both the Hamilton House and Vaughan Woods Memorial State Park from the river, pull out on the eastern shore, adjacent to the mansion.

Trip Description
This beautiful river has a delightfully rural quality. Despite its proximity to industry and a rapidly expanding urban population, much of the shoreline is composed of marsh, forest, and field. Along the eastern shore, there are opportunities to explore quiet trails beneath stately white pines at Vaughan Woods Memorial State Park, and to enjoy the

historic Hamilton House, a splendid Federal-style building, surrounded by magnificent gardens.

From the launch ramp south of ME 101, turn northeast and paddle under the bridge. The river sweeps left around a wide bend with marsh on both banks, before turning north. At approximately 1 mile, the southern edge of Vaughan Woods appears on the eastern shore, recognized by its steep banks, beautiful trees, and observation points overlooking the river. The Hamilton House can now been seen on a bluff above a small cove 0.75 mile ahead. Continue paddling beyond the cove to a section of tall reeds adjacent to the main structure. This is the best place to take out and explore the Hamilton grounds as well as Vaughan Woods via the trail that connects the two.

From here, the river narrows and turns northeast. At 2.25 miles, pass

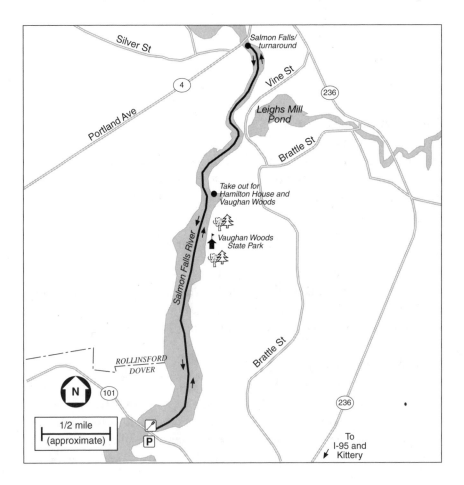

Leighs Mill Pond on your right and follow the river around bends to the left and right, past farms and pastureland. Continue north through a more developed area before reaching Salmon Falls at 2.9 miles. Turn around here and retrace your route.

Nature and History Notes

Native Americans knew these falls as *Quamphegan*, meaning "dip net falls." The reference was to the method used to collect salmon during their migratory run. Later, when settlers arrived, they harvested timber and harnessed the falls to power the first sawmill built in America. According to local legend, in 1634, a ship called the Pied Cow sailed up the river and landed the first cows to the area. The spot is now known as Cow Cove and is part of Vaughan Woods.

About 1785, Jonathan Hamilton built his magnificent house on a bluff overlooking the river. By 1898, when Emily Tyson, a wealthy Bostonian, bought the house, it had fallen into disrepair and the surrounding landscape was little more than brush and a small remnant forest. Tyson and her stepdaughter, Elizabeth Vaughan dedicated themselves to restoring the house, returning the formal garden to its full splendor, and nurturing the forest back to health. They succeeded on all counts. In

The falls on the Salmon Falls River powered the first sawmill in America.

1949, Elizabeth Vaughan bequeathed the forest to the State of Maine to be kept "in the natural wild state as the Vaughan Woods Memorial."

Today, Vaughan Woods is a testament to beneficent hands and the restorative power of nature. Majestic Eastern white pines and old growth hemlocks tower above shady bridle paths, beautiful walking trails, and scenic overlooks of the river. The river too seems healthy, as evidenced by the return of bald eagles in recent years. When I last paddled here, I spotted a mature eagle, settled on a branch of white pine, high above the river.

Other Options

An alternative trip on the Salmon Falls River to the north is described in the AMC's *Quiet Water Maine* book.

More Information

The Hamilton House is open Wednesday through Sunday from June 1 through October 15. There are tours on the hour from 11:00 A.M. to 4:00 P.M. and summer concerts most Sundays (there is an entrance fee to tour the house). The grounds are open from dawn to dusk. Call 207-384-2454 or visit the Society for the Preservation of New England Antiquities at www.spnea.org.

Vaughan Woods Memorial State Park is officially open from 9:00 A.M. to sunset, Memorial Day through Labor Day. Call 207-384-5160 or visit www.maine.gov/doc/parks/.

TRIP 9
YORK RIVER

Difficulty: Easy to moderate
Distance: 8.0–9.0 miles round-trip
Estimated Time: 3–4 hours
Location: York
Map: USGS York Harbor
DeLorme *Maine Atlas*, map 1

An inland paddle on a picturesque river steeped in New England history.

Directions

From I-95, take Exit 7 (formerly Exit 4) to Route 1. Turn right (south) on Route 1 and drive to Route 1A. Take Route 1A south to ME 103 (Lilac Lane) in York Village. Turn right on ME 103 and follow for 0.1 mile to a small parking area on the left across from Barrells Mill Pond.

Trail Notes

To access the river, carry your boat(s) across ME 103 to the causeway dividing the river from Barrells Mill Pond. Depending on the tidal flow, put in at the pond and paddle beneath the small suspension bridge, known locally as Wiggly Bridge, or launch directly into the river. Because of the river's strong current, it's best to paddle upriver on a rising tide and return on the ebb tide.

For a shorter, point-to-point trip of 4.5 miles, spot a second car at the Scotland Bridge on Scotland Bridge Road off Route 91.

Trip Description

This scenic river is a pleasure to paddle and a fine excursion from summer crowds along the coast. The York's swift current will carry you past several notable historic sites, beautiful shoreline houses, parks and preserves before branching off into marshland above the Scotland Bridge.

Depending on the tide, put in on either side of the Wiggly Bridge. This picturesque structure spans the inlet to Barrells Mill Pond and is purportedly the world's smallest pedestrian suspension bridge. The bridge leads to Steedman Woods, a 16-acre sanctuary left "forever wild" by the C. Roland Steedman family and now under the care of the Old York Historical Museum. The mile-long walk through the preserve is well worth the trip.

Begin paddling upriver (northwest). Soon, you'll site a small shack on your right adorned with an array of colorful lobster buoys. The little shack fronts an historic wharf that includes the John Hancock Warehouse and George Marshall Store. The structures, preserved by the Old York Historical Society, document 300 years of commercial life along the York River. Hancock, famed American patriot and signer of the Declaration of Independence, became part owner of the warehouse in 1780. He used the building to store traded merchandise he did not want taxed by the British government.

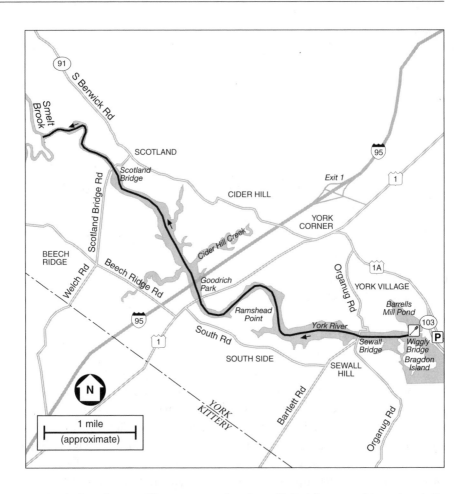

At 0.6 mile, you'll come to the Sewall Bridge, an historic civil-engineering landmark. Built in 1761, the pile-trestle bridge was so well constructed it remained in use until 1934 before being rebuilt in a similar design. Beyond the bridge to the left is a beautiful example of a colonial-era home. The dark red structure was built in the 1730s and situated close to the shoreline to accommodate river traffic.

At 1.8 miles, the river bends around Ramshead Point before reaching the US 1 and I-95 overpasses. Between the two bridges, there is a nice pullout on river right at The Grant House in Goodrich Park. Continuing upriver, you'll pass two large side creeks—Cider Hill and Bass Cove—before reaching the Scotland Bridge at 4.2 miles. Beyond the bridge, the river changes character as it opens to a beautiful expanse of marshland and diverges left from Smelt Brook. Paddling either tributary is interesting and worth exploration, given time and tide consideration. Otherwise, turn around here and catch the ebb tide for a quick ride back to the put-in.

Nature and History Notes

The town known today as York was the first "chartered city" established in America. It was originally called Agamenticus after its earliest known inhabitants. In 1641, Sir Fernando Gorges incorporated a 3-square-mile tract of land near the mouth of the York River. In 1642, Gorges, desirous of a suitable capital for his Province of Maine, replaced the town corporation to a chartered city, which he named Georgeana. The name York was appointed after the fall of the Loyalists under Cromwell in 1652, commemorating the town (York, England) in which Cromwell defeated the King's forces.

More Information

To learn more about the York River and surrounding watershed, visit the York Rivers Association website at www.york rivers.org. For more information about the historic sites along the York River, visit the Old York Historical Society's website at www.oldyork.org.

Kayakers enjoying a sunset paddle on the York River.

Rachel Carson

Rachel Carson loved Maine. After vacationing here in June 1946, she wrote to a friend, "At least I know now that my greatest ambition is to be able to buy a place here and then manage to spend a great deal of time in it—summers at least!" According to biographer Linda Lear, "Carson had found a place to which she gave her heart, one that was to have a lasting influence on both her life and her writing." Indeed, to research material for her 1956 book, *The Edge of the Sea*, Carson spent much of her time exploring and studying a small tide pool near Pemaquid Point. Today, the site is under the care of the Nature Conservancy and known as the Rachel Carson Salt Pond Preserve. Eventually, Carson did manage to buy a cottage on Southport Island.

Carson was born in Pennsylvania in 1907. She initially studied English in college, but later turned to zoology, and went on to teach at John Hopkins University and the University of Maryland. In 1932, she also took a part-time position as a science writer for the U.S. Bureau of Fisheries, which later was renamed the U.S. Fish and Wildlife Service. A few years later, she outscored all other applicants on a civil service exam to earn a full-time position with the Bureau (as a Junior Aquatic Biologist), only the second woman to do so up to that time. Her first significant work published outside the Bureau appeared in 1937 in *Atlantic Monthly*. The article, entitled "Undersea," was later expanded into book form as *Under the Sea-Wind*, published in 1941.

By 1949, Carson had advanced to Chief Editor of Publications for the Bureau, and continued to work on material for a second book. *The Sea Around Us*, a lyrical and meticulous study of the origins of oceans, appeared in 1951, and remained on the *New York Times* bestseller list for 86 weeks. The work also earned Carson a National Book Award, and the financial independence to pursue writing full time. *The Edge of the Sea*, her final book about ocean life, soon followed, and became another bestseller.

Carson's most famous book is undoubtedly *Silent Spring*, which is often considered one of the most influential works of the twentieth century. Published in 1962, the book describes the detrimental effects of man's broad application of synthetic pesticides upon the natural world: "As crude a weapon as a cave man's club, the chemical barrage has been hurled against the fabric of life." Of particular concern was the pesticide DDT, which was developed during World War II, and used with great effect to combat mosquitoes spreading malaria, typhus, and other insect-borne human diseases. However, DDT is persistent in the environment and, with *Silent Spring*, Carson sought to explain its unintended consequences and toxic effects as it accumulated through the food chain.

Controversy surrounded the book even before its publication. Carson's assertions were attacked by the chemical industry, and her publisher was pressured to suppress the book. Nonetheless, *Silent Spring* had an enormous impact, and quickly became a worldwide bestseller. Carson was later credited with igniting the modern environmental movement, prompting the creation of the Environmental Protection Agency, and providing the impetus for the 1972 ban on DDT.

To this day, the ban has proved to be a continuing source of controversy, and has, to some extent unfairly, clouded Carson's legacy. Critics argue that the ban has resulted in needless deaths around the world, and further research has failed to prove Carson's assertion that DDT is a human carcinogen. However, Carson never advocated for a complete ban of pesticides, including DDT. Rather, she encouraged responsible use, with an awareness of the chemicals' impact on the entire ecosystem. Appearing on a CBS documentary about *Silent Spring* in 1964, she remarked, "Man's attitude toward nature is today critically important, simply because we have now acquired a fateful power to alter and destroy nature. But man is a part of nature, and his war against nature is inevitably a war against himself."

Rachel Carson never lived to see the full impact of her work. She succumbed to breast cancer only two years after *Silent Spring*'s publication. The Rachel Carson National Wildlife Refuge in Wells, Maine, was dedicated to her memory in 1970. In 1980, she was posthumously awarded the Presidential Medal of Freedom, the highest civilian honor in the USA. In 1999, *Time* magazine named her one of the "100 Most Important People of the 20th Century."

TRIP 10
SCARBOROUGH MARSH

Difficulty: Easy
Distance: 3.0–4.0 miles round-trip
Estimated Time: 2 hours
Location: Scarborough
Maps: USGS Cumberland County
　　　　DeLorme *Maine Atlas*, map 3

A meandering paddle through Maine's largest salt marsh.

Directions
From US 1 in Scarborough, turn east onto Pine Point Road (also marked as Route 9 West). The Scarborough Marsh Nature Center and boat ramp are located 0.8 mile on the left.

Trail Notes
Be especially attentive to wind and tides before launching. The Audubon staff wisely recommends paddling out against the tide and allowing the incoming tide to assist your return. However, bear in mind, paddling against rising tides, strong currents, and high afternoon winds can be exhausting. Conversely, being stranded up a shallow-creek-turned-mud-flat at low tide is an invitation for frustration or worse. Aim for the half tide or higher, especially in the early morning when the light is soft, winds calm, and wildlife most active. An evening or full moon paddle can also be a safe and serene experience (Audubon offers several full-moon outings during the season).

Trip Description
Paddling through the heart of the Scarborough Marsh Estuary provides a unique opportunity to explore one of Maine's most productive ecosystems. Although salt marshes account for less than 1 percent of the state's landmass, they provide critical habitat for sustenance, refuge, and nesting to an abundance of wildlife. The estuary's broad, sweeping oxbows, serpentine bends, and shallow channels invite investigation and discovery.

This outing begins from the launch ramp adjacent to a small nature

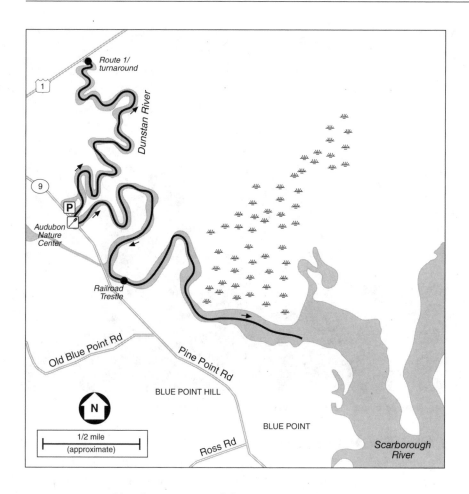

center operated by the Maine Audubon Society. The center is a great resource for more information about this unique habitat or for joining one
of the many interesting tours offered from late spring into fall.

From the launch, you can paddle in either direction depending on
conditions and your inclination. The trip north penetrates deep into the
marsh through a series of ever-narrowing twists and turns on the Dun-
stan River. At 2.2 miles, the river meets Route 1. Turn back here.

To the south, the river meanders in several directions before relaxing
and broadening into a generally southeast course. At 1.5 miles, a railroad
trestle crosses over the river. This is a good place to turn around and retrace your path if you are canoeing. Kayakers can venture farther south;
however, the river is subject to wind and waves, especially at the mouth
of the Scarborough River at Pine Point.

Canoeists enjoying a moonlight paddle at Scarborough Marsh.

Nature and History Notes

Remarkably, more than 70 percent of water-dependent birds identified statewide, including herons, egrets, terns, ibises, willets, and plovers, frequent this beautiful marsh. Tidal influences nourish the estuary with a mixture of fresh, salt, and brackish waters, sustaining a vital spawning ground and nursery to many species of fish.

Native Americans called these marsh environs *Owascoag*, "land of many grasses." Indeed, several species of grass thrive here. For years, early European settlers farmed the marsh for Spartina patens, commonly known as salt marsh hay, to feed their cattle. During the 1940s and 1950s, sections of the marsh were ditched and drained in an effort to rid the area of mosquitoes. The effort did not produce the desired end. Rather, it greatly affected other wildlife and the ecology of the marsh.

Today, 3,100 acres of Scarborough Marsh are preserved under the Wetlands Protection Act of 1972 and managed by the Maine Department of Inland Fisheries and Wildlife.

More Information

The Scarborough Marsh Audubon Center (207-883-5100) is open from 9:30 A.M. to 5:30 P.M. 7 days a week from mid-June through Labor Day. In addition to exhibits and a nature store, the center offers canoe rentals, walking trails, guided and self-guided tours, and a wide variety of special programs for all ages.

TRIP 11
CIRCUMNAVIGATION: GERRISH & CUTTS ISLANDS

Difficulty: Moderate
Distance: 8.5-mile loop
Estimated Time: 3 hours
Location: Kittery
Maps: USGS Kittery Quadrangle
DeLorme *Maine Atlas*, map 1

A spectacular introduction to kayaking the Maine coast.

Directions

From I-95, take Exit 2 (Route 236) toward Kittery. At the traffic circle, continue south on Route 236 for 1.2 miles then turn left on ME 103. Follow ME 103 1.5 miles to Frisbee's Market & Cap'n Simeons Galley. The wharf and launch ramp are located behind the restaurant. There is a launch fee during the season. Parking is available at a fee lot across the road from Frisbee's Market ($10).

Trail Notes

This trip is tide-dependent. At low tide, Chauncey Creek and the channel through the Rachel Carson National Wildlife Refuge are impassable. Aim for the top of the tide when starting. Portions of this trip are also exposed to the full force of the Atlantic Ocean as well as a section of the Piscataqua River (the third fastest-flowing navigable river in the United States), so be mindful of wind, waves, and current before committing to open water.

Trip Description

This trip is a gem. From launch to take-out, there's something for every-one: attractive coves, a serene creek and clear-water channel, the chal-lenge of surf and swell on the open ocean, historic forts and lighthouses, a magnificent salt marsh and wildlife refuge tucked into a beautiful har-bor. Did I mention the lobsters?

Launch into Pepperrell Cove, paddling east between Phillips Island and Gooseberry Island into Chauncey Creek. Make your way up the creek past charming waterfront dwellings and the tantalizing Chauncey Creek Lobster Pound (resist the temptation to haul out for a lobster feast. You can reward yourself after the trip!). Continue under a bridge that con-nects the mainland to Gerrish Island. The creek soon broadens into a small cove. Bear left and paddle through the tight culvert beneath the Seapoint Road Bridge.

You're now entering a beautiful tract of protected marsh within the Rachel Carson National Wildlife Refuge. The passage through the refuge

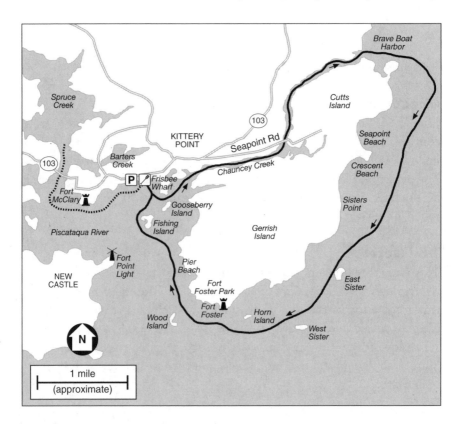

Paddling through a beautiful tract of the Rachel Carson National Wildlife Refuge.

is extraordinary. The creek narrows to a twisting channel of remarkably clear water for about a mile before opening up into Brave Boat Harbor.

Depending on tide and weather, exiting the harbor can be difficult and dangerous (hence, the derivation of the harbor's name). Several reefs line the outer harbor and breaking surf is the norm. The jetty to the south end of the harbor is a good place to beach your boat and scout conditions before attempting a passage.

From the outer harbor, turn southwest and continue down the coast for a beautiful 3-mile stretch of open ocean paddling. You'll pass two long, sandy beaches—Seapoint and Crescent, respectively—before reaching Fort Foster, a former garrison turned town park at the southern point of Gerrish Island. Round the point, paddling between Wood Island (notable for the large, red-roofed structure that once served as a Coast Guard life-saving station) and the large pier jutting out from Gerrish Island. A small beach, just beyond the pier, is a good spot to pull out for a picnic or to explore the fort's World War II bunkers and observation towers.

Beyond the point, Pepperrell Cove and the final leg of the trip are in full view. Paddle northwest along the eastern edge of the Piscataqua River, navigating around a few small islands before reaching the cove and take-out.

Nature and History Notes

From the wharf at Pepperrell Cove, there are sweeping views over mast and sail to the mouth of Portsmouth Harbor and beyond. Sturdy Whaleback Light, Maine's southernmost lighthouse, stands in the distance, guiding seafarers since 1872 through the notoriously squirrelly waters of the Piscataqua River. The green-beaconed lighthouse across the river in New Hampshire fronts historic Fort Constitution, now a U.S. Coast Guard station.

Other Options

An exploration of Spruce Creek (5.0 to 6.0 miles round-trip) is a great alternative when rough seas preclude venturing onto open water. Depart from Pepperrell Cove and turn west, following the shoreline toward Fort McClary. The Fort's hexagonal blockhouse design is easy to spot. Beyond the fort, round Hick's Point and turn north, entering the creek beyond the Route 103 Bridge.

TRIP 12
CAPE PORPOISE ARCHIPELAGO

Difficulty: Moderate
Distance: 10.0 miles round-trip
Estimated Time: 4–5 hours
Location: Kennebunkport/Cape Porpoise
Maps: USGS Kennebunkport
DeLorme *Maine Atlas*, map 3

An exceptional coastal paddle and island tour.

Directions

There are two launch options for this trip. For a fee, you can park and launch from the Kennebunkport Marina (they also rent kayaks) or park and put in at Colony Beach at the mouth of the Kennebunk River. The parking at Colony Beach is free; however, it fills up quickly during summer.

From the center of Kennebunkport, travel north on ME 9 for 0.1 mile. Turn right on Ocean Avenue. Travel 0.5 mile to the Kennebunkport

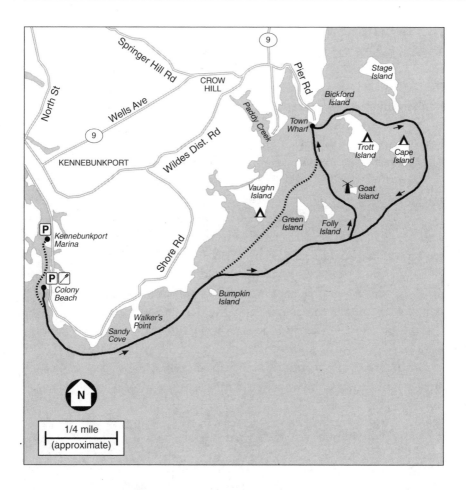

Marina on the right or continue another 0.4 mile to Colony Beach, also on the right, just beyond the Colony Hotel.

Trail Notes

This trip requires calm conditions or sturdy boating skills. Strong wind and seas can produce heavy surf at the mouth of the river and there are numerous ledges outside the archipelago. Time your trip with the top half of the tide as Cape Porpoise Harbor empties at low tide.

Paddlers setting off from the Kennebunkport Marina will have to negotiate potentially strong currents through the jetties at the mouth of the harbor. A departure from Colony Beach avoids this, but may encounter waves breaks at the beachhead.

Keep an eye out for poison ivy if you explore the islands on foot.

Trip Description

The Cape Porpoise Archipelago is an exceptionally beautiful cluster of small islands surrounding one of Southern Maine's most picturesque fishing harbors. Many of the islands are owned and preserved by the Kennebunkport Conservation Trust, which allows considerate day use and overnight camping (permit required). The trip begins in the quaint but tourist-beset village of Kennebunkport and travels along one of Maine's stateliest, exclusive shorelines before reaching the islands.

From the mouth of the Kennebunk River, paddle south then east, tracking the shoreline around Fort Point. Continue past Cape Arundel toward Walker's Point. Walker's Point is, of course, prominent as a seasonal residence of the Bush family. At present, there are no restrictions to recreational boaters passing by the "summer White House"; however, you are certain to invite scrutiny should you venture too close. If the president or former president is actually in residence at the time of your trip, you may have the company of the Secret Service and/or the U.S. Coast Guard as you pass by. Enjoy the opportunity to view the residence, but please exercise an appropriate respect for the owners' privacy.

Beyond the point, continue along the shoreline, passing several other stately homes along the way. At 1.8 mile, you'll approach small, treeless

The beach at the Cape Porpoise town wharf is a good spot to pull out for a break.

Bumpkin Island. There are numerous reefs around the island, so depending on the tide, use care when passing. Also, seals frequent the island to haul out or nurse their pups during the breeding season, so pass at a respectful distance.

Three of the islands that form the archipelago: Vaughn, Green, and Folly, come into view—north to south—just beyond Bumpkin Island. Vaughn is the largest island within the archipelago and an ideal spot for a picnic or camping. Green is a wildlife island, closed to the public during nesting season, April 1–August 30. Swing southeast of Folly Island and enter the mouth of the harbor west of the Goat Island Lighthouse. Alternatively, depending on the tide and current, you can paddle between Vaughn and Green islands toward Cape Porpoise Harbor.

Inside the harbor, there is a small beach to the right of the pier. Haul out here for a break and a bite to eat, or continue on, paddling between Bickford Island and the north tip of Trott Island. This section is not passable at low tide, so time your trip accordingly. On the southeastern side of Trott's, there is a lovely, protected stone beach and camping area. This is a good place to pull out and explore the island.

The trip continues around the northeast point of Cape Island; however, numerous rocks and reefs surround the island and the passage can be hazardous in heavy seas. Scout the conditions before venturing out to open water, or return the way you came. Safely south of Cape Island, turn west, paddle toward Goat Island, carefully cross the harbor entrance, and retrace your path to Kennebunkport.

Nature and History Notes

Goat Island Lighthouse has the distinction of being the last manned lighthouse in Maine. The original 20-foot stone lighthouse was built in 1833. In 1859, the tower was rebuilt and a dwelling added, with a covered walkway connecting the two. But, surly seas and hazardous rocks around the island continued to claim vessels, including 46 between 1865 and 1920. Incredibly, no lives were lost in any of the wrecks, partly due to the lighthouse keepers picking up survivors near the island.

During the blizzard of 1978, the island became partially submerged and the covered walk was blown away. The keeper's wife and two small children took refuge on the second floor of the house. The family was offered a transfer shortly after the ordeal and automation of the lighthouse seemed imminent.

However, when George H. W. Bush came into office in 1988, the Coast Guard decided to use the island as a security station and another keeper was assigned. Military and security helicopters frequently landed on the island, especially when foreign dignitaries visited. Apparently, the president himself would occasionally drop in on the keeper when out fishing from his speedboat. Nonetheless, the light was eventually automated in 1990.

The Kennebunkport Conservation Trust now owns Goat Island and maintains a caretaker there during the summer months. Visitors are not allowed on the island without the Trust's permission.

More Information

The Kennebunkport Marina (207-967-3411) is located at 273 Ocean Avenue, across from the Harbor Watch Inn. Camping and fire permits for the islands are available at the Kennebunkport Police Department at 101 Main Street in Cape Porpoise (207-967-2454). For more information about the islands, visit the Kennebunkport Conservation Trust website at www.kennebunkportconservationtrust.org.

TRIP 13
PORTLAND HARBOR/CASCO BAY

Difficulty: Easy
Distance: 2.5 miles round-trip
Estimated Time: 2–3 hours
Location: Portland
Maps: USGS Portland East
    DeLorme *Maine Atlas*, maps 3 and 5

An enjoyable introduction to the multitude of paddling opportunities in Casco Bay.

Directions

To reach the put-in, take Exit 8 (Washington Avenue/ME 26 south) from I-295 in Portland. From Washington Avenue, turn left onto Eastern Promenade and follow it to Cutter Street, which provides access to the

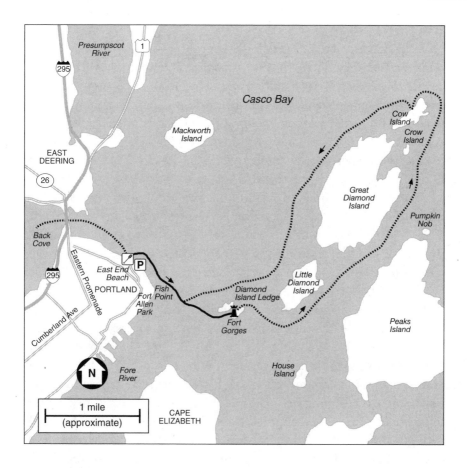

boat ramps and East End Beach. To view the route before launching, continue a short distance past Cutter Street to Fort Allen Park.

Trail Notes

Although this trip avoids the main shipping lanes in Portland Harbor, paddlers should use extreme caution when boating here. The harbor is one of the busiest shipping ports in New England. Major vessels as well as numerous recreational boaters frequent these waters.

For a fee, you can launch from the recreational boat ramp. Alternatively, the put-in is free at East End Beach, southeast of the rest rooms.

Fort Gorges, owned by the City of Portland, is only accessible by small boat. The fort is not maintained, so visitors are advised to enter the fort at their own risk.

Trip Description

An excursion to historic Fort Gorges from the Eastern Promenade is a wonderful introduction to the many paddling opportunities within Casco Bay. The sweeping views overlooking the bay from the Eastern Prom allow you to sight your destination before launching, and the trip plies relatively protected waters, avoiding the major shipping lanes within Portland Harbor. Once at the fort, there are endless nooks and crannies to explore (with care) and excellent views of the city and the entire bay from the fort's third-tier rampart.

From East End Beach, turn southeast and paddle along the shoreline toward Fish Point at the tip of the Eastern Prom. Beyond Fish Point, there is just under a mile of open water to paddle, so check for traffic, then point your bow towards the Fort and paddle away. Fort Gorges sits prominently atop Hog Island Ledge. There is a landing spot on a gravel beach near the fort's main entrance on the north side of the ledge.

Fort Gorges is an impressive, beautifully designed structure featuring elegant stone arches, massive gun casements, an interior courtyard and parade ground. Following the war of 1812, the U.S. Army Corps of Engineers proposed the fortification to support nearby Forts Preble and Scammel. Congress approved funding for the fort in 1857 and construction began the following year. The fort's thick granite walls were designed to be impervious to weaponry used up to that time. However, by 1864, with guns mounted and the fort nearing completion, long-range rifled cannons had already been developed to penetrate such fortifications. Despite attempts at modernization, Congress ultimately abandoned funding for the project in 1876. The fort was never manned.

To return to East End Beach, follow the same route from which you came.

Nature and History Notes

Casco Bay is a large estuary extending from Cape Elizabeth to Cape Small. It is one of 28 estuaries in the nation designated as an "Estuary of National Significance" by the U.S. Environmental Protection Agency. The bay supports more than 800 species of marine life as well as 150 species of waterfowl. The bay has so many islands they are often referred to as the Calendar Isles—one island for every day of the year. In actuality, there are more than 700 islands, islets, and exposed ledges within the bay, many of which are protected from development. Casco Bay marks

The view of Fort Gorges from Portland's Eastern Promenade.

the starting point of the Maine Island Trail (see essay page 81), a 325-mile-long waterway extending downeast to Machias Bay.

Other Options

There are endless opportunities to extend the trip described here. One alternative is to circumnavigate the Diamond Islands with a stop at Cow Island, via the passage between Peaks Island and the Diamonds (8.5 miles). Cow is a 26-acre island owned by the Maine Coast Heritage Trust and open to the public for low-impact recreational use.

Alternatively, time your trip to Fort Gorges with the outgoing tide so that when you return to East End Beach you can catch the incoming tide into Back Cove, a shallow but interesting sanctuary in the heart of the city.

More Information

For extended trip ideas throughout Casco Bay, check out the AMC's *Sea Kayaking Along the New England Coast* by Tamsin Venn. For information about the Maine Island Trail, visit the Maine Island Trail Association website at www.mita.org.

2

Midcoast

MAINE'S MIDCOAST IS A PREMIERE DESTINATION for outdoor enthusiasts. The exceptionally beautiful and intricate coastline provides an inexhaustible resource for paddlers, while the region's inland hills and magnificent islands offer outstanding hiking and biking opportunities. Here, the state's largest rivers—the Kennebec and Androscoggin—flow into the Gulf of Maine at Merrymeeting Bay (Trip 21), home to abundant waterfowl and the endangered short-nose sturgeon. Farther east, the "mountains meet the sea" in dramatic fashion above beautiful Penobscot Bay, Maine's largest bay. Featured trips in this region include outstanding hiking on Monhegan Island (Trip 14), a variety of trips within the Camden Hills (Trips 15, 16, and 18), a paddle to historic Eagle Island (Trip 22), and a kayaking excursion from the AMC's Knubble Bay Camp (Trip 23).

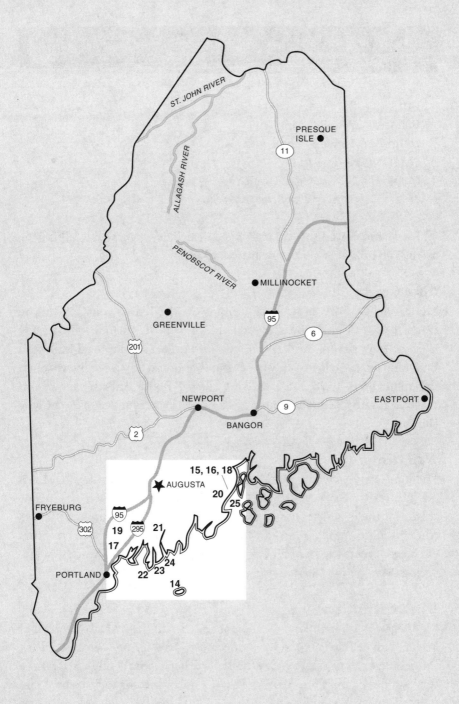

ST. JOHN RIVER

ALLAGASH RIVER

PENOBSCOT RIVER

PRESQUE
ISLE ●

11

MILLINOCKET ●

● GREENVILLE

95

6

201

NEWPORT

9

EASTPORT ●

BANGOR

2

15, 16, 18

★ AUGUSTA

20

25

FRYEBURG
●

95

19

295

21

302

17

24

PORTLAND ●

22   23

14

TRIP 14
MONHEGAN ISLAND

Difficulty: Easy to moderate
Distance: 3.0-mile loop
Estimated Time: 2–3 hours
Location: Monhegan
Maps: USGS Monhegan Island
    DeLorme *Maine Atlas*, map 8

From enchanted forests to rugged sea cliffs, spectacular hiking on one of Maine's most beautiful islands.

Directions

Monhegan Island is located 12.0 miles off the Maine coast. It can be reached via passenger boat from a choice of ports including Boothbay Harbor, New Harbor, and Port Clyde. From Port Clyde, the Monhegan Boat Line departs thrice daily in season (Memorial Day weekend through Columbus Day). To reach Port Clyde, take US Route 1 north past Thomaston to Route 131. Drive south on Route 131 for 14 miles to Port Clyde Harbor.

Trail Notes

There are nearly twenty trails on Monhegan Island with abundant opportunities to design your own trip. Trail maps are available at the few stores on the island or any of the several small hotels and guesthouses (there is no camping allowed). Because of the heavy influx of visitors during summer, the best time to explore Monhegan is definitely in late spring (May) or fall (September and October).

Trip Description

Monhegan is arguably one of the most enchanting destinations in all of Maine. Full of charm, yet devoid of pretense, the island seems to reflect the character of the state more than any other place. Though little more than a mile square, there are more than 7 miles of trails to discover, from quiet, captivating forest walks to rugged cliff jaunts with spectacular seaward views.

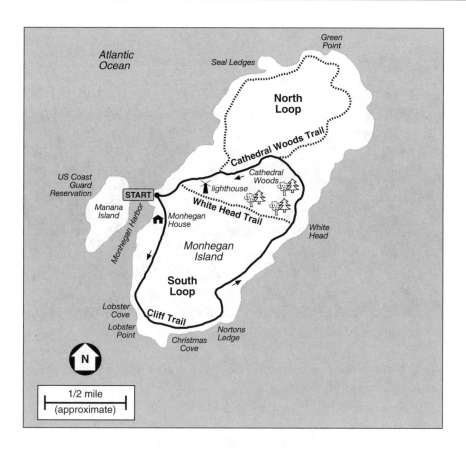

There are two major loops on the island including South Loop, which takes in Lobster Cove, Christmas Cove, Burnt Head, and White Head. The North Loop passes through a serene forest before emerging on Black Head and continuing around the island's northern reaches. This trip combines portions of both loops for a 3-mile exploration of Monhegan's most beautiful destinations.

Depart from the village, walking south past the Monhegan House and up the hill. The road passes several houses before turning to a grassy double-track trail, ending above Lobster Cove with expansive views westward. From here, locate Trail 1, the Cliff Trail, and travel south then east along the shoreline past Christmas Cove and Nortons Ledge toward Gull Rock.

The trail then follows the shoreline, climbs over open ledge and in and out of a weathered forest of spruce and balsam, passing Trails 3 (Underhill) and 4 (Burnt Head) along the way. The path continues around Gull Cove, passing Trails 6 and 1A before climbing to the height of land at

The cliff trails on Monhegan Island provide spectacular seaward views.

White Head. The views from this 160-foot perch over the seaward side of the island are simply spectacular.

To shorten the trip from here, you can take the White Head Trail (7) across the island, past Monhegan Lighthouse and back to the village. Otherwise, rest up, soak in the views, and continue on, following the Cliff Trail (1) north and east toward Little White Head.

The trail traces the height of land, passes the eastern end of Trail 1A, then turns inland. At approximately 2 miles, Trail 1 meets Trail 11, the Cathedral Woods Trail. Turn left (west) here. The path through this majestic, virgin stand of red spruce, balsam, and pine is nothing less than serene. Quietude abounds. As you walk, look closely for fairy houses at the base of trees. Islanders have been building them here for generations.

Emerging from Cathedral Woods, the trail ends at a junction with a tree-shaded gravel road. Turn left here and follow the path back to the village, or turn right and explore the north end of the island via the North Loop.

Nature and History Notes

Although Monhegan has been a popular artist's colony for more than a hundred years, its true heritage belongs to the mariners who have been working its fertile fishing grounds for centuries. In fact, some historians suggest that Viking sailors first visited the area as early as 1100. The theory derives from strange inscriptions found on Manana, Monhegan's sister island.

Whatever the case, European mariners had certainly arrived by the fifteenth century. By the seventeenth century, however, the French and British contested the island and, during the 1700s, Monhegan was all but abandoned and became a base of operation for pirates. Eventually, the island fell into private hands and was bought and sold several times. By 1824, just four years after Maine achieved statehood, the island's importance as a landfall for ships was substantiated when the Monhegan Lighthouse was built.

Today, Monhegan is home to roughly 75 year-round residents, many of whom work its fishing banks. But that number often swells to more than 1,200 in summer, when part-time residents, artists, and day-trippers arrive.

More Information

For information or to make reservations on Monhegan Boat Line, call 207-372-8848 or visit their website at www.monheganboat.com.

TRIP 15
MAIDEN CLIFF LOOP

Difficulty: Moderate
Distance: 2.0-mile loop
Estimated Time: 2 hours
Location: Camden
Maps: USGS Camden
　　　　　AMC's *Maine Mountain Guide*, 9th ed., map 4
　　　　　Camden Hills State Park Map
　　　　　DeLorme *Maine Atlas*, map 14

Magnificent views from a stunning precipice above Megunticook Lake.

Directions

To reach the Maiden Cliff trailhead, take Route 52 (Mountain Road) from US 1 just north of downtown Camden. The parking area and trailhead are 2.9 miles from US 1, adjacent to the southern end of Megunticook Lake.

Trail Notes

This short, moderately steep climb is one of the finest hikes in Camden Hills. It can also be combined with the Ridge, Tableland, and Mount Battie trails for an excellent point-to-point traverse. For additional trip options, refer to the AMC's *Maine Mountain Guide*, 9th ed., or pick up a map at Camden Hills State Park headquarters.

Be sure to carry plenty of water when hiking here, as there is no reliable water supply within the park.

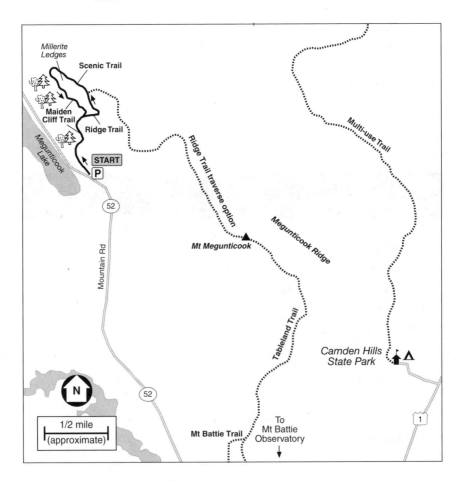

Trip Description

Justifiably described as "The Jewel of the Maine Coast," Camden (along with its sister towns of Rockport and Lincolnville) is second only to Acadia National Park as Maine's premiere destination for multi-sport adventures (see Trips 16, 18, and 24). Situated between the highest mainland mountain range on the Atlantic coast, and beautiful Penobscot Bay, the setting is an outdoor enthusiast's dream. This trip, with its sheer ledges and amazing views over Megunticook Lake, is an excellent introduction to some of the outstanding hiking the area has to offer.

From the parking area on ME 52, the Maiden Cliff Trail enters the woods beneath the dramatic rock face rising 700 vertical feet above the lake. The trail ascends steadily on an old logging road now shaded by a deciduous forest of mostly birch and beech trees. After crossing two small brooks, the trail continues climbing to the north and east beneath beautiful woods that are particularly attractive in fall. At 0.5 mile, you'll reach a trail junction. Bear right (east) here onto the Ridge Trail and begin the 0.3-mile climb to gain the ridge and reach the Scenic Trail. As you surmount the increasingly open ledges, there are excellent views overlooking the Megunticook Ridge and beyond to the Atlantic Ocean.

Megunticook Lake sparkles beneath the outlook atop Maiden Cliff.

At 0.8 mile, you reach a junction where the Ridge Trail turns south and the Scenic Trail turns sharply to the northwest (left). Follow the Scenic Trail over exposed Millerite Ledges as it makes its way to a junction with the Maiden Cliff Trail. Following the white blazes, the trail turns west and makes a slight descent to reach Maiden Cliff. A side path to the right descends to the open ledges high above the lake. Here you'll find a large white cross tethered to the edge of the cliff marking the point where 12-year-old Elenora French fell to her premature death in May 1864.

There are excellent places here to rest and enjoy the views. Across the lake, to the southwest rise Bald and Ragged mountains. Both mountains are within the Camden Hills range, have excellent views from their respective summits, and are well worth a visit. They are also part of a wonderful trail system called the Georges Highland Path, an extensive network of conservation trails within the Georges River watershed.

To make the return trip and complete the loop, return to the Scenic Trail/Maiden Cliff junction and turn south onto the Maiden Cliff Trail. The trail rises briefly along the ridge before descending into the woods, following a few switchbacks before reaching the Ridge Trail junction you took earlier. Continue down the Maiden Cliff Trail, crossing the brook and reaching the parking lot at 0.5 mile from the junction.

Nature and History Notes

According to the stone memorial atop Maiden Cliff, legend has it that Elenora French was a member of a "maying party" and fell to her death trying to catch her wind-blown hat.

Elenora's sister provided a more detailed account of the tragedy in an article (excerpted here) that appeared in *The Camden Herald* in 1915:

That day myself and the school teacher, Miss Hartshorn, were getting ready to drive to Lincolnville Center to see some friends, when little Elenora coaxed her mother to let her go with us. After dinner a young man, Randall Young, invited us to go up the mountain, and the four of us climbed Megunticook from the Lincolnville side.

We did not realize we were over the boldest cliff on the rock until Mr. Young told us so, and he said he would find a big rock and roll it down over. While he was looking for a rock, Miss Hartshorn and I were sitting down and little Elenora was rambling around us.

I remember exactly how she looked. Her hat had blown off and with it the net, and when I last saw her she was sitting on a rock near the edge of the cliff putting on her net. I turned to speak to Miss Hartshorn. I heard a scream. I looked where Elenora had been sitting and she was gone.

We were dazed for a moment and then ran to the edge of the cliff, but could not get near enough to look over. Mr. Young climbed down the face of the cliff to where Elenora had landed, nearly 300 feet they say from where she fell.

She was still alive and not a bone broken, but she was injured internally and died at 12:30 that night. I do not know how my sister came to fall. I shall always think that a puff of wind took her hat, and she fell over going after it.

More Information

For hiking and camping information within Camden Hills State Park, contact 207-941-4014 or visit www.state.me.us/doc/parks. For trail information about the Georges Highland Path, visit the Georges River Land Trust website at www.grlt.org. Maps are available at most trailheads.

TRIP 16
BALD ROCK MOUNTAIN

Difficulty: Easy to moderate
Distance: 3.6 miles round-trip
Estimated Time: 3 hours
Location: Camden
Maps: USGS Lincolnville
  AMC's *Maine Mountain Guide*, 9th ed., map 4
  Camden Hills State Park map
  DeLorme *Maine Atlas*, map 14

An excellent summit hike to open ledges with magnificent views overlooking Penobscot Bay.

Directions

To reach the trailhead, take Route 52 (Mountain Road) from US 1 just north from the center of Camden. At 4.6 miles, you'll reach the junction of Youngtown Road. Turn right on Youngtown Road and drive 2.6 miles to the trailhead at Stevens Corner.

Alternatively, depart from US 1 in Lincolnville (4.0 miles north of Camden) onto ME 173. Drive west for 2.3 miles and bear left at Youngtown Road. The parking area is immediately on the left.

Trail Notes

This trip approaches Camden Hills from the less visited north end of the park, avoiding some of the inevitable summer crowds. From the trailhead, a multi-use path bisects the park, accessing several trails and providing an opportunity to link trails for a longer point-to-point traverse. For additional trip options, refer to AMC's *Maine Mountain Guide*, 9th ed., or pick up a map from park headquarters.

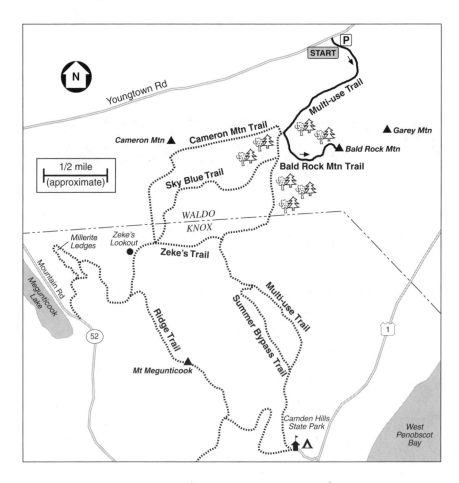

Enjoying the views from the summit of Bald Rock Mountain.

Be sure to carry plenty of water when hiking here, as there is no reliable water supply within the park.

Trip Description

Bald Rock Mountain's open, ledgy summit provides some of the best views within Camden Hills State Park. On a clear day, there are sweeping vistas of West Penobscot Bay from east of Camden to Deer Isle. At 1,100 feet, it is among the highest mountains in the park, yet the modest grade to the top makes it a perfect hike for families.

From the trailhead at Youngtown Road, follow the wide path known as the Multi-use Trail (11 on the park map) into the woods, heading south and west. This trail bisects the park and, when connected with the Summer Bypass Trail (20), is a fine (though challenging) way to explore the park on mountain bike (see Trip 18).

The path cuts through a nice stand of mixed hardwoods, ascending gradually to an elevation of 600 feet. At 1.3 miles, the path reaches a junction with the Bald Rock Mountain Trail departing to the left and the Cameron Mountain Trail on the right. Turn left here and begin the enjoyable 0.5-mile ascent to Bald Rock's summit ledges. The trail, once an old tote road, departs south and east through a cluster of tall pine trees. The path continues to rise steadily, winding over a succession of ridges and through attractive woods, before turning north then east.

At 1.7 miles, the trail turns due east and rises through a stand of conifers to the open ledges.

The views from the summit are magnificent. Vinalhaven sits southeast, Isleboro and North Isleboro to the northeast, and, on a clear day, Deer Isle can be spotted due east. An old shelter, adjacent to the summit ledges, is suitable for camping should you want to enjoy a sunrise from this magnificent vista.

To return, retrace your steps to the Multi-use Trail and turn north (right) for the 1.3-mile walk back to the parking lot.

Nature and History Notes

Camden Hills State Park was created during the Depression Era when the federal government instituted a program to develop state park systems nationwide. In the 1930s, the government purchased the area's farmland to help local farmers whose land was no longer productive. The park was designed by local landscape architect Hans Heistad and constructed by a Civilian Conservation Corps crew under the supervision of the National Park Service. The park is now one of the state's most popular areas with 5,700 acres, more than 30 miles of trails and full-service camping facilities.

Other Options

For an excellent point-to-point traverse, return to the Multi-use Trail after climbing Bald Rock Mountain, turn left and follow the path to the Sky Blue Trail (right). Take Sky Blue to Zeke's Trail (be sure to enjoy the views from Zeke's Lookout) and then onto the Ridge Trail. From here, you can turn left and traverse Megunticook Ridge to the campground or Camden Village, or turn right and follow the ridge to Maiden Cliff.

More Information

Camden Hills State Park is accessible to visitors year-round during daylight hours. The camping area is open May 15 through October 15. For more information, or to reserve a site, call 207-236-3109 or visit www.state.me.us/doc/parks.

TRIP 17
BRADBURY MOUNTAIN STATE PARK

Aerobic Difficulty: Moderate
Technical Difficulty: Easy to difficult
Distance: 6.5-mile loop
Estimated Time: 2–3 hours
Location: Pownal
Maps: USGS North Pownal
       DeLorme *Maine Atlas*, map 5

Fun, challenging riding, minutes from downtown Freeport, with excellent trails and beautiful summit views.

Directions
From I-295 in Freeport, take Exit 22. Turn north onto ME 125/136 and follow 0.1 mile to the T-intersection. Turn left onto Pownal Road and drive 4.0 miles to the four-way intersection with the blinking light at Pownal Center. Turn right here onto ME 9 and drive 0.5 mile to the park entrance on the left.

Trail Notes
The extensive network of trails on and around Bradbury Mountain has become a prime destination for mountain bikers. Please support the efforts of the park staff and many volunteers who have worked to make this a great place to ride by staying on bike-specific trails and using appropriate trail etiquette.

Trip Description
Bradbury Mountain was one of Maine's original state parks and the first to welcome mountain bikers. Today, the nearly 600-acre park has a wonderful system of diverse trails accessible to riders of every level. This ride features a beautiful woods loop, a brisk ascent to the mountain's 485-foot summit, and a challenging, technical descent.

Begin at the trail kiosk located in the northeast parking lot, next to the athletic field. You'll be returning to this spot to ascend the mountain, but first, turn south and follow the path known as the Link Trail,

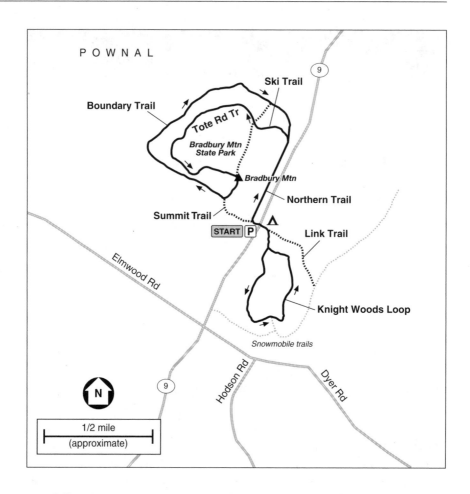

POWNAL

Ski Trail

Boundary Trail

Tote Rd Tr

Bradbury Mtn
State Park

Bradbury Mtn

Northern Trail

Summit Trail

START P

Link Trail

Knight Woods Loop

Snowmobile trails

Elmwood Rd

Hodson Rd

Dyer Rd

N

1/2 mile
(approximate)

carefully crossing Route 9 to reach the Knight Woods Trail. This fun, beautiful loop is suitable for all levels of riders and provides a good warm-up for the climb to the summit.

You can ride the loop in either direction, however, I suggest staying right at the trailhead and following the easier half-mile double-track section first. Acquired in 1991, Knight Woods is a beautiful, 100-acre tract of shaded forest. Along the route, the park has placed educational kiosks explaining local flora and fauna. At 0.6 mile, a snowmobile trail enters on the right. Stay left, following the white blazes as the path swings east and then north, completing the loop at 1.2 miles.

For the ride to the summit, retrace your route back across Route 9 to the trail kiosk next to the ball field. From here, pick up the blue-blazed

An old cattle pound along the Northern Trail at Bradbury Mountain State Park.

Northern Trail heading east and north. The path parallels Route 9 briefly, crosses several water bars, and passes a remnant "cattle pound" before turning north and west. At 1.0 mile, turn left onto the Ski Trail and begin a short climb to a four-way intersection with the Northern Trail and the Tote Road Trail. Continue straight onto the white-blazed Tote Road Trail as it winds around the northwest side of the mountain to the open summit.

To descend the mountain, you can retrace your route, follow the Northern Trail to the bottom, or pick up the more difficult Boundary Trail, described here. Marked with orange blazes, the Boundary Trail begins with a short, southeast descent from the summit over challenging terrain of loose rocks and exposed roots before reaching a sharp corner at a stone fence. Turn right here, and follow the Boundary Trail as it parallels the stone fence along the park's outer edge. The descent is sustained and tricky in spots, but otherwise straightforward.

As you descend, you'll pass a couple of spur trails on that connect to the Tote Road Trail. Continue on the Boundary Trail, crossing two small brooks, until you reach the Northern Trail junction. Stay left here to return to the parking lot and complete the descent.

Nature and History Notes

There are great views to the coast from Bradbury Mountain's glacier-sculpted, 485-foot summit and wonderful opportunities to observe hawks riding thermals during fall migration.

The cattle pound near Route 9 was built around 1800 to hold stray cattle, sheep, and pigs. The animals were held there until "picked up by their owners upon payment of poundage."

More Information

Most trails at Bradbury Mountain State Park are open to hikers, bikers, horseback riders, cross-country skiers, and snowmobiles in winter. The park also allows camping at its 41-site primitive campground. For more information, call 207-624-6080.

TRIP 18
CAMDEN HILLS STATE PARK

Aerobic Difficulty: Moderate
Technical Difficulty: Moderate with difficult sections
Distance: 10.5 miles round-trip
Estimated Time: 3 hours
Location: Camden and Lincolnville
Maps: USGS Lincolnville
  AMC's *Maine Mountain Guide*, 9th ed., map 4
  Camden Hills State Park map
  DeLorme *Maine Atlas*, map 14

A great ride through the heart of the park on a challenging multi-use trail, with a difficult section of single-track.

Directions

From downtown Camden, follow US 1 north for 2.0 miles to Camden Hills State Park. To reach the alternate start, take ME 52 (Mountain Road) from US 1 just north from the center of Camden. At 4.6 miles, you'll reach the junction of Youngtown Road. Turn right on Youngtown Road and drive 2.6 miles to the trailhead at Stevens Corner.

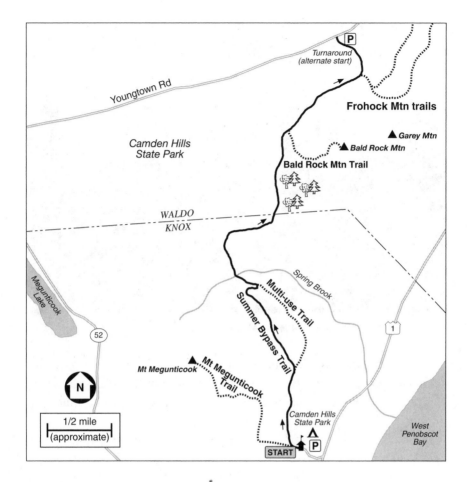

Trail Notes

Although this ride has little overall elevation gain, both its duration and degree of difficulty require a good level of fitness and bike-handling capabilities. To avoid the most challenging sections of the trip (especially, the Summer Bypass Trail), begin from the alternate start on Youngtown Road and follow the Multi-use Trail for an enjoyable out-and-back ride on the easier going gravel road.

Trip Description

Mountain biking is a great way to enjoy Camden Hills State Park. The Multi-use Trail extends from the park's campground to its northeastern reaches, providing miles of scenic, challenging riding and opportunities to link a bike trip with a summit hike. This trip covers the length of the

Fall riding on the Multi-use Trail at Camden Hills State Park.

trail from difficult single-track cut specifically for mountain bikers to smoother-going gravel paths. Depending upon your time and inclination, you can begin the trip from either end, ride point to point (5.3 miles), or out and back as described here.

From the parking area next to the park's check-in station, begin riding up the paved road toward the campground, following the signs for the Mount Megunticook and Multi-use trails. From the trailhead, the Mount Megunticook Trail (10 on the park map) turns left, and the white-blazed, Multi-use Trail (11) veers right toward a green water tower. Follow the trail around the tower and continue for about 1 mile of intermediate riding to reach the Summer Bypass Trail (20) on the left.

The Summer Bypass Trail was designed and cut by local riders in cooperation with park staff to avoid low-lying, water-prone sections of the Multi-use Trail. The terrain here is tight, twisty, and technical, hugging the northeast slope of Mount Megunticook over loose rocks, exposed roots, and runoff brooks, providing a thorough challenge for any rider.

At 2.2 miles, the Summer Bypass Trail rejoins the Multi-use Trail. Turn left here and enjoy more relaxed riding. Soon, you'll cross Spring Brook, pass the remains of an old cross-country ski shelter and, at 4.0 miles, reach the Bald Rock Mountain trailhead. Continue on the Multi-use Trail, over relatively smooth double-track to reach the Youngtown Road trailhead at 5.3 miles.

From here, turn around and retrace your path back to the campground.

Other Options

At the time of this writing, a new biking trail was being developed from the Frohock Mountain trailhead at the Youngtown Road end of the park. Riders who start from this end may enjoy combining this route with portions of the Multi-use Trail. Check with park staff for details.

TRIP 19
RUNAROUND POND

Difficulty: Easy
Distance: 4.0–7.0 miles round-trip
Estimated Time: 3–4 hours
Location: Durham
Map: USGS North Pownal
        DeLorme *Maine Atlas*, map 5

Quiet paddling on a beautiful, serpentine pond, teeming with wildlife, near Freeport.

Directions

From I-295 in Freeport, take Exit 22. Turn north onto ME 125/136 and follow 0.1 mile to the T-intersection. Turn left onto Pownal Road and drive 4.0 miles to the four-way intersection with the blinking light at Pownal Center. Turn right here onto ME 9, passing Bradbury Mountain State Park and continuing for another 3.0 miles to West Durham and Runaround Pond Road. Turn left and continue for approximately 1 mile to the parking lot and put-in.

Trip Description

This is a pleasant paddle to plan around a trip to Freeport or to link with a bike outing at Bradbury Mountain State Park (Trip 17). The pond is composed of two shallow, riverlike tributaries, both inviting and worth

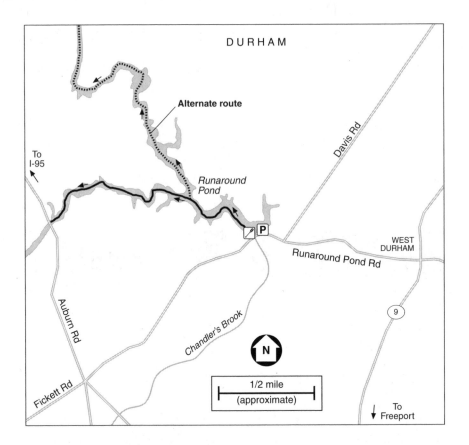

exploration. When I paddled here in early fall, I had the place to myself except for the beavers, osprey, kingfishers, herons, turtles, and numerous other wildlife that reside here.

From the put-in, stay left and begin paddling up the main channel. Because the pond is shallow, there are abundant varieties of colorful, aquatic plants growing here, including pickerelweed, water lily, pond lily, and bladderwort. The forested shoreline remains largely undeveloped and dense with beautiful trees including, pines, balsam, maple, and oak.

About 0.5 mile into the trip, the pond forks into two meandering streams. Both channels are similar in length, character, and beauty, though the right tributary is somewhat narrower and thicker with aquatic vegetation. The left channel, described here, is more exposed to wind, but also appeared to be more active with wildlife.

Turning west, paddle into an open body of water punctuated by a few inviting coves on the left. Interestingly, along this section of the pond,

A calm morning at Runaround Pond.

I counted more than half a dozen beaver lodges. Also, the day I paddled here, I observed several ospreys soaring overhead, or perched high above the shoreline scanning the pond for a meal.

Soon, the channel rounds a bend, narrows, and continues to meander along in a westward direction. At 1.75 miles from the put-in, the gap closes and reaches Auburn Road. Turn around here, making your way back to the fork to explore the right channel, or continue back to the put-in.

Nature and History Notes

Runaround Pond was created when Chandler's Brook was dammed in the eighteenth century. The water was harnessed to power a sawmill built to supply lumber to the coastal boat-building industry centered in Yarmouth and Freeport. Apparently, the pond's name derives from the overflow of water that spilled around either side of the dam, known as the "run round."

More Information

Additional information about this paddle can be found in the AMC's guidebook *Quiet Water Maine*.

TRIP 20
MEGUNTICOOK LAKE/FERNALD'S NECK PRESERVE

Difficulty: Easy
Distance: 3.0–7.0 miles round-trip
Estimated Time: 3–4 hours
Location: Camden
Maps: USGS Camden
    DeLorme *Maine Atlas*, map 14

**Picturesque paddling beneath the Camden Hills with a side
trip to a beautiful nature preserve.**

Directions

A boat launch is conveniently located adjacent to the Maiden Cliff Trailhead (Trip 15). From US 1 in Camden, take Route 52 (Mountain Road)
north for 2.9 miles. The launch and parking area are on the left, just beyond the southern end of the lake. For easier access to the western side
of the lake, put in at the public boat launch on Route 105, 3.5 miles from
downtown Camden.

Trip Description

With its stunning backdrop and attractive shoreline, Megunticook Lake
is a wonderful place to enjoy a leisurely paddle, especially after a hike up
Maiden's Cliff (Trip 15). On this trip, we'll paddle from beneath Maiden's
steep precipice on Megunticook's eastern shore and explore Fernald's
Neck, a wild and beautiful 315-acre Nature Conservancy Preserve that
juts into the heart of the lake.

From the boat launch, paddle north and west, paralleling Route 52
and the steep cliffs on your right. A couple of small, beautiful islands
lay ahead. Stay west here and turn towards larger Crane Island on your
left. Round Crane's northern tip and continue paddling west to reach the
eastern shore of Fernald's Neck.

There are nearly 3-miles of protected shoreline to explore around the
Neck. The cliffs along the western shore are particularly attractive. First,
though, turn north and track along the more wooded eastern shoreline.
Keep your eyes peeled for an unmarked trail about 0.1 mile beyond Crane

Island. You're searching for the short path to Balance Rock, a massive boulder that is a striking example of a glacial erratic. The trail lies just to the south of a large cove. From Balance Rock, you can continue inland to explore more of the preserve's beautiful trails.

Otherwise, return to your boat and make your way around the neck's southern tip. There are wonderful granite ledges along this section that make ideal spots to pull out, enjoy a picnic, or take in the beautiful views of Mount Megunticook.

Continuing around to the western shore, you'll come upon dramatic cliffs that, at points, rise more than 60 feet above the water. Farther along, a cove on the right fronts Great Bog, a part of the preserve rich in aquatic plants and bird life.

As you reach the end of Fernald's, you come to Wiley Neck and Narrows Island. You can continue here, looping around Kelly Island farther

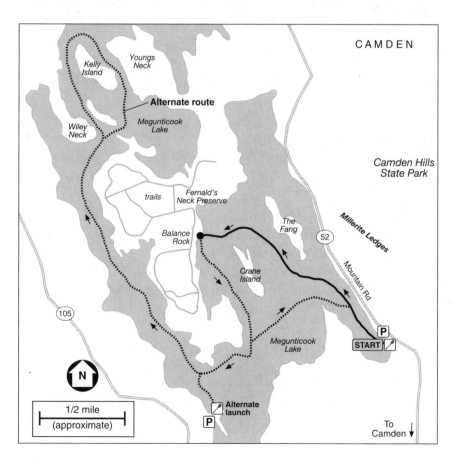

Balance Rock, a glacial erratic at Fernald's Neck Preserve.

still, or turn around and make your way around the southern tip of Fernald's and back to the put-in.

Nature and History Notes

Glacial erratics are common throughout New England and form part of the story of how this landscape was shaped. They can range in size from pebbles to massive boulders, like Balance Rock. An erratic is identified by the rock surrounding it as much as the rock itself. During the last Ice Age, advancing glaciers tore away chunks of bedrock. When the ice melted and the glaciers retreated thousands of years later, the erratics were left stranded in areas of different bedrock composition. The glaciers came and went at least four times in New England, leaving behind the erratics as well as Megunticook Lake and the beautifully sculpted Camden Hills.

Other Options

To explore Fernald's Neck Preserve on foot, drive north on Route 52 to Youngtown Corner. Just past the corner, turn left onto Fernald's Neck Road. Follow Fernald's Neck Road (which changes to dirt), bearing left at the fork (look for the TNC sign here). Continue into the hayfield to the parking area.

More Information

To learn more about Fernald's Neck Preserve, contact the Maine Chapter of The Nature Conservancy at 207-729-5181.

TRIP 21
MERRYMEETING BAY/SWAN ISLAND

Difficulty: Easy to moderate
Distance: 4.0 miles round-trip or 10.0-mile loop
Estimated Time: 3–5 hours
Location: Richmond
Maps: USGS Richmond
　　　　DeLorme *Maine Atlas*, maps 6 and 12

Excellent paddling on the Kennebec River at the head of Merry-meeting Bay with an excursion to beautiful Swan Island.

Directions

Take I-95 north to Exit 26 (Richmond/Litchfield). At the exit, turn right onto Route 197 and drive 3.5 miles to Richmond's town center. At the junction of Routes 24 (Front Street) and 197, turn left and then right to the town landing.

Trail Notes

There are 5-to-7-foot tidal fluctuations around Swan Island and currents can be swift through the narrows around either side. Planning your trip with the tide in mind will save you time and precious energy, especially if you intend to circumnavigate the island.

The Maine Department of Inland Fisheries and Wildlife limits access to Swan Island. Reservations and a (small) fee are required for day-use or camping. The department also provides ferry service (by reservation) to the island, located next to the Richmond town landing, for hikers, bikers, and campers.

Trip Description

This is one of my favorite discoveries in Maine. The paddling is relatively protected, the bay provides endless opportunities for exploration, and Swan Island is truly a nature lover's paradise. Add to that, options for camping and biking and the real possibility of sighting prehistoric-looking sturgeons unexpectedly leaping from the water in front of your bow, and you'll begin to understand my affinity for the place.

This excursion begins from the town landing in Richmond. Next to the all-tide boat ramp, you'll find the helpful folks at Kennebec Tidewater, an outfitter and guide service that rents bikes, boats, and even camping gear, and can provide you with additional information regarding trip options, local tide, etc.

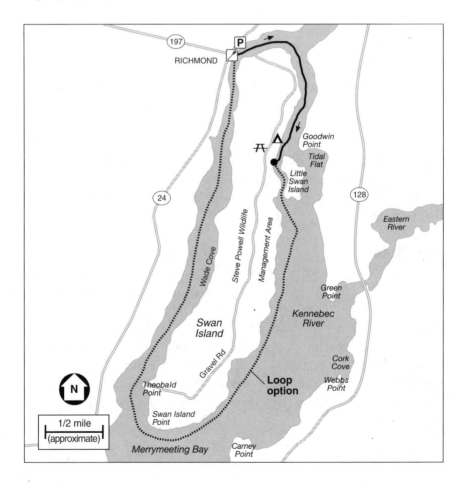

With your bow in the mighty Kennebec River, Swan Island seems close enough to touch. However, unless you take the ferry, the only authorized landing spot is on the eastern side of the island. Consider the tide and your level of interest in circumnavigating the island (10.0 miles) to determine the direction you take to get there. The short route, described here, can be paddled against a moderate tide, and is about 2 miles long. The southern route around Swan Island Point is 8.0 miles long, but you can scoot along on the lower half of an outgoing tide and ply your way north on the slack tide without too much effort.

Turning northeast, check for boat traffic and set off with a strong ferry to reach the island's western shore. Give yourself a wide berth around the northern tip of the island, as there are shallow sections and potentially strong crosscurrents. Turning south now, paddle downriver, staying close to the island's eastern shoreline. At approximately 1.7 miles, you'll approach Little Swan Island. Stay right here and enter the Little River. On the main island to the right, you'll see an open field with a few buildings clustered around its southern end. This is the access to the camping and picnic area and your pull-out to explore the island. Be sure to pull your boat out far enough that an incoming tide doesn't whisk it away!

There are miles of excellent trails to explore on Swan Island.

After enjoying the island, you can retrace your route back to Richmond, or continue down the Little River, paddling around the southern tip of the island and then upriver to the put-in. Either way, be sure to explore the section between the two Swans; it's beautiful, protected, and a great spot to enjoy a refreshing swim.

Nature and History Notes

The Steve Powell Wildlife Management Area encompasses over 1,700 acres of land including Swan Island, Little Swan, and surrounding tidal flats. The area is also a game preserve, providing refuge for migrating waterfowl and a beautiful herd of resident white-tailed deer. The abundant wildlife here, including deer, bald eagles, wild turkeys, and a host of other species are often visible and easily spotted along the network of trails that connect to the 4.5-mile gravel road that runs down the center of the main island. Recently, an observation tower was erected in one of the prime wildlife viewing areas in honor of the late Bill Silliker, Jr., one of Maine's best-known wildlife photographers.

There are ten campsites on the island featuring Adirondack-style shelters, fire pits, and picnic tables. The remnant buildings here are relics from what was once Perkins Township. Today, the remaining structures and the entire island are on the National Register of Historic Places.

The shortnose sturgeon, an ancient, federally (though, not state) endangered species, predates the dinosaur. It can be found in several Maine Rivers, especially the Kennebec. They are primitive-looking fish, with rows of bony, armor-like plates on their sides and a skeleton of cartilage rather than bones. Sturgeons are bottom-feeders; they suck plants and animals into their tube-like mouths. Like salmon, they are anadromous fish, returning to their natal rivers to spawn. When ready to spawn, the sturgeon migrate upstream and deposit their eggs over gravelly or rocky river bottoms in moderately deep water with strong current. Though rarely reaching more than 3 feet long, their cousins, the Atlantic sturgeon, also thrive here and can grow up to 7 feet long.

More Information

To learn more about Swan Island and the Steve Powell Wildlife Management Area or to reserve a campsite, contact the Maine Department of Inland Fisheries and Wildlife at 207-547-5322. Kennebec Tidewater can be reached at 207-737-2112.

Maine Island Trail

The 325-mile-long Maine Island Trail encompasses more than 100 islands, many of which remain wild and undeveloped, along a diverse and beautiful pathway that extends from Casco Bay to the Canadian Maritimes. The Maine Island Trail Association (MITA) manages the islands as well as mainland sites along the trail, and is the largest water trail organization in North America. MITA was "founded on the belief that recreational visitors can and should serve as stewards of Maine's wild islands."

The notion of a water trail along the Maine coast was initially conceived in the 1970s after a survey determined that the state held title to well over a thousand unclaimed islands, rocks, ledges, and water bars. A decade later, the state contracted the Island Institute to evaluate the recreational potential of these holdings. Forty of the islands were identified with the potential to support recreational access. By 1987, these islands became the inspiration for the nation's first formalized recreational water trail.

A year later, MITA was formed under the auspices of the Island Institute to manage the islands and encourage thoughtful, active stewardship through volunteer support and membership. In 1993, MITA became its own independent entity, and today, there are more than 138 islands and mainland sites along the trail supported by nearly 4,000 association members and hundreds of volunteers. MITA remains a model for similar organizations that support access to natural settings, but also strive to protect and conserve these ecological and cultural resources.

In addition to preserving Maine's coastal heritage, another benefit of membership to MITA is the opportunity to access many privately owned islands and mainland sites. Of the 138 islands along the Maine Island Trail, nearly half are privately owned. A cooperative partnership between MITA and landowners, supported by trust, stewardship, and respect for privacy, has sustained the trail's growth and new opportunities for exploration. Several private, non-profit organizations, including the Appalachian Mountain Club, have also provided MITA members access to their properties. Like the trail itself, these arrangements

Burnt Island lighthouse along the Maine Island Trail.

are fluid and change from year to year, with new islands added and others removed due to ownership transfers, sensitivity to nesting and wildlife habitat, or other circumstances.

MITA also provides members with the annual *Guidebook and Stewardship Handbook*, which provides a wealth of information about the trail, including stewardship responsibilities, coastal geology, flora and fauna, and detailed descriptions of the islands. The handbook is an essential companion for trip-planning, understanding the MITA mission, and discovering the vast opportunities available to boaters venturing onto Maine's coastal waters. For more information about the Maine Island Trail, or to become a MITA member, contact MITA at 207-761-8225 or visit the MITA website at www.mita.org.

TRIP 22
EAGLE ISLAND

Difficulty: Easy to moderate
Distance: 4.0 miles round-trip
Estimated Time: 3–4 hours
Location: Eastern Casco Bay
Maps: USGS South Harpswell
         DeLorme *Maine Atlas*, map 6

A short paddle to a beautiful island and the former summer home of Arctic explorer Admiral Robert Peary.

Directions
The launch site is located at Dolphin Marina in South Harpswell. From US 1 in Brunswick, take Route 123 south down Harpswell Neck for 11.7 miles. At the West Harpswell School, turn right onto Ash Point Road. Follow Ash Point Road for 0.2 mile to Basin Point Road. Turn right and continue for 0.5 mile to the marina. There is a small launch fee.

Trail Notes
Despite the short distance, this trip is subject to wind and waves, especially in summer when prevailing winds blow in from the south and west. Also, there are strong currents in the passage beyond Upper Flag Island and a fair amount of boat traffic.

Eagle Island is a state-owned historic site with a caretaker in-residence. It is restricted to day-use only, and visitors are charged a nominal fee during the season from June 15 through Labor Day. To protect nesting eider ducks, the island's trails may be closed until approximately July 15.

Trip Description
Long before setting his sights on the North Pole, famed explorer Robert E. Peary became captivated with a little island in Eastern Casco Bay. He first explored and fell in love with Eagle Island while on a camping trip during his high school years in Portland. After graduating from Bowdoin College in 1881, he purchased the island, reportedly for $500. This trip

takes you from the southern tip of Harpswell Neck out to the island where you can explore for yourself its natural beauty and tour Peary's spectacular summer home.

The journey begins from the all-tide boat launch at Dolphin Marina in Potts Harbor. Turning southwest, aim for Upper Flag Island and begin paddling toward its northeastern point. As you approach the island, take note of wind, waves, and boat traffic, and skirt to whichever side offers the most protection.

Upper Flag is an interesting, treeless island with beaches at both ends and pretty cliff formations along its western side. Beyond the southern point, you'll get your first glimpse of Eagle Island, less than a mile distant. The crossing is completely exposed to southerly winds and can be choppy, especially if there is a lot of boat traffic in the area. Make your way across the channel, aiming for the northeastern tip of Eagle Island.

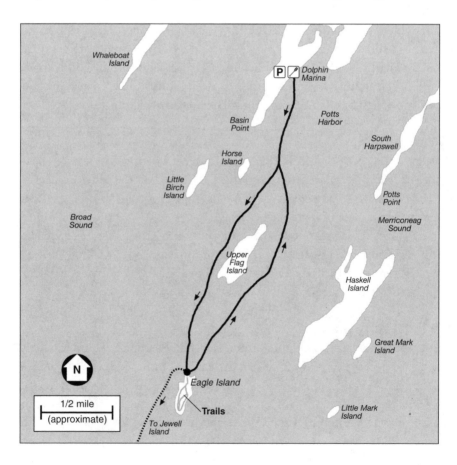

As you approach the island, the house looms high on a rocky bluff. Peary thought of the bluff as a ship's prow and built his home as the ship's pilothouse. Stay your course, and aim for a landing on the small sand and cobble beach at the island's northwestern tip. You can also pull out at a small pocket beach to the left, but avoid the area near the pier where larger watercraft land.

Safely on shore, be sure to pull your boat a good distance from the water's edge, or the tide may swallow it up while you're blissfully enjoying the island. There's a nice grassy picnic area next to the house and excellent nature trails to explore the island's 17 acres. The house itself is not to be missed. Much of the family's belongings remain, providing a fascinating glimpse into Peary's life.

To return, retrace your path, choosing the best course around Upper Flag to minimize your exposure.

Nature and History Notes

According to the island's archives, on the afternoon of September 6, 1909, two boats motored toward Eagle from South Harpswell. The first brought news from the Associated Press that Peary and his crew had become the first men ever to reach the North Pole. Apparently, Mrs. Peary

Visitors to Eagle Island can explore Robert E. Peary's former summer residence.

was none too excited, having heard many similar, though false, accounts before. However, the second boat was more encouraging. It brought South Harpswell's postmaster, who delivered to Peary's wife a telegram from her husband. It read simply, "Have made good at last."

Other Options

Advanced paddlers may choose to extend the trip by circumnavigating the island, though there is substantial exposure on the southeastern side. Or, you can continue southwest for 2.0 miles to reach Jewell Island, one of the most popular islands on the Maine Island Trail. However, be well advised that the passage is very exposed and fraught with ledges around Broken Cove. It should only be attempted when conditions are calm.

More Information

To learn more about Eagle Island and Admiral Peary, contact the Bureau of Parks and Lands Southern Region office at 207-624-6080, or visit the Friend's of Peary's Eagle Island website at www.pearyeagleisland.org.

TRIP 23
KNUBBLE BAY

Difficulty: Moderate
Distance: 10.0 miles round-trip
Estimated Time: 3–4 hours
Location: Georgetown Island
Maps: USGS Boothbay Harbor
      DeLorme *Maine Atlas*, map 7

Exploring the beautiful waterways around the AMC's Knubble Bay Camp.

Directions

Follow US 1 through Bath and across the Kennebec River Bridge. Just beyond the bridge, turn right onto ME 127 and proceed 5.8 miles to Robinhood Road on the left. Go 1.0 mile and turn left onto Webber Road

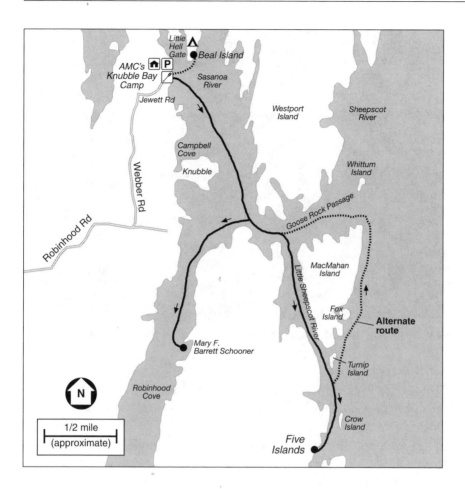

at the Robinhood Meeting house. Follow Webber Road for 1.2 miles to the first right turn at Jewett Road. There is an AMC marker on the Residents signpost. Follow Jewett Road 0.6 mile (turning right at each fork) to Knubble Bay Camp

Trail Notes

Caution: The Sasanoa River is subject to severe tidal rips, especially at Little Hell Gate and Lower Hell Gate on either side of Beal Island, and at Goose Rock Passage where it joins the Little Sheepscot River. Passage through these areas should only be attempted around the high and low water slack and never at night or in fog.

Kayakers enjoying an afternoon paddle near the AMC's Knubble Bay Camp.

Trip Description

The AMC's Knubble Bay Camp is perfectly situated for exploring the extraordinary paddling opportunities in this beautiful region of Midcoast Maine.

From Bath to Boothbay, there are a host of outstanding tidal rivers, bays, islands, and coves to discover. This outing introduces the area with a nice excursion into Robinhood Cove to see the remains of a five-masted schooner, followed by a visit to lovely Five Islands on the western side of Sheepscot Bay.

From the Knubble Bay Camp launch site, turn south and paddle out of Knubble Bay toward Robinhood Cove. Less than a mile into the paddle, you'll pass Knubble Point and Little Knubble on your right. From here, the Sasanoa River narrows, resulting in some fast moving water and potentially difficult rips through Goose Rock Passage. Before steering through this section, stay right and paddle into picturesque Robinhood Cove (if you prefer, you can visit this area on the return).

As you enter the cove, stay left. At approximately 1.5 miles from the camp you'll come upon the remains of the Mary F. Barrett, one of 29 five-masted schooners built in Bath around the turn of the twentieth century. She was 241 feet long and used mostly for coastal and deep-water trading, except during World War I when she was requisitioned to ferry supplies to Europe. Her last voyage was in 1927. In 1929, the hull of the ship was towed to a final resting place in the cove.

After visiting the Barrett and exploring more of Robinhood Cove, retrace your path and return to Goose Rock Passage. Your path through the passage will depend on the height of the tide and strength of the current. Just beware that the waters here can be extremely squirrelly with whirlpools, tidal rips, and strong eddy lines, so pass with caution.

Beyond the passage, turn south and paddle down the Little Sheepscot River. The river is easiest to negotiate around a slack tide, especially through the narrows at the southern end of the river. When you reach Turnip Island, stay right and continue south, reaching Crow Island, the first of the Five Islands, approximately 1.5 miles from Goose Rock Passage.

Five Islands is an extremely picturesque harbor that makes a perfect spot to stop for lunch or dinner. There's a great lobster pound and ice cream stand at the town dock. The best place to haul out is at the small beach tucked into a cove just south and west of the main dock.

For the return trip, catch an incoming tide and retrace your path, or take a slightly longer but equally interesting route around MacMahan Island, which provides great views across Sheepscot Bay and some interesting coves to explore along the island's northeast point.

Nature and History Notes

Knubble Bay Camp is a rustic, post-and-beam cottage that has bunk space for fifteen persons and is open year-round. There is a kitchen with stove, refrigerator, and cookware; an inside composting toilet; and woodstove. Water is provided from a hand pump outside the camp. Boat rentals are available through the registrar.

Beal Island is a short paddle from Knubble Bay Camp and is the AMC's only coastal island wilderness facility. The campground is situated in a large meadow overlooking the island's beautiful south beach. There is a great cooking area set up on the beach and a permanent fire ring (fires are only allowed on the beach). There is also 2-mile perimeter trail to explore the 64-acre island.

Other Options

Trip opportunities from Knubble Bay are limited only by your time and imagination. Several trips possibilities are posted at the camp. Also, check out the AMC's *Sea Kayaking the New England Coast* for details of a great trip from Knubble Bay Camp to the Maine Maritime Museum in Bath.

More Information
To find out more about Knubble Bay Camp and Beal Island, or to make reservations, visit the AMC's website at www.outdoors.org.

TRIP 24
MUSCONGUS SOUND/TODD WILDLIFE SANCTUARY

Difficulty: Moderate
Distance: 6.0–7.0 miles round-trip
Estimated Time: 3–4 hours
Location: Muscongus
Maps: USGS Louds Island Quad
　　　　 DeLorme *Maine Atlas*, map 7

Superb kayaking in an island-studded bay with a visit to an Audubon sanctuary.

Directions
To reach the put-in at Muscongus Harbor, turn south on ME 32 from US 1 in Waldoboro. Follow ME 32 for 11.0 miles to Muscongus Road (left). Continue on Muscongus Road for 0.2 mile to the parking area and launch ramp. There is a $5 parking and launch fee.

You can also put in at Round Pond 2.0 miles south of Muscongus Harbor off ME 32. From ME 32, turn left onto Back Shore Road. Turn right at the fork onto Anchor Inn Road and then right again onto Landing Road to reach the parking lot and all-tide ramp (fee).

Trail Notes
This section of Muscongus Sound and Muscongus Bay is relatively protected; however, east of Hog Island there is more exposure to wind and waves.

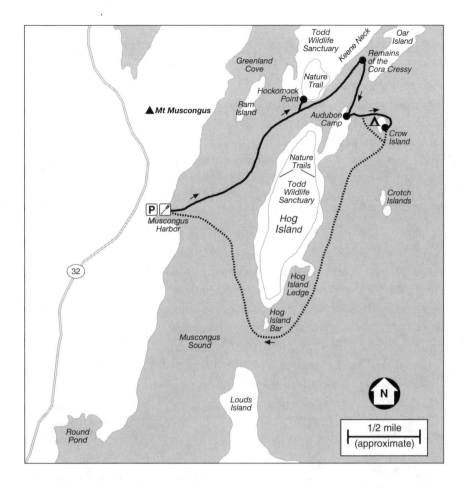

Trip Description

Muscongus Bay is one of my favorite places to paddle. Beautiful, accessible islands, abundant wildlife, and charming harbors combine to make it a perfect destination for day trips or extended outings. This trip introduces the western side of the bay with an easy paddle up Muscongus Sound, a visit to an Audubon sanctuary, a brief side trip to the remains of a 1902 schooner, and a lunch stop at popular Crow Island.

The trip begins from quiet Muscongus Harbor where there is a small parking area and all-tide ramp. As you arrive, you're sure to be greeted by Nelson Webber, who owns the harbor and collects the small fee for parking and launching. Before departing, you'll also want to visit with the folks at Sea Spirit Adventures who operate a boat rental and tour facility at the harbor and can provide helpful information about paddling options around the bay.

Alternatively, you can set off from beautiful Round Pond, which has an excellent lobster pound (not to be missed), but tends to see more traffic.

From either harbor, Hog Island lies due east. Begin paddling towards the island and then turn north as you enter Muscongus Sound. Continue tracking northeast and aim for Hockomock Point, which lies a mile distant, at the tip of Keene Neck.

As you approach Hockomock Point, the northern tip of Hog Island closes in from the southeast. The result is a channel known as "the narrows" that forms between the two points of land. Watch for swift water through this area.

The cluster of buildings visible at the tip of Hog is home to an Audubon Ecology Camp and part of the Todd Wildlife Sanctuary, which comprises 330 acres on the island and an additional 30 acres at Hockomock Point. Visitors are welcome at both sites; however, Audubon asks that boats be kept away from the boat houses and landing docks. At Hockomock Point, there is a visitors center and nature store and several nature trails to explore. To visit the island, paddle around the northern tip of Hog and land at the small pocket beach on the eastern shore. Sign in at the office and pick up a trail map.

Muscongus Harbor.

For an interesting side trip, continue north, paddling through the narrows between Keene Neck and Oar Island. After a short paddle, you'll come upon the massive hulk of the Cora Cressy, a stout, five-masted schooner built in Bath in 1902. In her heyday, she was known as the "Queen of the Atlantic Seaboard." However, in 1928 she lost her sails in a gale. The following year, a deckhouse was built over her main deck and she was turned into a nightclub, first in Gloucester, Massachusetts, and then in Providence, Rhode Island. In 1938, she was gutted and towed to her present home where she now sits as a breakwater to a lobster pound.

East of Hog Island, Muscongus Bay opens to a beautiful expanse of water dotted with several attractive islands, many of which are open to public use. Crow Island, which is part of the Maine Island Trail, is easiest to reach from the northern end of Hog Island and well worth the effort. The 4-acre island has nice pocket beaches on its eastern and western shores, tent sites, and some nice ledges on the southern end that make a great place to stretch out for lunch.

From Crow, you can retrace your route back to Muscongus Harbor, or continue around the eastern shore of Hog and circumnavigate the island before returning to the put-in. If you choose the longer route around the island, watch for the rich array of bird life active along the shoreline.

Nature and History Notes

Maine Audubon's Todd Wildlife Sanctuary is home to more than 150 species of birds, including heron, osprey, and a rich variety of songbirds. Mammals include red fox, raccoons, flying squirrels, and deer. The sanctuary was made possible through the conservation efforts of Mabel Loomis Todd, who purchased Hog Island in 1908 to prevent it from being logged. In 1936, Todd's daughter, Millicent Todd Bingham, continued her mother's inspiration and established the ecology camp in cooperation with the National Audubon Society. The sanctuary and camp are now operated by Maine Audubon, which continues to offer a wide variety of programs during summer.

More Information

To find out more about the Todd Wildlife Sanctuary and the Maine Audubon Camp on Hog Island, visit the Maine Audubon website at www.maineaudubon.org. For boat rentals or tours contact Sea Spirit Adventures at www.seaspiritadventures.com.

Project Puffin and the Seabird Restoration Program

Atlantic puffins (*Fratercula arctica*) are among the most beautiful and interesting birds that grace Maine's coastal waters and islands. These small, striking seabirds live on the open ocean for most of the year, and breed in colonies on rocky islands from Eastern Egg Rock to Machias Seal Island between April and mid-August. The puffin population thriving in Maine today is due in large part to Project Puffin, the National Audubon Society's ongoing effort to restore the birds to their former colonies after years of intensive hunting nearly led to their demise.

For almost 300 years, puffins and other Maine seabirds were hunted for their meat, eggs, and feathers. The seabirds' situation grew particularly dire during the latter half of the nineteenth century, when ladies' decorative feather hats became popular. In fact, by 1900, the thriving millinery trade had completely decimated several seabird species in Maine, including cormorants, eiders, gannets, murres, and Great black-back gulls. By 1902, just one pair of Atlantic puffins remained at Matinicus Rock.

Fortunately, at the same time, public outrage over the rapidly declining bird populations led to the formation of Audubon societies, which worked for the passage of protective laws. In 1901, Maine enacted its first bird protection law, and, in 1916, a federal treaty between the United States and Great Britain (on behalf of Canada) ensured further protection. By 1960, several seabird species had reclaimed their historic nesting sites, but more uncommon species like puffins, terns, Leach's storm petrels, and murres never recovered. Of the six islands in Maine once populated by puffins, only Matinicus Rock had a surviving colony.

In 1973, the National Audubon Society began Project Puffin in an effort to return the seabirds to their historic nesting sites in the Gulf of Maine. Young puffins, only 10 to 14 days old, were transplanted from Newfoundland to Eastern Egg Rock in Muscongus Bay, where they were banded for identification and reared until they fledged. Because puffins usually return to breed on the island where they hatched, the hope was that these puffins would return to Eastern Egg Rock after spending their first 2 to 3 years at sea. Between 1973 and 1986, 954 puffins were transplanted to Eastern Egg Rock and 914 of these successfully fledged. In June 1977, the first of the transplanted birds began returning to the island, and lingered there because of the surprising attractiveness of wooden puffin decoys placed around the boulders.

By 1981, five pairs had nested on the island, and in 2005, the colony of nesting pairs had increased to 71. Audubon, in cooperation with the Canadian Wildlife Service and the U.S. Fish and Wildlife Service, expanded the project in 1984 to Seal Island, which lies at the outer fringe of Penobscot Bay. By 2005, the colony there had grown to 300 pairs.

Throughout the project, Audubon biologists also began developing management techniques to help in the restoration of other threatened seabirds, including terns and petrels. As a result, among other successes, today Audubon's seven managed islands are home to more than 60 percent of the entire Common, Roseate, and Arctic tern population in Maine.

Audubon now manages seven research stations along the Maine Coast, including Stratton Island in Saco Bay, Jenny Island in Casco Bay, Pond Island National Wildlife Refuge near Popham Beach, Eastern Egg Rock in Muscongus Bay, Matinicus Rock, and Seal Island in Outer Penobscot Bay. The National Audubon Society owns Stratton Island where visitors are encouraged to come ashore, observe, and learn about Maine's seabirds. Other islands are managed in cooperation with various agencies including the U.S. Coast Guard, the U.S. Fish and Wildlife Service, and the Maine Department of Inland Fisheries and Wildlife. Several chartered boat services (some with Audubon naturalists aboard) are also available to take passengers around Eastern Egg Rock to view puffins and terns. Information on these cruises can be found on the project's website.

In fall 2005, Audubon opened the Project Puffin Visitors Center in Rockland (open seasonally from May through November). The center features live streaming video footage from the Matinicus Rock seabird colony, as well as a theatre, art gallery, gift shop, and bookstore.

To learn more about Project Puffin and the Seabird Restoration Project, visit the National Audubon Society's website at www.project puffin.org.

TRIP 25
ROCKPORT HARBOR TO CAMDEN HARBOR

Difficulty: Easy to moderate
Distance: 4.5 miles one-way; 9.0 miles round-trip
Estimated Time: 3–4 hours
Location: Rockport and Camden
Maps: USGS Camden Quad
　　　　DeLorme *Maine Atlas*, map 14

Classic shoreline paddling between two of Maine's most picturesque harbors.

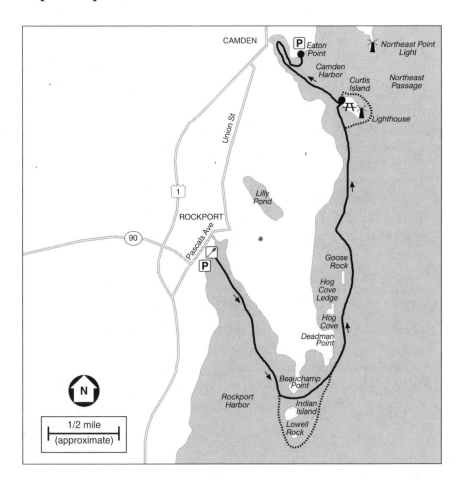

Directions

To reach the public boat launch at Rockport Harbor, go east on West Street at the junction of US 1 and ME 90. Turn left on Pascals Avenue, then right at the PUBLIC BOAT ACCESS sign onto Andre Street and down to the Rockport Marine Park. Parking is limited and there is a small fee to launch your boat.

For a point-to-point trip, spot a car at the all-tide ramp just north of downtown Camden. From the junction of US 1 and ME 52, go north on US 1 for 0.1 mile and turn right onto Sea Street. Continue for 0.3 mile and turn right onto Steamboat Landing Drive. There is very limited parking at the launch site; however, overflow parking is available on Avey Avenue, a short distance back from the put-in. To reach the Avey Avenue parking area, go back to Sea Street, turn right, and follow the road around a bend to the parking lot on the left.

Trail Notes

The shoreline here is exposed and subject to strong wind and waves, especially around Deadman Point. Check the forecast before launching. Also, in recent years, bald eagles have been nesting on Curtis Island, so the island may be closed to the public during the breeding season (usually through August 15).

Trip Description

With their picturesque harbors, mountain backdrop, and stunning shoreline, Rockport and Camden are justifiably two of the most attractive and popular destinations along midcoast Maine. For kayakers, the view from Penobscot Bay provides a unique vantage point to explore this beautiful setting away from summer crowds. This trip begins from Rockport and ventures up the coast with a stop at Curtis Island at the mouth of Camden Harbor.

From Rockport Harbor, paddle along the eastern shoreline to the mouth of the harbor. Depending on weather conditions, you can either paddle around Indian Island or between the island and Beauchamp Point. Indian Island lighthouse, at the eastern entrance to the harbor, is worth seeing, but privately owned and inaccessible to the public.

Turning north and east, follow the shoreline around Deadman Point, watching for any wind or waves that may kick up in this area. Beyond Deadman Point, stay east of the ledges at Hog Cove and paddle a safe

Camden Harbor is home to a fleet of historic windjammers.

distance from Goose Rock. As you continue along the shoreline, you'll pass by some of the most gorgeous estates along the Maine coast.

At 4.0 miles, you'll reach beautiful Curtis Island with its attractive lighthouse, excellent picnic area, and enjoyable trails. The island, now a town park, was named after Cyrus Curtis, a publishing tycoon and philanthropist who founded the *Saturday Evening Post*. To view the lighthouse from the water, paddle around the island to the south. Otherwise, follow the western shoreline to the small beach and take out at the northwest end of the island.

From Curtis, it's a short paddle to Camden Harbor. However, there is usually significant boat traffic here, so it's best to stay out of the main channel as you make your approach. Still, it's well worth exploring the harbor to view some of the splendid vessels that moor here during summer, especially the magnificent fleet of Maine windjammers.

The town dock, at the head of the harbor, is a good (though, often crowded) spot to pull out and explore the village. Alternatively, you can paddle east of the harbor around Eaton Point and pull out at the all-tide boat ramp there. This is also the best spot to take out if you plan to make this a point-to-point trip. Otherwise, weave your way out of the harbor and enjoy the return trip to Rockport.

Nature and History Notes

During the nineteenth century, Rockport was known as the "lime capital of the world." More than 100,000 tons of limestone were annually mined from local quarries and shipped via narrow-gauge railroad to nearby kilns. The lime produced from the kilns was then shipped out of Rockport Harbor aboard sturdy sailing schooners. Because lime catches fire when wet, it was important to keep it dry during transport. Nonetheless, several ships were lost because of the volatility of the material. Today, visitors to the Rockport Marine Park can view a steam locomotive and limekiln from the period.

Rockport is probably best known for its famous summer resident, Andre the seal. Abandoned as a pup, the harbor seal was rescued and trained by Rockport resident Harry Goodridge and remained a family friend for the rest of his life. Andre spent his winters at the New England Aquarium, but each spring, when he was let loose in Boston Harbor, he faithfully returned to Rockport to visit with the Goodridge's. Andre died in 1986 at the age of 25, but his story lives on in books and film as well as a commemorative statue at the Marine Park.

3

Downeast

IN DOWNEAST MAINE, OCEAN MEETS LAND along rocky shores and rugged cliffs that have inspired travelers for generations. "Downeast" is a maritime term that refers to sailing downwind in an easterly direction with the summer winds. This is a region of superlative scenery, from spectacular Acadia National Park, the nation's second most popular park, to remote Quoddy Head State Park, the easternmost point in the United States. Within Acadia, there are miles of hiking trails and carriage roads, serene forests, freshwater streams, ponds, lakes, and mountains, including Cadillac Mountain, the highest point on the eastern seaboard north of Rio de Janeiro. Farther east, picturesque working harbors are nestled among dazzling archipelagos, stunning seaside cliffs, and beautiful bays. Highlighted trips for this region include a variety of outings within Acadia (Trips 26–29, 31, 32, and 34), exceptional paddling opportunities from the Deer Isle Archipelago (Trip 36) to Cobscook Bay (Trip 38), and a remote ride within Moosehorn National Wildlife Refuge (Trip 33).

TRIP 26
THE BUBBLES—ACADIA NATIONAL PARK

(Excerpted from the AMC's *Discover Acadia National Park* by Jerry and Marcy Monkman)

Difficulty: Strenuous but short
Distance: 1.6 miles
Estimated Time: 1.5 hours
Location: Acadia National Park
Maps: AMC's *Discover Acadia National Park Map*: E7
      USGS Southwest Harbor Quad
      USGS Acadia National Park and Vicinity

A short but irresistible climb to the summits of Jordan Pond's distinctive mountains.

Directions
From the Acadia National Park Visitor Center, drive south on the Park Loop Road for 6.3 miles. Be sure to continue straight at the intersections marked Sand Beach and Cadillac Mountain. The Bubble Rock parking area will be on your right, 1.1 miles south of Bubble Pond.

Trip Description
The Bubbles are two well-rounded granite hills that stand at the northern end of Jordan Pond. Their shape and location are so distinctive, it is hard to imagine Jordan Pond without them. At an estimated 770 feet and 872 feet, they are far from being the tallest mountains in the park, but they do provide good views of the pond and the taller surrounding peaks. South Bubble is also home to perhaps the most well known rock in the state of Maine: Bubble Rock, perched precariously over the steep eastern slope of the mountain, is a perfect example of a glacial erratic.

This hike starts at the Bubble Rock parking lot, which is about 1.1 miles south of Bubble Pond on the Park Loop Road. From the parking lot, follow the Bubble-Pemetic Trail west for a short distance to a junction with the North Bubble Trail and the Jordan Pond Carry Trail. Go straight

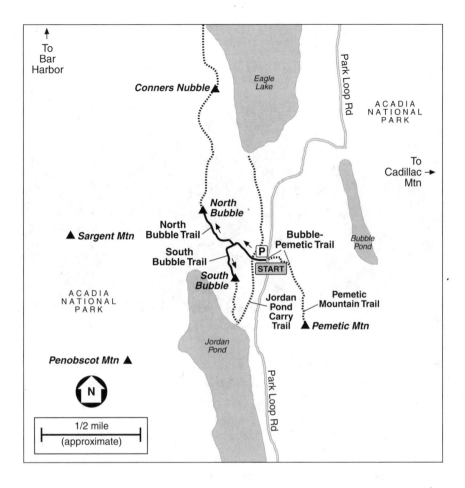

on the North Bubble Trail. The footpath is wide and level as it passes through one of the few true northern hardwood forests on the island.

The trail turns left and climbs up a set of stairs to a junction with the South Bubble Trail. From here, the summit of South Bubble is 0.3 mile to the left, while the summit of North Bubble is 0.3 mile to the right. For this hike, stay to the right on the North Bubble Trail, which soon begins a steep climb over granite ledges. Scree walls (small rock walls), built by the park's trail crew, line the trail in an attempt to keep hikers on the footpath. Like most trails in Acadia, this one is heavily used. It is very important to stay on the trail in order to assure that the surrounding vegetation remains healthy.

Views begin to open up as thick forest gives way to pitch pines and

The view of Jordan Pond from South Bubble. Photo by Jerry and Marcy Monkman.

blueberry bushes. The summit is reached 0.6 mile from the parking lot. The view takes in Jordan Pond and the surrounding group of Mount Desert's highest peaks—Cadillac, Pemetic, Penobscot, and Sargent.

To go to South Bubble, head back down the North Bubble Trail toward the parking lot. At the junction with the South Bubble Trail, turn right. The trail is fairly level for 0.1 mile until a trail junction, where going straight will bring you down to the northern end of Jordan Pond. Turn left for a moderate 0.2-mile ascent to the summit of South Bubble. Although lower than North Bubble, this summit has better views of Jordan Pond. Bubble Rock, which lies just to the east of South Bubble's summit, is the most conspicuous example of a glacial erratic on Mount Desert Island.

Nature and History Notes
The northern hardwood forest here is dominated by birch and American beech. Search the forest floor for beechnuts, a favorite food for bear, turkey, and other animals. With the demise of the American chestnut, which was decimated by a fungus in the early twentieth century, beechnuts became an even more important food source for the animals of

eastern North America. Now, the American beech is being attacked by the combination of a fungus and a scale introduced by the importation of European beech trees. Without the natural defenses necessary to fight off this threat, it is possible that the American beech could go the way of the American chestnut.

TRIP 27
THE BEEHIVE AND THE BOWL—
ACADIA NATIONAL PARK

(Excerpted from the AMC's *Discover Acadia National Park* by Jerry and Marcy Monkman)

Difficulty: Difficult (for steepness and exposure)
Distance: 1.3 miles round-trip
Estimated Time: 1 hour
Location: Acadia National Park
Maps: AMC's *Discover Acadia National Park Map*: E9
    USGS Seal Harbor Quad
    USGS Acadia National Park and Vicinity

A challenging climb up iron rungs to spectacular views and a visit to a quiet and beautiful mountain pond.

Directions
From Downtown Bar Harbor, drive south on Maine Route 3 for 2.1 miles and turn right at the Sieur de Monts Spring entrance to the Park Loop Road. Follow the signs for Sand Beach. The Sand Beach parking area is on the left, 3.25 miles south of the Sieur de Monts Spring entrance. The Bowl Trail is across the road from the parking area.

Trail Notes
Caution: This hike is very steep and traverses the cliffs of the Beehive using iron rungs and ladders. This hike is very dangerous in wet weather. People who have a fear of heights should consider climbing the Beehive

from the Bowl instead of up the Beehive Trail. It is not recommended for people with small children, and those with older children should consider hiking it without kids first to determine if it is an appropriate hike for the family.

Trip Description

The challenging nature of this hike up the Beehive makes it one of the most popular hikes in the park. The fact that it is just across the road from Sand Beach and has good views probably adds to its popularity as well. The Bowl is a beautiful pond nestled between the Beehive and Champlain Mountain and is one of the two ponds in the park that are accessible only by foot (Sargent Pond is the other).

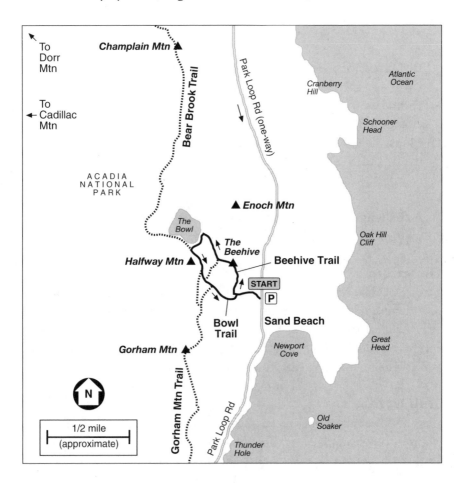

Begin this hike on the Bowl Trail, which is across the Park Loop Road from the Sand Beach parking area. The Beehive Trail is the first trail junction, 0.2 mile from the road. Turn right to follow the Beehive Trail toward the 350-foot cliffs of the Beehive.

The trail quickly rises to meet the cliff wall and begins to climb almost straight up. The iron rungs and ladders alternate with stretches of granite ledges. Views of the Atlantic Ocean, Sand Beach, and Champlain Mountain get better and better as you climb, but be sure of your footing before you look over your shoulder! While strenuous, the climb up the Beehive is relatively short, and most hikers can finish the 0.5-mile hike to the summit in about 30 minutes. The views of the ocean are good, but the view toward the interior of the island is one of the prettiest mountain views in the park. While looking over the Bowl toward Dorr

Climbing the iron ladders of the Beehive Trail. Photo by Jerry and Marcy Monkman.

and Cadillac Mountains, you see no sign of man, no Park Loop Road, no carriage roads, no power lines.

To hike down to the Bowl, a small 9.5-acre pond, follow the Beehive Trail northwest, away from the cliffs. A side trail leads left back to the Bowl Trail but bypasses the Bowl. Continue straight on the Beehive Trail to reach the Bowl, a good example of a glacial tarn, which is a deep, typically circular lake that forms when an alpine glacier melts. The Bowl is a quiet place with a unique view of Champlain Mountain.

To finish the hike, follow the trail to the left, along the southern end of the pond. In the middle of a set of wooden puncheons built to protect the boggy shoreline, the Bowl Trail comes in from the left. Turn left on the Bowl Trail and follow it 0.6 mile back to the Park Loop Road.

Nature and History Notes

Like most of the mountains on Mount Desert Island (as well as many of the islands surrounding it), the Beehive has a gradual-sloping north face and steep cliffs on the south face. Glaciers during the last ice age created this landscape feature. The pressure of the ice caused water to fill the cracks on the south face of the peaks. The rock weakened as the water went through repeated cycles of freezing and thawing. As the glacier moved forward, it sheared off these weakened pieces of granite, creating the cliffs.

Acadia National Park

From its picturesque cobblestone beaches to its windswept granite peaks, Acadia National Park is one of the most diverse and dramatic natural settings in all of Maine. Although it occupies a mere 47,000 acres, and is one of the country's smallest national parks, it consistently ranks as one of its most visited, attracting more than 3 million tourists annually. Here you'll find an alluring landscape of rugged mountains, serene woodlands, deep glacial ponds, quiet coves, and spectacular seaside cliffs. Acadia is also home to an abundance of flora and fauna with 500 plant species and more than 300 species of birds, including bald eagles, osprey, and peregrine falcons.

For outdoor enthusiasts, Acadia offers more than 100 miles of hiking trails from easy ocean-side walks to steep cliff-side climbs and exposed ridge hikes with sweeping views. Over 50 miles of gravel carriage roads built by John D. Rockefeller, Jr., in the 1920s and 1930s provide bikers an excellent means to explore the park. For boaters, there are numerous ponds and lakes to paddle, and excellent sea kayaking opportunities including the Mount Desert Narrows, Frenchman Bay, and spectacular Somes Sound, the only fiord on the eastern seaboard.

While Acadia stretches from remote and beautiful Isle au Haut to the rugged and secluded Schoodic Peninsula, most of the park is located on

Mount Desert Island, the largest coastal island in Maine. Desert is pronounced "dessert," from the French *mont desert*, or "bare mountain." Among the many glacially scoured peaks on the island is 1,532-foot Cadillac Mountain, the highest peak on the North Atlantic Seaboard.

The Wabenaki Indians called the Mount Desert Island "Pemetic," meaning "sloping land." Archeological evidence suggests that Native Americans were living on the island at least 6,000 years ago. The French explorer Samuel de Champlain is generally given credit for "discovering" the island when he ran aground near Otter Point in 1604. In his journal he wrote, "The mountain summits are all bare and rocky. . . . I name it Isles des Monts Desert." In 1613, French Jesuits established the first French mission in America on what is now Fernald Point, near the entrance to Somes Sound. Although the local Wabenaki welcomed them, the Jesuit's plans were soon thwarted when an English ship captained by Samuel Argall destroyed their fledgling settlement.

In 1688, Antoine Laumet immigrated to "New France" with the ambition of establishing a feudal state in the New World. Having arrived, he soon bestowed upon himself the grand title Sieur de la Mothe Cadillac, then asked for and received 100,000 acres of land along the Maine coast from Louis XIV. Cadillac briefly settled on Mont Desert Island, but soon abandoned his plans and moved on. He would later gain lasting recognition as the founder of Detroit. For decades after, the island fell into limbo, and was little more than a landmark for seamen while the French and English fought for territorial rights in the New World.

The English began settling Mount Desert Island after their victory in the French and Indian War in 1759. By 1850, word had spread about Mount Desert's beauty. Visitors from the big cities on the East Coast soon arrived, and by 1871 Bar Harbor had eleven hotels and was visited by four tourist-laden steamships a week. The 1880s saw the beginning of the building of summer "cottages" by America's wealthy elite. Many of these seasonal retreats had 50 or more rooms, and were staffed by 10 to 15 servants. Among the prominent families who resided here were the Rockefellers, Fords, Carnegies, Astors, and Morgans. These families also bought up huge pieces of the most desirable real estate on the island.

By the turn of the twentieth century, there was concern that the tranquil beauty of the island might be compromised by the invention of the portable sawmill. Notable residents, including the Vanderbilts and Kennedys, came together to form a non-profit organization under the leadership of George Dorr called the Hancock County Trustees of Public Reservations. The organization's sole purpose was "to acquire by devise, gift, or purchase, and to own, arrange, hold, maintain, or improve for public use lands in Hancock County, Maine, which by reason of scenic beauty, historical interest, sanitary advantage, or other like reasons may become available for such purpose."

For years, Dorr worked tirelessly to persuade landowners to donate land to the Trustees. By 1913, 6,000 acres had been acquired, and in 1916, the land was given to the federal government for the creation of Sieur de Monts National Monument. In 1919, the national monument became Lafayette National Park, the first national park east of the Mississippi River. Dorr was hired as the park's first superintendent. By 1929, the park's official name was changed to Acadia National Park.

The era of wealthy summer cottages came to an abrupt end in 1947, when a disastrous fire swept over the island. The fire burned 17,000 acres—10,000 acres within Acadia—aided by gale force winds that, at one point, swept the flames over 6 miles in less than 3 hours and burned 67 summer cottages in the section of Bar Harbor known as Millionaire's Row. The fire also dramatically altered the park's natural landscape. Spruce and fir, trees that once dominated the landscape, were heavily burned, inviting other species, such as birch and aspen to flourish. Today, a mixed forest has reclaimed the burned areas of the park, and Acadia now contains a more diverse mix of flora and fauna than it did before the fire.

For a complete description of Acadia National Park's fascinating history and excellent outdoor opportunities, check out the AMC's popular guidebook *Discover Acadia National Park*, by Jerry and Marcy Monkman. Trips to Acadia featured within *Discover Maine* are excerpted from that book, which features more than 45 hiking, biking, and paddling opportunities and thorough descriptions of the park's flora and fauna, and natural history.

TRIP 28
PENOBSCOT AND SARGENT MOUNTAINS—
ACADIA NATIONAL PARK

(Excerpted from the AMC's *Discover Acadia National Park* by Jerry and Marcy Monkman)

Difficulty: Difficult
Distance: 5.2 miles round-trip
Estimated Time: 3.5 hours
Location: Acadia National Park
Maps: AMC's *Discover Acadia National Park Map*: E9
   USGS Seal Harbor Quad
   USGS Southwest Harbor Quad
   USGS Acadia National Park and Vicinity

A strenuous hike to two of Acadia's highest peaks, with long periods of hiking on open ledges with spectacular views.

Directions
From the Acadia National Park Visitor Center, drive south on the Park Loop Road for 7.3 miles. Be sure to continue straight at the intersections marked Sand Beach and Cadillac Mountain. The Jordan Pond parking area will be on your right.

Trip Description
The cliffs of Penobscot Mountain rise steeply from the western shore of Jordan Pond and provide habitat for one of Acadia's nesting pairs of peregrine falcons. This hike provides an alternative to the Jordan Cliffs Trail, which is often closed due to the nesting falcons. Sargent Mountain is the second highest peak on Mount Desert Island, and its flat, wide-open sub-alpine summit provides some of the island's best views of Somes Sound, the Cranberry Islands, and western mountains.

This hike starts on Penobscot Mountain Trail, which is located behind and to the left of the Jordan Pond House. The trail crosses a carriage road in about 50 yards. Cross the stream on the other side of the carriage road

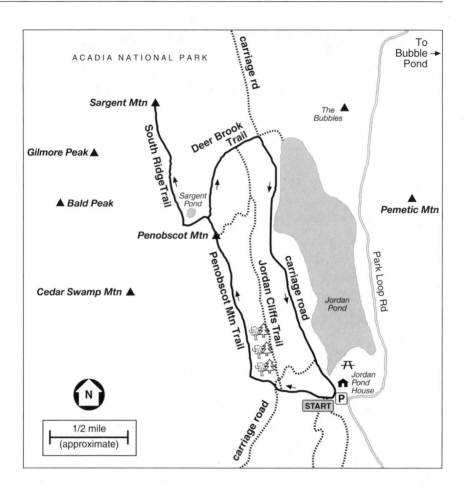

where there is a trail junction. The trail to the left is the Asticou Trail. This hike continues straight on the Penobscot Mountain Trail, which you will follow for 1.6 miles to the summit of Penobscot Mountain.

The trail rises and falls gently through a mixed hardwood and conifer forest to the west of Jordan Pond. After crossing another brook, the trail begins a steep ascent up a well-built set of rock steps. These steps are a good example of how proper trail maintenance can prevent severe erosion on a trail that receives a lot of use. Just before crossing another carriage road, the Penobscot Mountain Trail turns left at its junction with the Jordan Cliffs Trail. After crossing the carriage road, the trail makes a very steep ascent up the cliffs of Penobscot Mountain. There are a few iron rungs on this section of the hike as the trail squeezes through narrow cracks in the granite cliff face.

The steep climb ends at about 0.5 mile from the Jordan Pond House. Here the trail emerges from the trees and turns sharply right in order to make a moderate ascent of the south ridge of Penobscot Mountain. The walk up the south ridge is over open granite ledges with good views of most of the mountains in the park and of the Atlantic Ocean. The environment is sub-alpine with prostrate trees and plants from the heath family like sheep laurel and rhodora. Lowbush blueberries are very common on this trail.

Looking north from the summit you will see Sargent Pond and the summit of Sargent Mountain, second only to Cadillac Mountain in height. Cadillac Mountain is to the east, beyond Pemetic Mountain. The summit is a good place to watch for ravens and hawks riding the thermals of air warmed by the sun-baked granite peaks. You should be able to spot the peregrines if they are nesting on Jordan cliffs.

Continuing north from the summit, the trail descends quickly to the

Hiking on Sargent Mountain. Photo by Jerry and Marcy Monkman.

col between Penobscot and Sargent Mountains. At this col, the Deer Brook Trail enters from the right. Stay to the left and you will soon reach Sargent Pond. Sargent Pond is fairly typical of ponds in the boreal forests of Maine—a bowl of water surrounded by spruce forests with blueberry bushes and rhodora clinging to its banks. From the pond, the trail rises moderately to a junction with the Sargent Mountain South Ridge Trail.

Turn right on the Sargent Mountain South Ridge Trail. From here, the trail ascends very gradually for 0.8 mile to the summit of Sargent Mountain. This part of the hike is reminiscent of the Tableland plateau on Maine's Mount Katahdin, although at a much lower elevation. The summit of Sargent Mountain is surrounded by an extensive area of relatively flat, open terrain filled with sedges, wildflowers, stunted versions of spruce, cedar, and birch. On the way to the summit, two more trails come in from the left. Continue straight at these junctions to keep on track for the summit cairn. The views from the summit are excellent.

To return to the Jordan Pond House, walk back down the Sargent Mountain South Ridge Trail to the Penobscot Mountain Trail and turn left towards Sargent Pond. After passing Sargent Pond again, the trail rises to meet the Deer Brook Trail. Turn left on the Deer Brook Trail, which goes down toward Jordan Pond. This trail descends steadily and has very rough footing over wet rocks and tree roots. The trail follows a stream, which overflows onto the trail after heavy rains.

After 0.5 mile, the trail reaches a carriage road. Turn right on the carriage road for an easy 1.5-mile walk back to the Jordan Pond House. Shortly after leaving the Deer Brook Trail, the carriage road passes through a boulder field below Jordan Cliffs. There are good views of the pond and the Bubbles from here. The rest of the walk is through northern hardwood forest. At the only intersection, stay to the left.

TRIP 29
CADILLAC MOUNTAIN—ACADIA NATIONAL PARK

(Excerpted from the AMC's *Discover Acadia National Park* by Jerry and Marcy Monkman)

Difficulty: Moderate
Distance: 7.0 miles round-trip
Estimated Time: 4 hours
Location: Acadia National Park
Maps: AMC's *Discover Acadia National Park Map*: D8, E8
      USGS Seal Harbor Quad
      USGS Acadia National Park and Vicinity

A relatively long hike over open ledges to the summit of Mount Desert Island's highest mountain. There are great views during most of this hike.

Directions
The trailhead for the Cadillac South Ridge Trail is just west of the entrance to Blackwoods Campground on Maine 3, 5.6 miles south of Bar Harbor.

Trip Description
Although this hike is not a loop, the south ridge of Cadillac Mountain, with its open forest of pitch and jack pine, is worth experiencing twice in the same day. This hike starts on Maine Route 3 near the entrance to Blackwoods Campground and makes a moderate, enjoyable climb to Cadillac's busy summit over a leisurely 3.5 miles. While the summit may not be the wildest spot in the park, with its gift shop and parking lot full of tourists, the south ridge of Cadillac is relatively quiet and full of excellent views.

The Cadillac South Ridge Trail starts on the north side of Maine Route 3, about 50 yards west of the entrance to the Blackwoods Campground. It is legal to park on the shoulder of the highway. The first mile of this hike rises gently, then moderately, through a forest predominated by

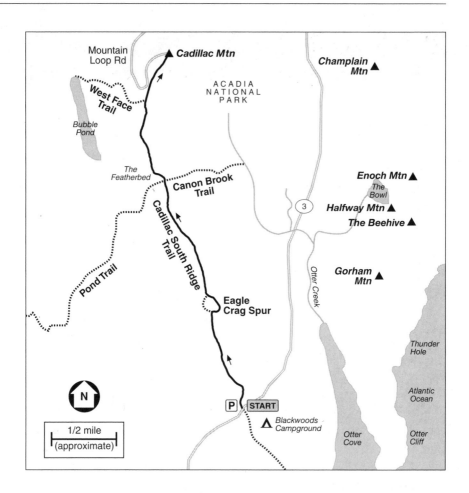

white pine and spruce. At the 1-mile mark, a spur path leads 0.1 mile to the right to an overlook called Eagle Crag, which has good views of Otter Creek and the Atlantic Ocean. This is a worthwhile destination for families staying at the campground who are not up for the full hike to the summit.

The spur path loops around to reconnect with the main trail after a total of about 0.2 mile. Turn right to head toward the summit. Almost immediately, the hike enters a forest of pitch pine spread over granite ledge, taking on an open, airy feeling. The occasional boulder among the gnarly and twisted trees contributes to the forest's look of a grown-up Japanese bonsai garden. Of course, this is the real forest, and wind and water are the gardeners. From here, there are good views of the island and the surrounding waters for most of the way to the summit. The trail then passes

Jack pine on Cadillac Mountain. Photo by Jerry and Marcy Monkman.

through one of the few pockets of jack pine on the island before it makes a short descent to the Featherbed.

The Featherbed is a boggy area 2.3 miles from the trailhead. This is one of the highest wetlands in the park. The trail crosses the Canon Brook Trail, which leads east to Dorr Mountain and west to Jordan Pond. Continuing straight on the Cadillac South Ridge Trail, the hike soon reaches its steepest climb. A trail junction 0.5 mile below the summit marks the Cadillac West Face Trail, which leads west to Bubble Pond. At this point, the trail nears the summit road before making its final ascent toward the summit.

Shortly before reaching the summit, the trail descends into a thick spruce-fir forest, which stands in marked contrast to the open pine forest of the last 2.5 miles. This forest grows in an area protected from the strong summit winds, and it collects just enough soil and water to allow the spruce-fir forest to thrive. The trail crosses a fire road and reaches the summit parking area just below the actual summit, which is marked by a set of interpretive signs describing the views extending in all directions of Frenchman Bay, the Schoodic Peninsula, the islands to the west, and even Katahdin, 115 miles to the north.

To complete your hike, walk back down the trail to your car.

Nature and History Notes

Sixteen species of hawks, eagles, and falcons live in or migrate through Acadia. In fall, Cadillac Mountain's location and elevation make it an excellent spot to watch for migrating raptors, especially when the wind is out of the north. Check with the Acadia National Park visitors center for information about hawk-watching programs run by park naturalists throughout September and early October.

TRIP 30
THE BOLD COAST—CUTLER PRESERVE

Difficulty: Moderate to difficult
Distance: 5.8-mile or 9.8-mile loop options
Estimated Time: 4–7 hours
Location: Cutler
Maps: USGS Cutler Quadrangle
　　　　Maine Bureau of Parks and Lands—Cutler Coast
　　　　Cobscook Trails Booklet—Quoddy Regional Land Trust
　　　　DeLorme *Maine Atlas*, map 27

A remote hike along a wild and windswept coastal headland, with spectacular seaward views from steep, jagged cliffs.

Directions

From Machias, take Route 1 north to Route 191. Turn right toward Cutler, and follow Route 191 for 16.9 miles to a small parking lot and trailhead on the right. For reference, the trailhead is 4.0 miles from Cutler Harbor.

Trail Notes

Caution: In many cases, the precipitous cliffs along the coastal section of this hike are completely exposed. Additionally, because this is a maritime environment, sections of the trail and cliff outcrops are often wet and slippery. A fall from the headlands would most certainly result in serious injury or worse. Moreover, the hike's remote location would preclude any opportunity of a timely rescue.

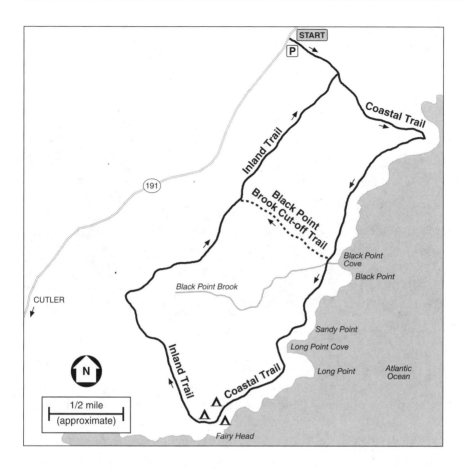

This area is home to a diverse and fragile ecosystem. Please ensure that the environment is not adversely affected by your presence by staying on marked trails and observing all primitive camping rules and regulations. Open fires are prohibited.

Trip Description

Along the Bold Coast, land meets sea in a spectacular crash of wild Atlantic surf and sheer, jagged cliffs. This is the "other" Maine, and in some ways, Acadia's alter ego: rugged, remote, and spare, but equally impressive. This loop hike explores a diverse landscape of barrens, bogs, and maritime forest, as well as a dramatic jaunt along the coast's windswept, precipitous edge.

Pick up a map at the trailhead kiosk, and then drop into the trail fol-

Enjoying the views atop the Bold Coast's exposed, 100-foot cliffs.

lowing a southeast course. The path cuts through a thin spruce-fir forest before reaching the first junction at 0.4 mile. Here, the Inland Trail turns right (west), a path we'll follow on the return, and the Coastal Trail continues straight.

Stay on the Coastal Trail, which crosses over a cedar swamp at 0.7 mile, then meanders through a beautiful and rare maritime forest, sometimes referred to as a "fog forest," of spruce and fir. At 1.4 miles, the sound of the sea begins to filter through the trees. At 1.5 miles, the trail rises over a rocky knob and reaches the barren headland in dramatic fashion. Below you, the cliffs plunge more than 100 feet to the sea. To the south, there are sweeping views across the Grand Manan Channel to Grand Manan Island, and to the west, spectacular vistas along the rugged cliffs to Black Point. In late summer and early fall, look for whales passing through the channel. Humpback, finback, northern right, and minke whales have all been sighted here.

The Coastal Trail continues right, tracking along the headland in a southwestern direction. For the next 1.5 miles, the path follows the cliff top, rising and dropping across steep knobs and winding in and out of the forest. Along the way, there are dozens of scenic vistas outward across the Atlantic Ocean and to pocket coves and cobble beaches far below.

You'll reach the Black Point Brook Cut-off 3.0 miles from the trailhead. To complete the 5.8-mile loop, turn right here. The trail turns northwest and crosses the wooded interior over a series of rocky knobs before arriving at the Inland Trail in 0.8 mile. At the junction, turn right (east) to reach the Coastal Trail at the first junction you passed on the way in. From there, turn left to reach the parking area in 0.4 mile.

To complete the longer loop of 9.8 miles, continue on the Coastal Trail at its junction with the Black Point Brook Cut-off. The trail crosses a 100-yard-long cobble beach at Black Point Cove, then rises and dips across the ledges at Black Point, where there are excellent views back to the cliffs you just walked and farther eastward to the Bay of Fundy. The trail continues across open ledges marked by rock cairns, passes over Sandy Point, and reaches Long Point Cove at 4.2 miles, where a stairway provides access to the 150-foot-long cobble beach.

The Coastal Trail ends at Fairy Head, 5.3 miles from the trailhead and parking area. Here, the Bureau of Parks and Lands has set up three primitive campsites, which are available on a first-come, first-served basis. Facilities include tent sites and pit toilets. The Bureau asks that you please stay on designated sites, as the low-lying vegetation in the area is extremely fragile.

The final leg of the longer loop turns away from the sea and follows the Inland Trail north and west over rolling terrain. The rocky path crosses a series of rises that provide excellent views of the surrounding forest, open meadows and ocean, as well as a large beaver pond about half way between Fairy Head and the Black Point Brook Cut-off Trail. Heading east now, the trail crosses over a freshwater marsh via a series of bridges and arrives at the Black Point Brook Cut-off Trail 2.5 miles from Fairy Head.

The final section of the Inland Trail continues over easy terrain, passing through freshwater marsh, forest, blueberry barrens, and peat bogs before arriving at the Coastal Trail Junction in 9.4 miles. From here, turn left for the 0.4-mile walk out to the trailhead and parking area.

Nature and History Notes

The 12,000-acre Cutler Coast Preserve protects a diverse environment that provides important habitat for a rich variety of flora and fauna. Several species of owl have been sighted here, including saw-whet, boreal, and short-eared. Bald eagles, ravens, and falcons may also be seen, as well as guillemots and eiders along the coast. Among the many unusual plant species to be found are dragon's mouth orchid, pearlwort, Hooker's iris, and baked-apple berry.

More Information

For maps, camping guidelines, or other information about the Cutler Coast Preserve, call the Maine Bureau of Parks and Lands at 207-827-1818 or visit their website at www.state.me.us/doc/parks. For a complete guide to trails and sites along the Bold Coast and around Cobscook Bay, contact the Quoddy Regional Land Trust at 207-733-5509 or visit their website at www.qrlt.org.

TRIP 31
JORDAN POND–BUBBLE POND LOOP—
ACADIA NATIONAL PARK

(Excerpted from the AMC's *Discover Acadia National Park* by Jerry and Marcy Monkman)

Aerobic Difficulty: Moderate
Technical Difficulty: Moderate
Distance: 9.0-mile loop
Estimated Time: 2.5 hours
Location: Acadia National Park
Maps: USGS Acadia National Park Quadrangle
USGS Southwest Harbor Quadrangle
AMC's *Discover Acadia National Park Map*: D7, E7, E8

A moderate ride next to the dramatic scenery of Jordan and Bubble ponds.

Directions

From the Acadia National Park Visitor Center, drive south on the Park Loop Road for 7.3 miles. Be sure to continue straight at the intersections marked Sandy Beach and Cadillac Mountain. The Jordan Pond parking area will be on your right. The carriage road for this trip begins across the street from the Jordan Pond Gatehouse.

Trip Description

Jordan Pond is arguably the most scenic pond in Acadia National Park, with its deep blue waters reflecting the steep cliffs of Penobscot Mountain and the graceful curves of the Bubbles. Bubble Pond is smaller and more intimate, with dramatic scenery of its own as the steep west face of Cadillac Mountain rises above its eastern shoreline. This is one of the longer rides in the carriage-road system, but its grades are never steep. For this reason, it makes a great day trip for a family with older children who are comfortable spending the day on bikes. Of course, following your ride, you can recharge your system with tea and popovers at the Jordan Pond House.

Begin this trip by turning onto the carriage road across the street from the Jordan Pond Gatehouse. Turn right at Post 16 and go straight

Biking the carriage roads next to Jordan Pond. Photo by Jerry and Marcy Monkman.

at Post 15. At 0.3 mile, a small bridge crosses the outlet to Jordan Pond as the carriage road climbs up to Post 14 at 0.5 mile, where you should continue straight. The road continues its upward trek through a mixed forest until Jordan Pond and the Bubbles come into view at 1.25 miles. The road crosses a huge rockslide where giant boulders line the steep east face of Penobscot Mountain.

George Dorr, the first superintendent of Acadia National Park, feared that constructing a road through such a treacherous rockslide was a risky proposition. John D. Rockefeller, Jr., and his contractor managed to assure Dorr that no one would get hurt, and they were allowed to proceed. The views from this stretch of the carriage road are fantastic. The pond is about 150 feet below the road, and you can see the Bubbles as well as the entire south ridge of Pemetic Mountain. You can also look straight up at Jordan cliffs, home of Acadia's nesting pairs of peregrine falcons.

As you re-enter the forest, you are rewarded with a crossing of Deer Brook Bridge. This bridge, with its pair of tall, narrow arches, gives you a close-up view of Deer Brook as it cascades in a waterfall over large slabs of pink granite. After the falls, the ride levels out as you pass the north end of Jordan Pond and head toward Eagle Lake. At 2.5 miles, turn right at Post 10. At 2.7 miles, turn right again at Post 8. At this point, you are about 500 feet up to the west of Eagle Lake behind a small peak called Conners Nubble. At 3.2 miles, you cross a hiking trail that you can use to walk quickly up to the summit for a nice view of Eagle Lake.

After passing Conners Nubble, the road makes a long descent to the southern end of Eagle Lake, which is surrounded by thick spruce forest. This forest is a great place to look for finches such as red crossbills, white winged crossbills, pine siskins, and common redpolls. Except for redpolls, all these finches breed in the park, but their numbers are highly variable. These finches of the boreal forest tend to migrate in waves depending on the severity of the weather and the abundance of seed crop, so their numbers in any one area can change greatly from year to year.

At 4.5 miles, turn right at Post 7 to ride toward Bubble Pond. You will cross the Park Loop Road at 4.8 miles and pass by the northern end of Bubble Pond. You then pass over a bridge that seems to extend over nothing but forest. The bridge was built to cross the Park Loop Road, which was subsequently relocated because it passed too close to the pond. Bubble Pond Bridge was constructed of compressed rock, as opposed to the granite blocks used for the rest of the bridges in the park. After crossing the bridge, the road turns left and follows the shoreline of Bubble Pond. Pemetic Mountain rises steeply to the west. Across the pond to the east is the steep west face of Cadillac Mountain. Cedar and paper birch grow on the shoreline as well as on the ledges of Cadillac. During the spring and fall migrations, you can see hawks, eagles, falcons, and vultures riding the thermals above Cadillac. Turkey vultures are known to use the huge boulders at the southeastern end of the pond as a resting spot. They blend in well with the gray rocks, so you may need binoculars to spot them.

After rounding the southern end of the Triad, go straight at Post 17 (7.7 miles). The road then climbs for 0.5 mile as it traverses the west side of the Triad behind Wildwood Stables to views of the Cranberry Islands. From here, it is an easy coast back down to the Jordan Pond Gatehouse.

TRIP 32
AROUND THE MOUNTAIN LOOP—
ACADIA NATIONAL PARK

(Excerpted from the AMC's *Discover Acadia National Park* by Jerry and Marcy Monkman)

Rating: Difficult
Distance: 12.0-mile loop
Estimated Time: 4 hours
Location: Acadia National Park
Maps: USGS Acadia National Park Quadrangle
       AMC's *Discover Acadia National Park Map*: D6, D7, E6, E7

This ride has it all: three waterfalls, mountain and ocean views, and seven major bridge crossings.

Directions

From the Acadia National Park Visitor Center, drive south on the Park Loop Road for 7.3 miles. Be sure to continue straight at the intersections marked Sandy Beach and Cadillac Mountain. The Jordan Pond parking area will be on your right. The carriage road for this trip begins across the street from the Jordan Pond Gatehouse.

Trip Description

It is not clear which mountain the person who named this loop had in mind, for it actually loops around six: Penobscot Mountain, Cedar Swamp Mountain, Bald Peak, Parkman Mountain, Gilmore Peak, and Sargent Mountain. It begins and ends next to the deep blue waters of picturesque Jordan Pond. For 12.0 miles, it rises and falls through almost every forest type in the park, passes steep cliffs and waterfalls, and climbs to dramatic views of the areas surrounding Acadia National Park. It is long by carriage-road standards and gains more elevation (1,000 feet) than any other loop in the park. Nevertheless, strong riders can still complete it in less than half a day. However, it is easy to spend the entire day studying details of nature and soaking in the long distance views.

Begin this trip by turning onto the carriage road across the street from the Jordan Pond Gatehouse. Turn right at Post 16 and go straight at Post 15. At 0.3 mile, a small bridge crosses the outlet to Jordan Pond, as the carriage road climbs up to Post 14 at 0.5 mile, where you should turn left. A short but steep climb brings you to the modest West Branch Bridge with its single, tall narrow arch spanning a small stream tumbling down Penobscot Mountain. Continue to climb 1.2 miles, where you will reach the 230-foot-long Cliffside Bridge, which has the style of a fortress from the Middle Ages. Two large viewing turrets invite you to look out at Pemetic and Day Mountains, as well as the Triad. Maples and other hardwoods dominate the foreground, while spruce and fir cling to the distant mountains.

As you round the southern end of Penobscot Mountain, you come to Post 21, where you should continue straight toward the Amphitheater.

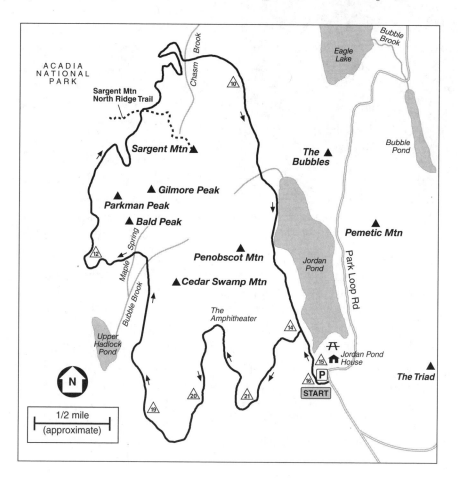

A rider takes a break on Waterfall Bridge.
Photo by Jerry and Marcy Monkman.

The road gently rises through a mosaic forest, and views of the rounded ridges that make up the Amphitheater soon come into view. At 2.2 miles, you'll reach the head of the Amphitheater and the 235-foot-long bridge that crosses the small gorge there. Walking down the trail at the west end of the bridge will take you down to Little Harbor Brook, where you can look through the arch in the bridge to a small waterfall.

Continuing past the bridge, turn right at Post 20 for a gradual climb up to views of the Cranberry Islands. As you ride toward Post 19, notice the variety of lichens that grow on the rocks lining the road. Green target lichens grow in concentric rings. Brown-and-black rock tripe looks like lettuce gone bad clinging to the rocks. Reindeer lichen grows in bunches, its greenish white branches looking like antlers. It is actually eaten by reindeer and caribou in the arctic environments where they live. There are also large clumps of rhodora, an evergreen shrub that grows in bogs and other areas with acidic soils. When you reach Post 19 at 3.6 miles, turn right. At 5.0 miles, you'll reach a pair of magnificent bridges that span Hadlock Brook and Maple Spring. Waterfall Bridge looks out at Hadlock Brook as it tumbles over 40 feet of granite. Hemlock Bridge spans Maple Spring, which is lined with tall hemlocks and white pines. An enchanted feeling creeps in as you ride over these intricate bridges through tall trees surrounded by the sounds of water and bird song. The road then climbs to views of Upper Hadlock Pond and the Cranberries at Post 12 (5.5 miles). Turn right to begin one of the longest climbs in the carriage road system.

The carriage road goes up for most of the next 1.8 miles, reaching an elevation of 800 feet. The road traverses the western shoulder of Parkman Mountain, rising through a forest of pitch pine on its way to extensive views to the west and north. Somes Sound, the only fiord in the eastern United States, can be seen just to the west of the road, with Acadia Beech and Bernard Mountains rising up to the west of the sound. As you get higher and round the northern end of Sargent Mountain, the wind gets a little stronger and the air a little colder. At this point, the views open up to include Mount Desert narrows and northern Maine.

Once you pass the Sargent Mountain North Ridge Trail at 7.3 miles, you are rewarded with a long, winding downhill coast that will take you back to Jordan Pond. It is easy to pick up a lot of speed on this stretch. Try to control your speed, because it is fairly likely that someone will be stopped on the road, hidden behind a curve. You will have good views to Eagle Lake on the way down. Notice how the forest is sharply demarcated between spruce-fir and paper birch. Spruce-fir forests dominated the island before the great fire of 1947. After the fire, pioneer species such as aspen, birch, and other hardwoods grew back in place of the spruce and fir. In this area, thin soil has made it hard for trees to return, and the paper birch that are growing are very thin and spindly. By identifying the different forest types, it is easy to see where the fire did its damage.

At 8.7 miles, cross a small bridge over Chasm Brook, which falls about 40 feet over the rocks to the south of the bridge. At 9.2 miles, go straight at Post 10. A slight incline brings you to another waterfall and the Deer Brook Bridge at 10.0 miles. The north end of Jordan Pond begins to come into view through the trees on the left. Continuing south, you will break out into the open as you pass by a massive rockslide on the east face of Penobscot Mountain. Here you will have a great look at Jordan Pond, the Bubbles, and Pemetic Mountain. Looming above you are Jordan Cliffs. At 11.3 miles, bear left at Post 14, which completes the loop. To finish your trip, stay to the left at Posts 15 and 16.

TRIP 33
MOOSEHORN NATIONAL WILDLIFE REFUGE

Aerobic Difficulty: Easy to moderate
Technical Difficulty: Easy to moderate
Distance: 10.0-mile loop
Estimated Time: 3 hours
Location: Baring, south of Calais
Maps: USGS Calais Quad
 USGS Meddybemps Lake East Quad
 DeLorme *Maine Atlas*, map 36

An enjoyable ride through woods, meadows, wetlands, and streams in a wild and remote national wildlife refuge.

Directions

The Baring Division of Moosehorn National Wildlife Refuge is located off US 1 southwest of Calais. It can be reached from US 1 north or south, or from Route 9, east of Bangor. From Calais, follow US 1 for 3.3 miles across Magurrewock Stream to Charlotte Road. Turn left onto Charlotte Road and drive for just over 2 miles to the refuge headquarters entrance. Turn right at the entrance and follow the dirt road to the headquarters parking area.

Trail Notes

Maps of the refuge are available at the main office during operating hours, Monday through Friday from 7:30 A.M. to 4 P.M. A self-serve information kiosk across from the parking area includes maps and other information if you are visiting the refuge after hours or during the weekend. Restroom facilities and a water fountain are accessible throughout the day and on weekends.

Trip Description

Moosehorn National Wildlife Refuge comprises nearly 25,000 acres of woods, wetlands, meadows, and streams and is home to an array of mammals including moose, deer, bear, and beaver. It is the easternmost refuge in the Atlantic flyway, a migration route that follows the east coast

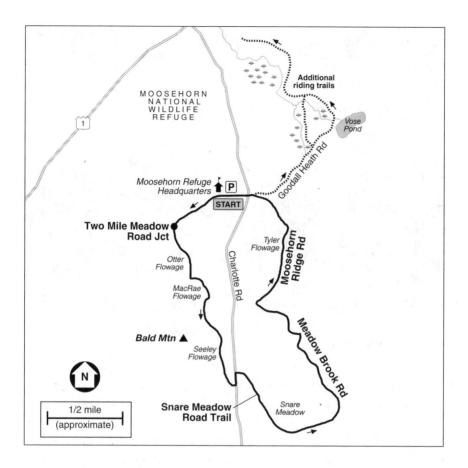

of North America. More than 125 species of birds come here to breed, including the elusive and endearing American woodcock, which the refuge is specially managed to support. With more than 50 miles of dirt roads and trails, biking is an excellent way to explore Moosehorn and observe its fascinating ecosystem and abundant wildlife.

This trip begins from refuge headquarters in the Baring Division of Moosehorn (the smaller Edmunds unit is located next to Cobscook Bay State Park). If you come here during office hours, be sure to stop in and pick up a map of the refuge and inquire about recent wildlife sightings. The route follows dirt roads and a series of flowages along the southwestern portion of the refuge, then crosses over Charlotte Road to pick up the trail on the eastern side of Moosehorn to complete the loop. Except for a few moderate rises and some rocky terrain along the eastern portion of the ride, the trail is well graded and accessible to all ability levels.

Riding past one of the many pondlike streams known as "flowages" at Moosehorn National Wildlife Refuge.

From the parking area, turn west and ride down the dirt road (gated) that departs behind the refuge headquarters. Follow the level, graded path beneath a mixed hardwood forest and along open meadows to the junction of Two Mile Meadow Road at 0.7 mile. Turn left (south) here. At 1.0 mile, the trail reaches the first in a series of pond-like streams known as "flowages." This one is called Otter Flowage and is marked with a sign that reads "Otter." When I arrived here, I assumed it described the body of water, but had second thoughts when, seemingly on cue, a river otter appeared at the water's edge. This was the first of several wildlife sightings I would have during the ride.

Continuing, the path bends to the left around MacCrae Flowage and reaches a T-junction at One-Mile Bridge Road. Turn right here and continue south through a mixed forest at the northeastern foot of Bald Mountain. Soon you'll reach another junction where a road leaves right. Stay straight to reach Seeley Flowage, a large, beautiful pond strewn with lily pads and fringed by wildflowers during summer. From here, the path cuts through a recently harvested section of woods before arriving at Charlotte Road, 3.5 miles from refuge headquarters.

To continue, cross Charlotte Road and turn north, pedaling on the pavement for 0.2 mile to reach the Snare Meadow Road Trail entrance. The trail turns south and east and travels along the western edge of Snare Meadow, reaching its beautiful beaver pond in 1.0 mile from Charlotte Road. Moosehorn is home to an estimated 300 beavers, and evidence of their work and presence is plainly visible at this pond.

From Snare Meadow, the road climbs east and then swings north onto Meadow Brook Road through a fairly long section of second-growth forest. This is the most difficult part of the trail, with short climbs that require a bit more work. Yet, like most of the refuge, it is worth the effort and full of surprises. When I came through, I was gathering speed on the backside of a short climb, rounded a bend, and was greeted by a large black bear in the middle of the road.

At 7.5 miles, the road reaches a junction with Moosehorn Ridge Road at a height of land. There is no sign here except for a cross-country ski marker. Turn right onto Moosehorn Ridge Road. If you stay straight on Meadow Brook Road, a short descent quickly brings you to Charlotte Road. From Moosehorn Ridge Road, the trail continues for 1.2 miles passing Tyler Flowage before reaching a sharp left. From here, it is just over a half-mile to a junction with Goodall Heath Road. Turn left here for the short ride to Charlotte Road and across to refuge headquarters.

Nature and History Notes

Moosehorn is a great place to watch ospreys and bald eagles, which are easily seen from the roadside observation platform on Route 1 or along Charlotte Road north of the refuge headquarters. The refuge is also home to a large population of American woodcocks. Woodcocks, also known as Timberdoodles, are reclusive shorebirds that have evolved and adapted to the eastern forests. They spend their days in dense thickets, using their long bills to locate and extract earthworms from the ground. Male woodcocks are well known for their spectacular aerial courtship displays, which they perform in open fields in spring and early summer. At dusk and dawn, the male sits in his chosen territory and begins to sing a nasal *peent* every few seconds. After several *peents*, he takes flight, spiraling high into the sky. As he flies higher and higher, he warbles a plaintive song to awaiting females. Then, he plunges back to earth, returning to the same spot, and repeats the display, intent on attracting a mate.

Unfortunately, the woodcock population along the Atlantic Flyway has steadily declined over the past two decades, primarily due to loss of habitat. Moosehorn is the only refuge in the nation specifically managed for woodcocks. The refuge has pioneered efforts to understand their biology and developed a variety of management techniques to support these interesting and whimsical birds.

Other Options

To extend this ride, you can take Goodall Heath Road east and north to Popple Flowage and Vose Pond and then onto Magurrewock Road along the eastern side of Magurrewock Marsh, home to bald eagles and ospreys. The road eventually reaches Route 1, where you can retrace your path or turn left onto Route 1 and ride to Charlotte Road and then back to refuge headquarters from there.

More Information

For more information about Moosehorn National Wildlife Refuge, contact the Refuge Manager at 207-454-7161, or visit the refuge website at www.fws.gov/northeast/moosehorn.

TRIP 34
EAGLE LAKE—ACADIA NATIONAL PARK

(Excerpted from the AMC's *Discover Acadia National Park* by Jerry and Marcy Monkman)

Difficulty: Moderate
Distance: 4.0 miles round-trip
Estimated Time: 3 hours
Location: Acadia National Park
Maps: USGS Quadrangles: Southwest Harbor, Seal Harbor,
      Salsbury Cove, and Bar Harbor
      AMC's *Discover Acadia National Park Map*: D7
      DeLorme *Maine Atlas*, map 16

A moderate paddle on a scenic lake with mountain views and wild shorelines.

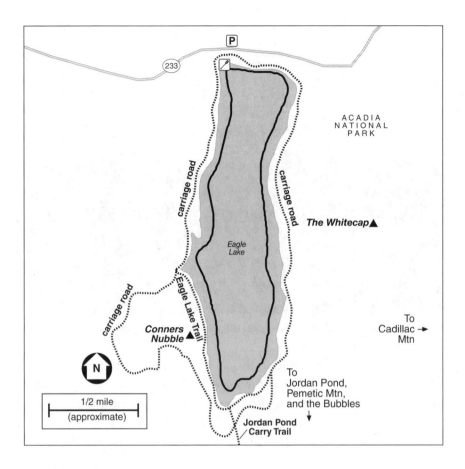

Directions

From the intersection of Route 3/233 in Bar Harbor, take Route 233 west toward Cadillac Mountain. The parking area for Eagle Lake is at 2.1 miles on the left.

Trail Notes

Because Eagle Lake is the water supply for Bar Harbor, swimming in the lake is prohibited.

Trip Description

Eagle Lake is the largest lake on the eastern side of Mount Desert Island and is a popular spot due to its proximity to Bar Harbor. All of Eagle Lake is part of Acadia National Park, giving it a wild shoreline with none of the cottages and camps you find on most other lakes on the island. Its views

Cadillac and Pemetic mountains across Eagle Lake. Photo by Jerry and Marcy Monkman.

of Cadillac and Pemetic Mountains, as well as the Bubbles, are breathtaking. It is 4.0 miles around the edge of the lake, making it possible to spend a leisurely day taking in the scenery and watching for loons, mergansers, and ospreys. Carriage roads circle the lake and connect with hiking trails, creating the opportunity to spend the whole day in the area, paddling, hiking, and biking.

A paddling trip on Eagle Lake begins at the north end of the lake, at the Eagle Lake parking area on the north side of Maine Route 233. Motorboats are allowed on the lake, but there is a 10-horsepower limit on motors. Motorized vehicles on the lake are most likely slow-moving boats of fisherman dropping their lines into the 110-foot-deep water, trying to hook the salmon and trout that thrive in the lake's cold water. These fish make up the diet of the common mergansers and loons that nest around the lake. The fish are also what draw ospreys to the wild southern end of the lake. Ospreys are impressive fisherman, diving into the water talons first and emerging with a fish more than 50 percent of the time. It is no wonder bald eagles often spend their time harassing ospreys in an attempt to get them to drop their prey.

Paddling Eagle Lake can take as much or as little time as you want. The shoreline is wooded and rocky, with just a few coves and inlets to explore.

Either follow the shoreline for a 4-mile paddle or paddle straight across to the southern end of the lake, 1.75 miles away. As on all bodies of water on Mount Desert Island, a wind out of the north can create some large waves at the southern end of the lake. On a windy day, keep in mind the fact that you will have to paddle against these waves on the return trip. At the southern end of the pond, directly opposite the put-in, is a shallow gravel area, which makes it easy to land your boat and take a break on the shore. The Eagle Lake Trail can be found here. Hiking the trail to the right makes for a flat 0.5-mile walk along the southwestern shore of the lake. Following the trail to the left can connect you to the Jordan Pond Carry Trail, which is a 1.1-mile footpath through northern hardwood forest that ends at the northeastern shore of Jordan Pond. These trails also connect with the extensive system of gravel carriage roads.

Whether you follow the shoreline back or paddle down the middle of the lake, see if your hearing is as keen as that of painter Thomas Cole, who first visited Eagle Lake in 1844. According to *Mount Desert Island and Acadia National Park: An Informal History* by Sargent Collier, Cole named the lake for the bald eagles that soared over his easel, and he once remarked that at Eagle Lake "one may fancy himself in the forests of the Alleghenies, but for the dull roar of the ocean breaking the stillness." The ocean is 3.0 miles away.

Nature and History Notes

Eagle Lake was saved from development before Acadia National Park existed. In 1908, a prominent Bar Harbor summer resident quietly made plans to build a summer home on the high ground to the west of Eagle Lake. When word of his plans became public and it was learned that outflow from the house had nowhere to drain but Eagle Lake, concerned citizens sprang into action. George Dorr, unquestionably the father of Acadia National Park and its first superintendent, rallied his wealthy and prominent friends to publicize the harmful sanitation effects of such a project on the pristine lake. His efforts convinced the state of Maine to pass legislation condemning the watersheds of Eagle Lake and Jordan Pond, effectively preserving the water quality and preventing development on either body of water. Eagle Lake achieved federal protection with the creation of the Sieur de Monts National Monument in 1916. Today, Eagle Lake is the largest body of water on the island without any buildings on its shoreline.

TRIP 35
DONNELL POND

Difficulty: Easy to moderate
Distance: 6.0 miles round-trip
Estimated Time: 4 hours
Location: Franklin
Maps: USGS Sullivan Quadrangle
DeLorme *Maine Atlas*, map 24

A pleasant paddle on a deep, clear-water pond with sandy beaches and access to panoramic views atop nearby peaks.

Directions
From Ellsworth, drive east on US 1 to ME 182. Turn left onto ME 182 and go 7.8 miles to Donnell Pond Road. Turn right, and drive 1.4 miles to a fork in the road. Stay left and drive another 0.2 mile to the launch site, parking area, and restroom facilities.

Trail Notes
Although Donnell Pond is largely undeveloped and personal watercraft (Jet Skis, etc.) are not allowed here, there may be significant motorboat traffic during summer weekends. Spring and fall are the best times to visit, or mid-week in summer.

Authorized campsites at Donnell Pond are available on a first-come, first-served basis with no fees or permits required. Campsites have a table, fire rings, and nearby pit toilet. Except in day-use areas, visitors may camp elsewhere on the unit, but they may not build fires.

Trip Description
The 15,000-acre Donnell Pond Reserve is one of 29 Public Reserve Lands spread across Maine. The reserve is tucked between two scenic byways (US 1 and ME 182) and encompasses a constellation of crystal-clear lakes, secluded ponds, and accessible mountains with panoramic views across the region, including Acadia National Park's prominent peaks. Donnell Pond's undeveloped eastern shoreline features sandy beaches, pocket coves, picnic areas, fourteen authorized campsites, and access to

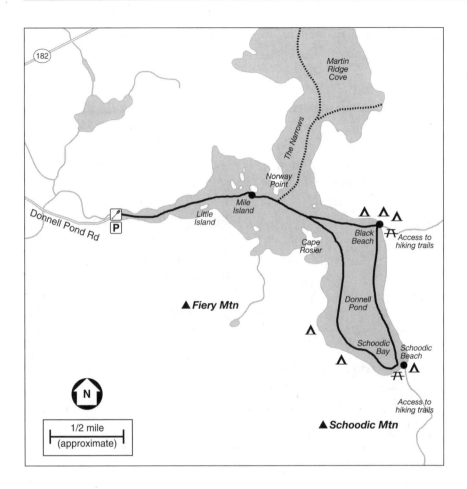

more than 15 miles of hiking trails. This is an excellent place for a family outing, or to explore the picturesque downeast landscape when visitors overwhelm Acadia.

Donnell's boat launch is located next to the tumbling waters of Alder Brook, the pond's western outlet. Although this section of Donnell is populated with camps and cottages, the majority of the 1,100-acre pond lies within Maine Public Reserve Land, and is otherwise wild and uninhabited. Paddling out from the pond's western arm, you'll have a direct view to Black Mountain, one of three peaks within the reserve that rise to over a thousand feet.

At 0.7 mile, you'll pass Little Island. Continue east for 0.3 mile to reach a cluster of islands at the head of a large cove. Mile Island, so named for its distance from the put-in, is the largest of the islands within the group and a good spot to pull out for a swim, picnic, or to explore its beautiful granite shoreline.

Beyond Mile Island, the pond opens to two large coves, with Martin Ridge Cove to the north, and Schoodic Bay to the south. Continue paddling east past Norway Point and toward the pond's eastern shoreline. At 2.0 miles, you'll approach Black Beach (also known as Redman's Beach), a long, sandy beach with a picnic area, campsites, and trail access through dense forest to the cliffs and open summit of Black Mountain.

From Black Beach, Donnell Pond extends for another mile south to picturesque and popular Schoodic Bay and Schoodic Beach. There are campsites here, a picnic area, and trails from the west end of the beach leading to Schoodic Mountain (2.5 miles round-trip). From Schoodic's bald summit, there are excellent views in all directions including south to Frenchman's Bay and Mount Desert Island.

To return, follow the western shoreline from Schoodic Bay around Cape Rosier and back to the put-in, or continue north through The Narrows to explore Martin Ridge Cove.

Nature and History Notes

Like other lakes and ponds in the area, Donnell Pond is oligotrophic, a body of water with very low nutrient levels. However, the scarcity of aquatic plants and algae, and low levels of phosphorous and chlorophyll result in excellent water quality and clarity. In fact, nearby Tunk Lake is reputedly the clearest lake in Maine. Donnell Pond supports a diversity of fish species including land-locked salmon, lake trout, and perch. In turn, the fish sustain osprey, bald eagle, and common loon.

Two noncontiguous areas within the reserve totaling nearly 6,000 acres have been designated as "Ecological Reserves" due to the presence of several "exemplary natural communities" as identified by the Maine Natural Areas Program. In addition, the bald summit of Schoodic Mountain is home to a rare plant species (mountain sandwort), and has been identified as an exemplary Low Bald Summit natural community.

The forests within the reserve support a mosaic of tree species including heath-krummholz summits, intact spruce-fir broom-moss forests on steep slopes, drier oak-pine forests on south facing slopes, and early successional hardwoods. There is also an ecologically significant stand of old growth red spruce near Black Mountain. Several trees within the 20-acre stand are more than 250 years old, with one tree dating to 1692.

Setting out on a fall afternoon for a quiet paddle on Donnell Pond.

Other Options

Schoodic Beach and the hiking trails to Schoodic Mountain and Black Mountain Cliffs can also be accessed from ME 183, 12.0 miles north of Ellsworth. Turn left onto Route 183 from US 1 in East Sullivan. Drive 4.5 miles, and turn left onto a gravel road (Public Lands sign) after crossing the railroad tracks. Follow the gravel road for 0.3 mile to a Y. Turn left on Schoodic Beach Road to the Schoodic Beach parking area (the right branch leads to Black Mountain and Caribou Mountain). A longer trail to the summit of Schoodic Mountain departs east of ME 200 in East Franklin. For a complete description of this route, consult the AMC's Maine Mountain Guide, 9th ed.

More Information

To learn more about recreational opportunities at the Donnell Pond Reserve, visit the Bureau of Public Lands website at www.maine.gov/doc/parks.

Lighthouses of Maine

For more than 200 years, Maine lighthouses have been guiding mariners home through treacherous waters and craggy coast. Sixty-eight such beacons grace Maine's 3,500 miles of rugged, convoluted shoreline. Fifty-four of these are still active today.

Portland Head Light was the first lighthouse built in Maine. When it was first proposed in 1784, Maine was still part of Massachusetts, and Portland, then known as Falmouth, was among America's busiest ports. That year, 74 merchants petitioned the Massachusetts government for a light to mark the entrance to the harbor. In 1787, when two people died in a shipwreck near Portland Head, the Commonwealth acceded and appropriated $750 for a lighthouse. However, the project was delayed by insufficient funds and didn't progress until 1790 when the United States government took over responsibility for all lighthouses and Congress allocated an additional $1,500 for the lighthouse. The original tower measured 72 feet from base to lantern deck and was lit with 16 whale oil lamps. It was first lit on January 10, 1791. President George Washington appointed the lighthouse's first keeper.

Portland native Henry Wadsworth Longfellow was a frequent visitor to the lighthouse. His poem "The Lighthouse" was inspired in part by his many hours spent there:

> The rocky ledge runs far out into the sea,
> And on its outer point, some miles away,
> The lighthouse lifts its massive masonry,
> A pillar of fire by night, of cloud by day.

In 1806, Thomas Jefferson signed the order authorizing construction of a lighthouse at West Quoddy to safely guide seafarers through the Quoddy Narrows, between the United States and Canada. The picturesque and distinctive lighthouse stands on the easternmost point of the United States, catching the mainland's first rays of morning light. It is one of only two lighthouses in the country painted with horizontal red and white stripes. The practice, more common in Canada, was meant to help the lighthouses stand out against the snow.

Pemaquid Point Lighthouse.

Cape Neddick Lighthouse in York, also known as Nubble Lighthouse, is among Maine's most famous and often photographed lighthouses. In 1977, when NASA launched the Voyager space probe, the craft was outfitted with photographs of Earth's most prominent landmarks in the event the probe was intercepted by "intelligent creatures." Among the pictures included were the Great Wall of China, the Grand Canyon, and Nubble Lighthouse.

TRIP 36
DEER ISLE ARCHIPELAGO

Difficulty: Moderate
Distance: 10.0-mile loop
Estimated Time: 6 hours
Location: Stonington
Maps: USGS Deer Isle Quad
      USGS Stinson Neck
      DeLorme *Maine Atlas*, maps 15 and 9

An island-to-island tour of Maine's premiere kayaking destination.

Directions
Presently, the only public launch site available in Stonington is a small, all-tide ramp behind the ferry service on Bayview Avenue. However, there is no parking at the launch site, and in-town parking is limited to 2 hours. The best option is to launch into Webb Cove from the all-tide ramp (fee) provided by Old Quarry Ocean Adventures (207-367-8977) on nearby Buckmaster Neck in Oceanville. Old Quarry caters to kayakers and can provide just about everything you might need, including the launch site, parking, boat rentals, shuttle service, trip suggestions, camping, equipment, and even registered guides.

To reach Old Quarry Ocean Adventures, look for the "Kayak Launch Site" sign at the junction of Route 15 and Oceanville Road, approximately 3 miles south of Deer Isle. Turn left onto Oceanville Road and travel 0.9 mile to a second sign at Fire Road 22. Turn right here and follow the road to the entrance.

Trail Notes
Boat traffic and fog are the principal safety issues to consider when paddling here. The Deer Island Thorofare is utilized by a variety of vessels including the Stonington fishing fleet, and is especially congested in summer. Merchant Row is the principal passage for larger vessels as well as ferries, schooners, sailboats, and other craft. Fog is frequent here and can develop quickly, severely limiting visibility.

Trip Description

The Deer Isle Archipelago is often referred to as the East Coast's premiere paddling destination. With its cluster of 65 beautiful islands set amidst a glimmering blue-green sea, it's no wonder why. For kayakers, few other places offer such an extraordinary combination of dazzling scenery, relative protection from the elements, and interesting trip options. Many of the islands are open to the public, and more than a few of these feature designated campsites, providing nearly unlimited opportunities for day trips or extended outings.

If there is one drawback to this extraordinary setting, it is that it sometimes suffers from its own popularity. In mid-summer, the islands are often crowded and the waterways congested with an array of vessels, not the least of which are kayakers (a matter of ongoing concern amongst

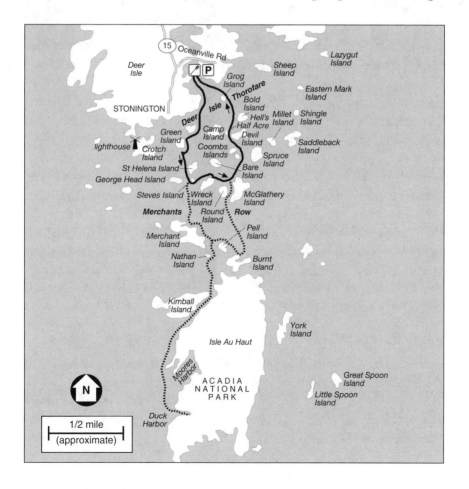

Looking out to Crotch Island from Stonington Harbor.

more than a few locals). Nonetheless, the archipelago is well worth a visit, especially if you can plan a trip outside of the high-season months of July and August.

With so many compelling islands to choose from, perhaps the only other difficulty in paddling here is deciding where to go. This day trip departs from the launch site at Old Quarry Ocean Adventures in Webb Cove and forms a suggested loop with optional visits to some of the most interesting islands, including Green, Wreck, and Hell's Half Acre (which, by the way, is neither Hell, nor a half-acre). However, with some helpful guidance from the folks at Old Quarry, you can easily chart your own course, and are encouraged to do so if weather is a consideration when you visit the area.

Departing from Webb Cove, paddle south and west to reach the southeastern tip of Deer Isle in Stonington. From here, check for traffic, and carefully ferry across the Deer Isle Thorofare to the northeastern tip of Russ Island, which is owned by the Island Institute, and has excellent views from its open hilltops. Once across, paddle around to the southern end of the island (there is a beach landing here if you want to explore Russ), and on toward Green Island. Like the majority of islands within the archipelago, Russ and Green are composed of beautiful stands of spruce and open meadows atop course-grained granite. During the nineteenth century, many of the islands, including Green Island, were quarried for their beautiful stone and used for public building projects in major eastern U.S. cities. Crotch Island, west of Green, is the site of the only remaining working quarry factory in Maine. The granite supplied from Crotch Island was used for the Boston Museum of Fine Arts as well as John F. Kennedy's memorial at Arlington National Cemetery.

Paddle down the eastern shore of Green Island to reach its southeastern tip, where there is an inviting stone beach that provides a great place to haul out for a break and enjoy the views. From Green, head due south to the western shore of St. Helena Island. Paddling between St. Helena and Georges Head Islands, aim for small, but popular, Steves Island, which has attractive coves and is among several islands here along the Maine Island Trail.

East of Steves Island is beautiful Wreck Island, owned by the Island Heritage Trust. This 60-acre island preserve is open for day-use only, but well worth exploring its pocket beaches, forest, and open meadows (the best landing site is on the eastern end of the island, which affords more protection). South of Wreck Island lies a mile of open water known as Merchant Row, which is exposed to wind, waves, and boat traffic. Across the passage, there are several interesting islands including Harbor, Wheat, and fabulous Isle au Haut, which is part of Acadia National Park. However, exploring the archipelago's outer fringe demands and deserves a multi-day excursion.

To complete the day trip, turn southeast from Wreck Island to reach Round Island, then paddle north and east across the top of McGlathery Island. Continue paddling north between Coombs Island and Spruce Island, then skirt around Devil Island to reach Hell's Half Acre. This popular island actually encompasses 2 acres and, with its sloping granite shoreline, is one of the most accessible destinations within the archipelago. The final leg of the trip requires a passage back across the Deer Isle Thorofare, around Grog Island, to Webb Cove.

Other Options

Excellent hiking and biking opportunities abound on Acadia National Park's Isle au Haut. Old Quarry Ocean Adventures offers a charter service (as well as bicycle rentals) for day-trippers who would like to explore the island by pedal and/or on foot.

More Information

For more information about the Deer Isle Archipelago and other trip options, refer to the AMC's *Sea Kayaking Along the New England Coast* by Tamsin Venn. For more information about Isle au Haut, check out the AMC's *Discover Acadia National Park*.

TRIP 37
GREAT WASS ISLAND

Difficulty: Moderate to difficult
Distance: 10.0 miles round-trip
Estimated Time: 5–6 hours
Location: Jonesport
Maps: USGS Jonesport Quad
USGS Great Wass Island Quad
DeLorme *Maine Atlas*, maps 17 and 26

An enjoyable paddle along the rugged shoreline of Maine's southernmost landmass with an excursion to a spectacular Nature Conservancy Preserve.

Directions

There is an all-tide public boat ramp in Jonesport located on Sawyer Square Road. From Route 1, take ME 187 into Jonesport. Toward the east end of town, turn south on Sawyer Square Road at the sign for Sawyer Square and follow to the launch site.

Trail Notes

Caution: Although the route described here is relatively protected, the crossing from Jonesport to Great Wass Island across Moosabec Reach is subject to swift tides and strong eddies, and is heavily traveled by fishing boats and other craft. Additionally, the archipelago is frequently beset by fog, wind, and waves. The southern tip of Great Wass Island, at Red Head, is particularly exposed and dangerous, and should only be attempted by experienced paddlers who possess advanced boating skills and sound judgment.

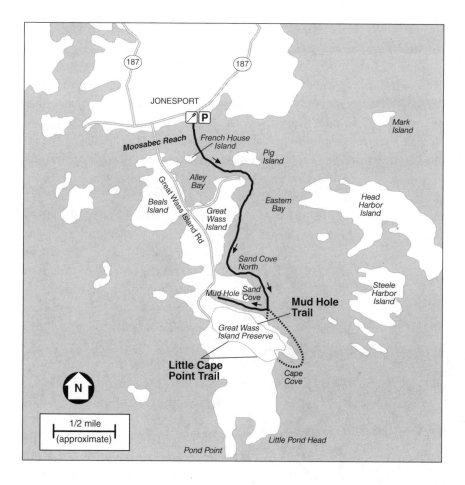

Trip Description

The Great Wass Archipelago, a magnificent collection of rugged, wind-swept, ecologically important islands, lies at the heart of Downeast Maine, where the waters from the Gulf of Maine collide with the Bay of Fundy. The cool maritime climate produces a rich and unusual assortment of flora, including arctic and sub-arctic plants that reach their southern limits here. The Nature Conservancy (TNC) and the U.S. Fish and Wildlife Service have acquired and protected several sensitive areas, including TNC's spectacular 1,500-acre preserve on Great Wass Island. For paddlers, the archipelago presents some major challenges. Fog is frequent in summertime, and much of the area is exposed to a beautiful but very rugged shoreline, as well as extremes of wind, waves, and tide.

Nonetheless, this is one of the state's most majestic settings and well worth the trip for experienced boaters.

This excursion departs from Jonesport, a quintessential Maine fishing community packed with lobster and fishing boats, and ventures across Moosabec Reach, through Pig Island Gut to the eastern shoreline of Great Wass Island. From here, we'll follow the varied shoreline to Mud Hole, a shallow, serene inlet that reaches well into the middle of the island at high tide. At Mud Hole Point, you can pull out to walk the beautiful trails into the heart of the Great Wass Island Preserve, or continue south to Cape Cove and pick up the trail from there.

Strong tides and heavy boat traffic warrant sound judgment before setting off into Moosabec Reach. The current floods to the east and ebbs west, and can reach 8 knots at times, making a paddle against an opposing tide difficult and tiring. The swift tides can also produce strong eddies and sharp eddy lines that may be unsettling for inexperienced boaters. Time your trip to avoid the middle of the tide when the current is strongest.

From the boat launch, ferry south across the reach toward the eastern end of French House Island. From there, turn east and south toward Pig Island Gut, which lies between Pig Island and the northern tip of Great Wass and exits into Eastern Bay. Beware that there is frequent boat traffic through this narrow passage. Once through, watch for offshore ledges outside the gut as you turn south toward Great Wass's eastern shoreline.

Continuing south, follow Wass's shoreline down the western edge of the bay. To the east, look for seals hauled out on the numerous ledges

The rocky shore of Great Wass Island.

and islands that dot the bay. About a mile and a half from Pig Island Gut, you'll reach Sand Cove North. From here, the shoreline juts to the east and south around a point and between ledges before reaching Sand Cove. The inlet to Mud Hole lies just south of Sand Cove, a little more than 4.0 miles from the launch site in Jonesport.

Mud Hole is a quiet, exceptionally beautiful inlet that marks the northern edge of the Great Wass Island Preserve. When I was here on a midsummer day, I sighted two immature bald eagles. At high tide, you can make your way about a half-mile into the cove. Otherwise, as the name suggests, Mud Hole turns to mud about two-thirds of the way in.

There are two options for exploring the inner part of the preserve. Just inside Mud Hole, at the tip of Mud Hole Point, you can haul out onto the rocks (be sure to pull your boat well above the water line) and walk up the bank to reach the Mud Hole Trail. There are faint but visible blue blazes marking the way. Or, you can continue paddling to an easier take-out inside Cape Cove south of Little Cape Point. At Cape Cove, a cairn marks the trail. The Mud Hole Trail (3.0 miles round-trip), skirts the edge of the inlet through beautiful woods before turning inland and crossing open ledges interspersed with large stands of jack pine trees. The longer Little Point Cape Trail (4.0 miles out and back) cuts across the heart of the preserve over interesting swamps and bogs, open ledges, jack pine stands, and a lush spruce-fir forest. Along the granite-strewn shoreline, a pathway, marked by blue blazes, connects both trails.

Beyond Cape Cove lay the rugged cliffs and deep inlets that form Wass's southern shore. Here, the scenery is even wilder and more beautiful, especially at Red Head and Pond Point. However, the exposure is extreme, and a challenge for even the most skilled paddlers. The steep, rocky shore provides little to no protection from offshore winds, large swells, and strong currents.

For the return, follow the same route, once again mindful of boat traffic within Pig Island Gut and currents and traffic across Moosabec Reach.

Nature and History Notes

Despite a challenging climate marked by frequent fog, salt spray, and wind, several rare plants manage to thrive on Great Wass Island's exposed headlands. Here, you'll find the beautiful beach head iris as well as marsh felwort, and bird's eye primrose. Amongst the ancient and rare coastal raised bogs along the Little Cape Point Trail, you may see carnivorous pitcher plants and sundews. Within the preserve's interior is one of Maine's largest stands of jack pine, a tree at its southern limit here. These stunted, gnarled, and twisted trees reflect the extremes of their environment, yet somehow manage to survive and reproduce in the thinnest of soils and, even more interestingly, without fire. Jack pines are considered fire-dependent, requiring the heat of fire to open their cones. Yet, the trees on Great Wass appear to be reproducing successfully, not only in the absence of fire, but amidst cool, humid, oceanic conditions.

Other Options

To reach the Great Wass Island Preserve by car, cross the bridge over Moosabec Reach from Jonesport to Beals Island. Continue through Beals to Great Wass Island, then follow the dirt road for three miles to Black Duck Cove where there is a parking area and kiosk on the left.

Jonesport is also a departure point for puffin-watching tours on Machias Seal Island. Norton of Jonesport leads daily tours from May through August. For more information, visit www.machiassealisland.com.

More Information

To learn more about the Great Wass Island Preserve, contact the Maine Chapter of The Nature Conservancy at 207-729-5181, or visit their website at www.tnc.org.

TRIP 38
COBSCOOK BAY

Difficulty: Moderate to difficult
Distance: 8–10 miles round-trip
Estimated Time: 4–5 hours
Location: Edmunds/Whiting
Maps: USGS Whiting Quad
       USGS Pembroke Quad
       DeLorme *Maine Atlas*, maps 27 and 37

An exceptional paddle through the "boiling tides" of one of the state's most remote, wild, and beautiful bays.

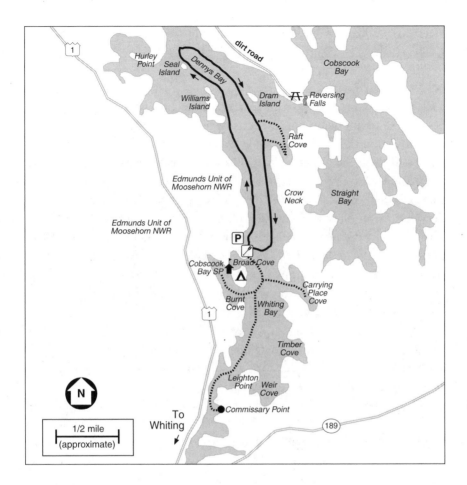

Directions

The all-tide launch ramp into Whiting Bay is located a short distance beyond the entrance to Cobscook Bay State Park. From Whiting, follow US 1 north for 4.3 miles to the park entrance sign. Turn right and drive past the park entrance to the launch site reached in 1.2 miles from US 1.

Trail Notes

Caution: With tidal averages of 24 feet, strong currents, associated whirlpools, eddies and falls, Cobscook Bay can be extremely difficult and dangerous for inexperienced paddlers. At Reversing Falls, a huge volume of water is squeezed between the narrows creating currents that exceed 10 knots along with standing waves and long drops.

A thorough knowledge of current tidal information is imperative. It is best to paddle here with the tide to avoid working against the brunt of the flow.

Trip Description

This trip explores the western reach of Cobscook Bay, one of the most beautiful and imposing natural settings in all of Maine. The bay derives its name from the Passamaquoddy word *kapscook*, which means "waterfalls." But, as author Fannie Hardy Eckstorm writes in *Indian Place Names of the Maine Coast*, "these are not ordinary waterfalls; they are the boiling tide over unseen rocks." Indeed, "boiling tide" is perhaps the more fitting description for the bay's turbulent waters and phenomenal tidal flow. The average tide here exceeds 20 feet, and can rise a foot every fifteen minutes. At the center of the bay, huge volumes of water are squeezed through a narrow gap known as Reversing Falls, creating currents in excess of 10 knots, standing waves, whirlpools, boils and massive eddies. The falls are so impressive that a park has been established near the water's edge so onlookers can witness the show. For boaters, Cobscook can be daunting to say the least. Yet, with sound judgment, appropriate skills, and a thorough understanding of the tides, paddling the bay can also be an enjoyable and serene experience.

Whiting and Dennys bays comprise Cobscook's western arm. Although both bays are subject to the extremes of tide and current, they are relatively protected and provide the best opportunity to enjoy Cobscook's natural beauty and abundant wildlife. Of the two, Whiting Bay is the most sheltered and appropriate for the least experienced paddlers.

From the all-tide ramp near Cobscook Bay State Park, you can turn north, following the shoreline to Birch Island. From Birch Island, continue on to Hallowell (a.k.a. Williams Island), a beautiful island owned by U.S. Fish and Wildlife and part of Moosehorn National Wildlife Refuge. Although there are no trails here, the island is open to the public for day use, and there are places to pull out and enjoy the bay. North of Hallowell, between Wilbur Neck and Hurley Point is a tiny island, named Seal Island, where you are very likely to see seals.

Turning around at Seal Island, paddle down the bay west of Dram Island. East of Dram is the narrows that lead to Reversing Falls. Be careful to avoid this area, especially in the midst of an outgoing tide. South of Dram is Crow Neck, a wooded Peninsula with several interesting coves, including Raft Cove at the northern tip of the neck and Carrying Place

Cove 3.0 miles farther south. Both coves are worth exploring, but beware that both empty at low tide. From Carrying Place Cove, it's a little less than a mile's paddle back across the bay to the launch ramp.

To explore the southern end of Whiting Bay, catch the flood tide and follow the western shoreline from the ramp toward Broad and Burnt coves. Both of these coves lie within the state park. From Burnt Cove, you can paddle across the bay to Carrying Place Cove, or travel farther south to explore Timber and Weir coves. Farther south, the bay narrows at Leighton Point. From here, you can travel into Leighton Cove, or continue on to Commissary Point, a 400-acre tract owned by the Maine Department of Inland Fisheries and Wildlife and managed to protect waterfowl habitat and nesting sites for bald eagles. Careful day-use is allowed. The round-trip from the ramp to Commissary Point and back is approximately 6 miles.

Nature and History Notes
Cobscook Bay's 200 miles of rugged, intricate shoreline remains largely undeveloped, making it one of the most pristine estuaries on the eastern seaboard. With its strong tides, cold, nutrient-rich waters, and extensive tidal flats, the bay is a rich environment for a wide diversity of marine species and prime habitat for sea scallops, sea urchins, and soft-shelled clams. The marine life, in turn, supports an abundance of other wildlife including a healthy population of osprey, bald eagles, migratory shorebirds, and waterfowl. The bay is home to 25 percent of Maine's wintering black duck population, and an important nesting habitat for bald eagles. Falls Island, a 140-acre Nature Conservancy preserve at the heart of the bay, is one of the most productive bald eagle nesting sites in the state, having produced 19 eaglets in the last 20 years.

Other Options
There are several hiking trails within Cobscook Bay State Park, and bicycle-friendly dirt roads at the Edmunds Division of Moosehorn National Wildlife Refuge, which is located off US 1 across from the park.

To visit Reversing Falls Park, follow US 1 from Cobscook Bay State Park toward Pembroke. Turn right at the extension of Route 214 (unmarked), which is located at a stop sign just before the post office. From 214, take an immediate left up a small hill, onto Leighton Point Road (a.k.a. Leighton Neck Road). Continue 3.3 miles and turn right onto a

Looking south from Cobscook Bay State Park at slack tide.

paved road, where a wooden marker indicates the park. At the end of this road, turn left onto a dirt and gravel road and travel for 1.5 miles to the park entrance.

For more information about other outdoor opportunities around Cobscook Bay, pick up a copy of the *Cobscook Trails Guide* published by the Quoddy Regional Land Trust (207-733-5509).

More Information

For information about camping at Cobscook Bay State Park, call 207-726-4412 or visit the Maine Bureau of Parks and Lands website at www.state.me.us/doc/parks.

For more about paddling opportunities in Cobscook Bay, consult the AMC's *Sea Kayaking Along the New England Coast* by Tamsin Venn.

4

Western Lakes & Mountains

THIS REGION'S IMPRESSIVE MOUNTAIN RANGES and vast watershed provide limitless opportunities for exploration and discovery. From Evans Notch to the imposing Bigelow Range, hikers will find an unmatched diversity of terrain from peaceful woods walks to steep scrambles and exposed ridge hikes. Here, paddlers can trace historic Native American waterways from Umbagog Lake, with its abundant wildlife (Trip 49), to Flagstaff, the state's fourth-largest lake, and beyond. The Rangeley Lakes Region alone includes more than 100 interconnected ponds, lakes, streams, and rivers. Featured trips include a demanding hike through Mahoosuc Notch (Trip 42), considered "the most difficult mile along the entire Appalachian Trail," an enjoyable scramble to a pleasant alpine tarn atop Tumbledown Mountain (Trip 43), a beautiful bike ride along the Carrabassett River (Trip 47), and a serpentine paddle in the heart of moose country (Trip 50).

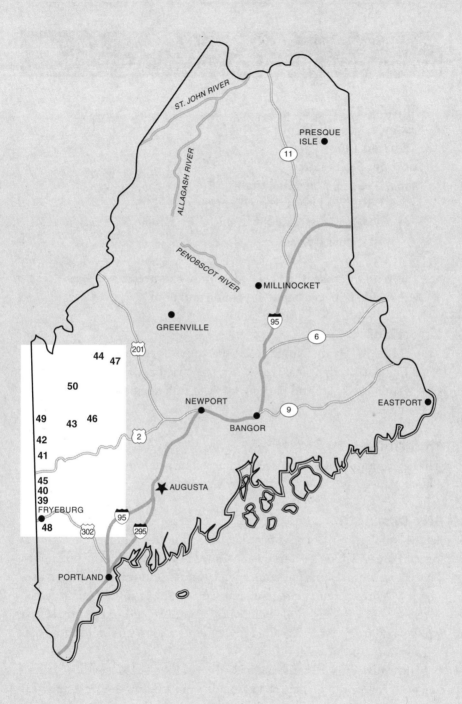

TRIP 39
EVANS NOTCH—BLUEBERRY MOUNTAIN LOOP

Difficulty: Moderate
Distance: 4.5-mile loop
Estimated Time: 3 hours
Location: Evans Notch
Maps: USGS Speckled Mountain
　　　　USGS Wild River, New Hampshire
　　　　AMC's *Maine Mountain Guide*, 9th ed., map 8
　　　　DeLorme *Maine Atlas*, map 10

A loop hike across Blueberry Mountain's impressive ledges with a side trip to a beautiful flume and pool.

Directions
From ME 113 (Evans Notch Road) 0.7 mile north of the AMC's Cold River Camp, turn right (east) onto Stone House Road. Drive for 1.1 miles to the padlocked gate and parking lot. The trail begins on the other side of the gate.

Trail Notes
The beginning of this trail passes by a private residence (the Stone House). Please respect the owner's privacy by walking clear of the property.

Trip Description
Evans Notch is probably the best-kept secret in the White Mountain National Forest. Though often overshadowed by better-known notches in New Hampshire, Evans has some of the finest hiking and most spectacular views throughout the region, and, during fall, is simply unsurpassed for sheer beauty. This loop explores the southern end of the notch, just up the road from the AMC's Cold River Camp, and is a great hike for first-time visitors to the area.

The trail begins from the padlocked gate at Stone House Road. Traveling east, follow the gravel road through a mixed-growth forest and past an open field. At 0.3 mile, you'll pass the White Cairn Trail on the left. This will be your return route. For now, continue east on the gravel road

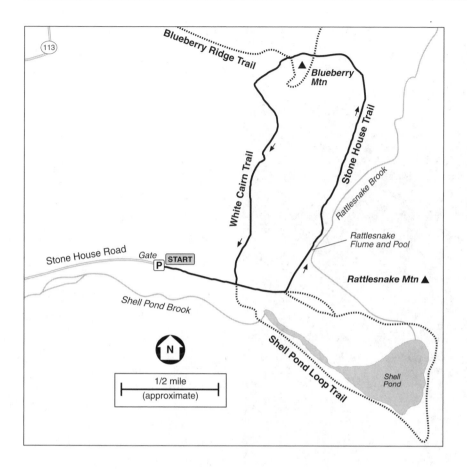

for another 0.2 mile to reach the Stone House Trail, which departs from the left just beyond a small white shed.

At the trailhead, the path turns northeast and follows an old logging road into the woods. At 0.2 mile, the trail merges with a private road. Continue right and look for the spur path that leads right to a bridge overlooking Rattlesnake Flume, a small, beautiful gorge that should not be missed.

Back on the main trail, continue heading northeast to reach a second spur at 0.5 mile from the Stone House trailhead. This spur leads, in 0.1 mile, to a small, attractive swimming hole known as Rattlesnake Pool. The pool sits at the bottom of a small cascade shaded by hemlocks and is an excellent spot to idle away an afternoon on a hot summer day.

Beyond Rattlesnake Pool, the main trail enters the White Mountain National Forest and ascends steadily, passing a fine grove of balsams

Rattlesnake Flume on the Blueberry
Mountain Loop.

before turning west for the summit push at 1.2 miles. From here, the trail climbs steeply up Blueberry Mountain's eastern slope, reaching the Blueberry Ridge Trail at 1.5 miles.

Follow the Blueberry Ridge Trail across the summit to the high point at the Summit Loop Trail Junction. You can walk the loop, but the best views are from the mountain's western ledges. To reach the ledges, continue west on the Blueberry Ridge Trail as it descends into the woods before emerging onto open granite and reaches the junction for the return route down the White Cairn Trail. Straight ahead, there are spectacular views to the notch and beyond including East and West Royce Mountains and the Baldfaces.

When you're ready to descend, pick up the White Cairn Trail heading south as it continues along the crest of the cliffs, passing two springs along the way. At 0.7 mile from the Blueberry Ridge Trail, the path makes a couple of sharp descents before moderating. The trail continues south and west, passing a series of logging roads and an upland meadow before emerging onto Stone House Road. Turn right here for the 0.3-mile walk back to the parking area.

Nature and History Notes

A flume is generally defined as a narrow ravine or gorge with water running through it. According to the Flume Gorge Visitor's Center in Franconia Notch, the name derives from a combination of the Latin word *fluere*, meaning "to flow," and the French word *flumen*, meaning "stream" or "river." The term was also applied to manufactured channels that diverted water. To early American settlers, flumes were the wooden chutes, or troughs, built to transport logs down mountainsides, or to channel water to power gristmills.

Other Options
This loop is equally enjoyable in reverse, and may be the preferred option for those who want to have a refreshing (if not, chilly) dip in Rattlesnake Pool at the end of the hike.

More Information
For additional trail information in the Evans Notch Region, consult the AMC's *Maine Mountain Guide*, 9th ed., or contact the White Mountain National Forest Ranger District in Bethel, Maine, at 207-824-2134. For information about the AMC's Cold River Camp visit the AMC website at www.outdoors.org.

TRIP 40
EVANS NOTCH—THE ROOST

Difficulty: Easy
Distance: 1.2 mile round-trip
Estimated Time: 1 hour
Location: Hastings Township
Maps: USGS Speckled Mountain
　　　　AMC's *Maine Mountain Guide*, 9th ed., map 8
　　　　DeLorme *Maine Atlas*, map 10

An enjoyable jaunt to an excellent perch with commanding views across the Wild River valley.

Directions
The northern trailhead is located on the east side of ME 113, north of Hastings Campground and 0.1 mile beyond Wild River Road. The trail starts just north of the bridge where Evans Brook joins the Wild River. The southern trailhead lies just south of the campground, 0.5 mile from the northern trailhead.

Trail Notes

Parking for this route is limited to either side of the road south of the bridge over Evans Brook, or at the trailhead for the Highwater Trail across ME 113 off Wild River Road.

Trip Description

If you like your hikes short and sweet, you'll love the Roost. The spectacular perch at the end of this enjoyable, half-mile jaunt provides some of the finest views in Evans Notch, and one of the best places in the region to enjoy fall colors. For families, this is an excellent route to introduce children to the joys and rewards of hiking.

The trail enters the woods at the northern edge of the bridge over Evans Brook. The path begins with a short, steep scramble over a 30-

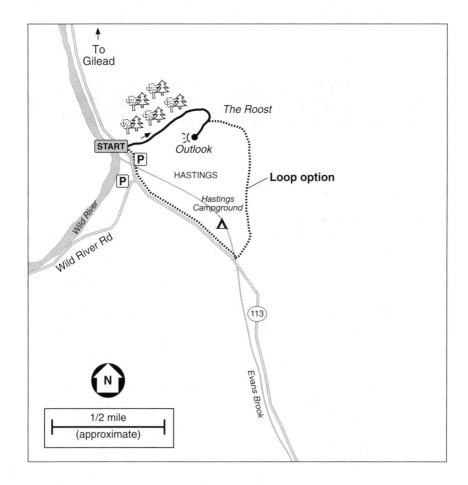

Enjoying the views over the Wild River valley from an outlook atop the Roost.

foot bank before turning east and moderating. The trail makes a steady, gradual ascent through a beautiful stand of mixed hardwoods and stately white pines and reaches a small brook crossing at 0.3 mile.

From here, the trail rises more steeply and swings briefly to the southeast to reach the first of two granite outcrops that form the Roost. There are decent views here, but for a truly spectacular panorama, continue west down the short spur trail that leads to more open ledges. The spur path makes a sharp descent down a granite fissure before easing off and reaching the cliff's edge at 0.1 mile.

Looking west, the outlook takes in the spectacular Wild River valley. The river shimmers 400-feet below as it cuts through the notch on its way to the Androscoggin River. To the south, there are good views of the Royce's and to the northwest you can make out Baldpate and the peaks that comprise Grafton Notch and the Mahoosuc Range. During fall, the palette of colors visible from this 1,200-foot perch is simply magnificent.

To return, retrace your steps up the spur path to the first granite outcrop. From here, you can go back the same way you came, or choose the longer loop option by following the southern route, which leads to ME 113 just south of Hastings Campground in 0.7 mile. To reach your car from here, turn north and walk along the edge of ME 113 for 0.5 mile.

Nature and History Notes

Whether you're hiking or simply enjoying the views from the comfort of your vehicle, Evans Notch is a must destination during the peak of fall foliage. The principal experience here is that of intimacy, a feeling of being enveloped by the kaleidoscope of colors, especially as you wind your way through the notch beneath the tight canopy above ME 113. Panoramas from the height of land, such as those from the Roost, are no less spectacular. Indeed, there are few other places in New England with more impressive views.

More Information

For information about camping at Hastings Campground, contact the Evans Notch Ranger District of the White Mountain National Forest at 207-824-2134.

TRIP 41
GRAFTON NOTCH—TABLE ROCK

Difficulty: Moderate to difficult
Distance: 2.5-mile loop
Estimated Time: 1.5–2 hours
Location: Grafton Notch State Park
Maps: USGS Old Speck Mountain
  AMC's *Maine Mountain Guide*, 9th ed., map 7
  DeLorme *Maine Atlas*, map 18

A short but demanding hike to a wonderful granite-ledge overlook with terrific views of Grafton Notch.

Directions

The trailhead departs from the Appalachian Trail on the eastern side of Route 26 in Grafton Notch State Park. It is located approximately 2.5 miles north of Screw Auger Falls, opposite a large parking area with a sign that reads "Hiking Trail."

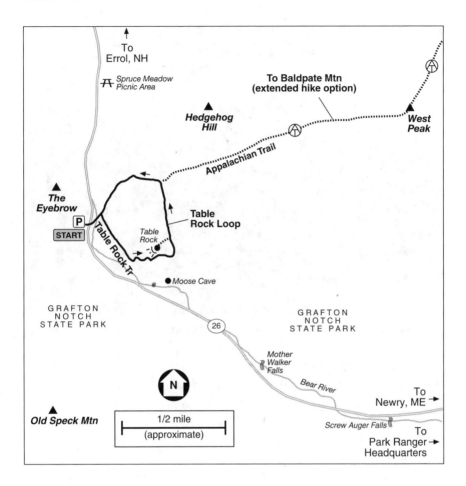

Trail Notes

Despite its relatively short length, this hike is relentlessly steep and demanding on the ascent and is not suitable for young children. To avoid the most difficult section, ascend via the Appalachian Trail to the Upper Table Rock Trail Junction (the descent described below).

Trip Description

Grafton Notch is as wild and remote as Evans Notch is intimate and inviting. While there are a host of accessible, roadside spectacles to savor within Grafton Notch State Park, including beautiful Screw Auger Falls and the deep flume known as Moose Cave, the region is best known for

There are great views across Grafton Notch to Old Speck Mountain from Table Rock.

its imposing terrain. Here, the Appalachian Trail cuts through what many thru-hikers consider the trail's most difficult section (see Trip 42).

Despite its relatively short length, this hike provides a taste of the area's demanding terrain with a steep 1-mile, 900-foot vertical ascent. Yet, it also rewards your effort with interesting caverns to explore and amazing views from the spectacular outlook known as Table Rock.

From the parking lot, cross Route 26 and pick up the white-blazed Appalachian Trail (AT), heading north. Follow the AT into the woods for 0.1 mile until you reach the junction for the Table Rock Trail (hikers seeking the easier route should continue along the AT for 0.9 mile and pick up the upper section of the Table Rock Trail). Turn right (south) at the junction, and follow the trail as it rises gently along the hillside.

At 0.4 miles, the trail begins to climb steadily through a stand of mature hardwoods, reaching a rock-strewn area known as the Boulder Patch at 0.6 mile.

From here, the trail ascends steeply along several rocky switchbacks to a deep ravine between two rock faces. Bear right at the top of the ravine to a prominent outlook at 0.8 mile. At 0.9 mile, the path reaches the ledges that form the base of Table Rock. Here, a series of slabs form an interesting array of cavelike alcoves that are worth exploration (*Caution:* Some of these alcoves are quite deep, and a fall could result in a serious injury). This area is possibly the largest "slab-cave" system in the state.

Beyond the caves, continue south around the bottom of Table Rock. At 1.0 mile, you'll reach the blue-blazed trail that marks Upper Table Rock Trail and your eventual descent. For now though, turn left on a spur path to reach the incredible Table Rock Overlook in 20 yards. The views from this broad, flat slab of granite take in most of the notch and provide a great look at Old Speck Mountain directly south.

After you've recovered from the ascent and soaked in the amazing views, pick up the blue-blazed trail heading north. After 0.5 mile of easy walking, you'll reach the junction with the Appalachian Trail. Turn left here to complete the loop and return to the parking area, or turn right and follow the AT to the Baldpates as described in the option below.

Other Options

To extend this trip into a backcountry excursion, consider a hike out to the west and east peaks of Baldpate Mountain along the AT. The views from East Peak are especially good. Combined with the Table Rock Loop (which, if you choose this option, is best taken on the return from Baldpate), this trip is 8.5 miles long and should take 6 to 7 hours.

More Information

For information about Grafton Notch State Park, contact the Maine Department of Conservation Bureau of Parks and Lands at 207-824-2912.

Grafton Loop Trail

The Grafton Loop Trail (GLT) is the AMC's first newly constructed trail in the North Country since 1976 and a major achievement among the diverse parties that worked cooperatively to complete the project. The final portion of the 38.6-mile loop was completed in the fall of 2005, connecting a series of scenic peaks and other natural features in the Grafton Notch region of Maine, including the east and west peaks of Baldpate Mountain, Old Speck, and Sunday River Whitecap. The project brought together private landowners, a host of nonprofit organizations, and the state of Maine with the goal of developing multiday hiking opportunities that offer alternatives to heavily used sections of the Appalachian Trail (AT). Environmentally, the trail will protect sensitive mountain resources and ease heavy use along a nearby portion of the AT.

The eastern half of the GLT was completed in 2003, and consists of a 21-mile section that leaves Route 26 in Newry, Maine, and returns to the road in Grafton Notch State Park. Seventeen miles within this section are newly constructed trail, which traverse four mountain peaks and include five primitive campsites; the final 4.0 miles to Route 26 in Grafton Notch are via the AT. Approximately two-thirds of the trail's length is on private lands with the remainder located on public lands managed by the Maine Bureau of Parks and Lands. Construction of this leg of the trail involved many individuals and organizations, including the Maine Appalachian Trail Club (MATC), the Hurricane Island Outward Bound School, the Maine Conservation Corps, and the AMC.

The western half of the GLT was completed in the fall of 2005. Its 17.6 miles of trails includes 12.9 miles of new trail that leave Route 26 in Newry, Maine, 0.6 mile south of the trailhead parking area. It connects to existing trails at the summit of Old Speck at a junction with the Mahoosuc Trail. At present, there is one designated campsite located on Sargent Brook, 5.4 miles west of Route 26, and 7.5 miles south of the Old Speck summit. Additional campsites may be constructed in the future. The highlight of the trail is the open, alpine summit of Sunday River Whitecap, which gives an outstanding view of most of the Grafton Loop Trail's route. The trail was constructed over a 4-year period using the AMC's professional and volunteer trail crews and the Maine Conservation Corps.

For more information about the trail, and a complete description of the route, visit the AMC's website at www.outdoors.org/trails/resource, or visit the website of the Maine Appalachian Trail Club at www.matc.org.

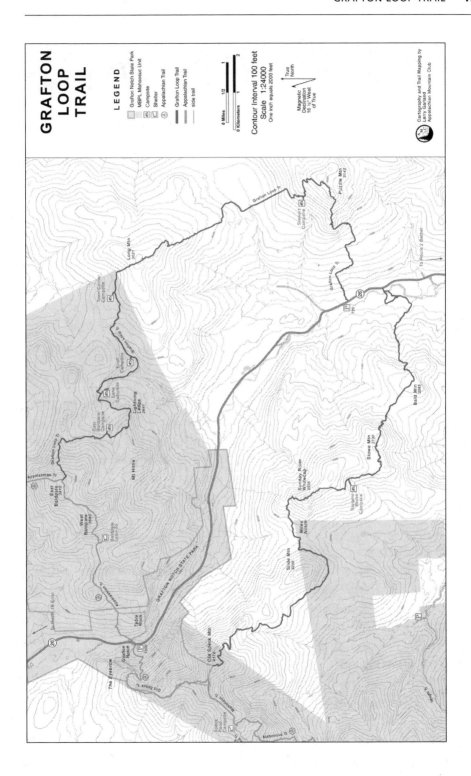

TRIP 42
MAHOOSUC NOTCH

Difficulty: Difficult
Distance: 6.5 miles round-trip
Estimated Time: 5–6 hours
Location: North Newry
Maps: USGS Old Speck Mountain
       AMC's *Maine Mountain Guide*, 9th ed., map 7
       DeLorme *Maine Atlas*, map 18

A difficult, rewarding traverse of the "hardest mile on the Appalachian Trail."

Directions

The Mahoosuc Notch Trail begins from Success Pond Road, a private logging road north of Berlin, New Hampshire. The road is not maintained in winter, and may be impassable during mud season.

From the junction of US 2 and Route 16 in Gorham, drive north on Route 16 for 4.5 miles. Turn east on Cleveland Bridge Road in Berlin and cross the Androscoggin River. Bear left on Unity Street, and then turn right onto Hutchins Street. Drive 0.8 mile and make a sharp left past the paper company mill yard. In 0.3 mile, turn right onto Success Pond Road. Follow Success Pond Road for 11.0 miles to the Notch Trail trailhead and parking area.

Trail Notes

The mile-long passage through Mahoosuc Notch is extremely difficult and is not recommended for young children, pets, or hikers bearing large, heavy packs. Plan on extra time to traverse the notch, especially early in the season.

Trip Description

Of all the notches in New England, perhaps none is more alluring or intimidating than Mahoosuc Notch. Often referred to by thru-hikers as the hardest mile of the entire 2,175-mile Appalachian Trail (AT), this difficult passage through jumbled granite slabs and shadowy caverns has

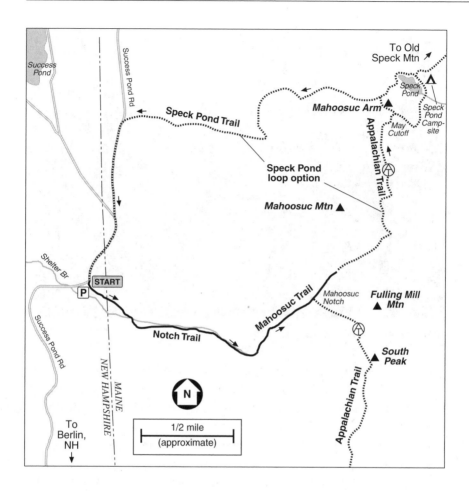

been known to frustrate more than a few ill-prepared or unsuspecting hikers. To make your way here, you'll have to crouch, crawl, jump, and climb over slippery terrain that is often snowbound well into June.

Yet, despite its fierce reputation, the notch is also a wildly beautiful place that never ceases to surprise. Walk the trail in late spring and delicate pink lady slippers will show the way. Come on a hot summer's day, and you'll delight in the cool, refreshing air that issues from the snow and ice clinging to life deep within the Notches' maw.

From the Notch Trail trailhead, cross a small brook and walk south and east along an old tote road. Soon, you'll cross a second brook and pass through a clearing. The trail makes a sharp left beyond the clearing and continues eastward along a moderate grade.

At 2.2 miles, the path reaches a junction with the AT at the Mahoosuc

Lady slippers along the Notch Trail.

Trail. Turn north onto the Mahoosuc Trail, and begin the descent into Mahoosuc Notch. The traverse through the notch requires constant vigilance, especially if the area is wet from recent rains or winter snowmelt. Carefully follow the white blazes that mark the AT, and pick your way across the maze of moss-covered slabs, boulders, and caverns.

The mile-long scramble through the notch ends at a small brook south and east of Mahoosuc Mountain. To complete the hike, turn around and retrace your steps. Alternatively, you can continue on, climbing over Mahoosuc Arm to Speck Pond (see the loop option below).

Nature and History Notes
Out west, they're known as "passes," to the south, "gaps," but here in New England, we call them "notches." From Evans to Grafton, Crawford to Franconia, these dramatic clefts of earth, sliced to picturesque perfection by the forces of time and ice, beckon us to explore their precipitous heights and hidden treasures.

The name derives from a term used by early North American settlers who chopped V-shaped cuts, or notches, into the trees they would fell to build their log cabins. Once down, the trees were stripped and hewed, and similar cuts were placed at either end of the log to keep the walls tight and the elements out. As pioneers moved further inland, they discovered comparable U- and V-shaped passages through the mountains and the name was applied.

Like other notches, Mahoosuc was cut by glaciers thousands of years ago. As the river of ice receded, it sheared a narrow, precipitous valley between Mahoosuc Mountain and Fulling Mill Mountain. Successive winter freezes tore massive blocks of rock from the cliffs, which tumbled into the valley floor, forming the cluttered passage seen today.

Other Options

To avoid traversing Mahoosuc Notch twice, you can extend this day trip into an even more challenging 11.0-mile loop that follows the Mahoosuc Trail to Speck Pond (shelter), then picks up the Speck Pond Trail (west) for the return back to Success Pond Road. From here, it's a 1.5-mile walk (south) along the road to reach your vehicle.

TRIP 43
TUMBLEDOWN MOUNTAIN LOOP

Difficulty: Difficult
Distance: 5.4-mile loop
Estimated Time: 4 hours
Location: Township 6—Weld Region
Maps: USGS Tumbledown Mountain Quadrangle
   AMC's *Maine Mountain Guide*, 9th ed., map 6
   DeLorme *Maine Atlas*, map 19

A thrilling ascent to one of Maine's prettiest mountain settings, with rugged cliffs, spectacular views, and a picturesque alpine tarn.

Directions

The Loop Trail departs from Byron Notch Road, 5.8 miles west of Weld Corner. From ME 142 in Weld Village, travel 2.0 miles northwest to Weld

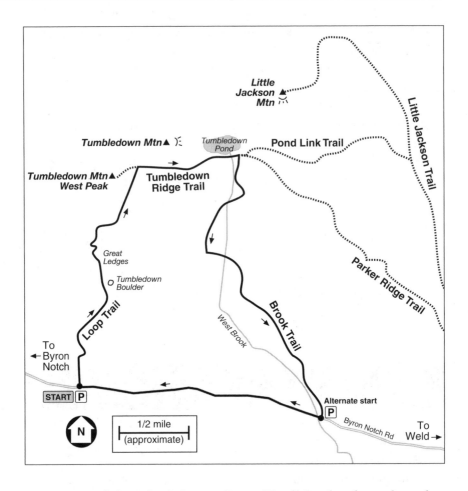

Corner. Turn left at the fork onto Byron Notch Road and travel another 0.5 mile to a second fork. Stay right here and follow the gravel road for 2.3 miles, past the Mountain View Cemetery, to another right turn. From here, it's 1.6 miles to the Brook Trail and 3.0 miles to the Loop Trail trailhead.

Trail Notes

The loop hike described below is difficult in sections, with steep climbing and scrambling over boulders and rock faces near the upper ridge. Some sections are inaccessible for pets, and may not be suitable for inexperienced hikers or children. For an easier, more direct route, opt for the Brook Trail to and from Tumbledown Pond.

Approaching beautiful Tumbledown Pond from the Tumbledown Ridge Trail.

Trip Description

For good reason, Tumbledown Mountain is one of Maine's most popular hikes. The ascent is one of the most exhilarating scrambles in the state, and the mountaintop setting is simply spectacular, with more than a half-mile of open ridgeline and a picturesque alpine pond nestled beneath peaks on three sides. Tumbledown is also one of the state's most geologically fascinating places, with an interesting variety of bedrock formations and a magnificent 700-foot cliff on its south face.

Begin on the blue-blazed Loop Trail, which starts opposite the dirt parking lot on Byron Notch Road. Entering the woods, travel due north along a modest grade that crosses over a brook twice before reaching a boggy depression. The trail soon begins climbing more steeply, and reaches massive Tumbledown Boulder at 1.0 mile.

From here, the path makes a very steep ascent of 0.3 mile to surmount the ridge known as Great Ledges, a flat table beneath Tumbledown Cliffs with excellent views of the 700-foot south face of the mountain. A large cairn on the ledges marks the junction of the Loop Trail and the defunct Chimney Trail. Be sure to stay right here, following the Loop Trail north and east into a ravine.

The trail soon turns north and begins climbing steeply out of the ravine. Near the top of the ravine, a side trail leads right to a fissure cave known as "Fat Man's Misery." Above the cave, an opening through the boulders marks the final passage to the saddle between the East and West Peaks. The challenging scramble through this, often wet, section is aided by a series of iron rungs.

The path reaches the Tumbledown Ridge Trail 1.9 miles from the trailhead. From here, there is a 0.1-mile spur trail (left) to gain the West Peak and views to the Swift River valley. To continue the loop, turn right and follow the Tumbledown Ridge Trail, which reaches the East Peak in 0.2 mile and your first glimpse of beautiful Tumbledown Pond.

From the East Peak, the Tumbledown Ridge Trail traverses mostly open ledges and descends to the edge of the pond in 0.4 mile. Unless it's crowded (which is increasingly common), there are countless places to stretch out and enjoy the pond and the tremendous views.

To descend, pick up the Brook Trail at the pond's southeast outlet. The upper portion of the trail is quite steep and requires hands and feet in places, but is otherwise straightforward. At 0.5 mile, the path moderates and joins an old logging road that continues for another mile before reaching Byron Notch Road. To complete the loop, turn right onto the road and walk the 1.4 miles back to the Loop Trail trailhead and parking area.

Nature and History Notes

As you scramble up the boulder-strewn Loop Trail, or gaze upon the mountain's scarred south face, it's easy to see how Tumbledown got its name. Like much of Western Maine, Tumbledown is composed of metamorphic rock and granite intrusions, which were formed from successive layers of sand and mud when the area lay at the edge of an ocean basin. About 400 million years ago, molten rock formed and moved through the layers, cooling into solid rock below the earth's surface. Eventually, the rock formations were exposed by the forces of erosion, chiefly glaciers.

When the glaciers moved across the landscape, they gouged earth and rock, polishing northern slopes and shearing broken rock from southern slopes, a process that is readily apparent on Tumbledown. Another indication of glacial activity here is seen in the many scratches left on the summit by rocks imbedded in the base of the advancing glaciers.

TRIP 44
BIGELOW PRESERVE

Difficulty: Difficult
Distance: 12.0-mile loop
Estimated Time: 8 hours
Location: East of Stratton
Maps: USGS "The Horns" Quadrangle
USGS Sugarloaf Mountain Quadrangle
AMC's *Maine Mountain Guide*, 9th ed., map 2
DeLorme *Maine Atlas*, map 29

A fantastic ridge hike along the Appalachian Trail within one of Maine's most prominent and beautiful wilderness preserves.

Directions
From ME 16/27, turn right onto Stratton Brook Road (dirt), 3.2 miles northwest of Sugarloaf Mountain Road (0.5 mile after the Appalachian Trail (AT) crosses the road at the Crocker Mountain trailhead), and 4.5 miles east of Stratton. The road is located directly after the sign marking the Bigelow Preserve if you're coming from Sugarloaf.

Follow Stratton Brook Road, which is rough in places, for 1.8 miles to a parking area and kiosk near Stratton Brook Pond.

Trail Notes
The circuit hike described here is rated "difficult" both for its overall length and steep climbing. For a less demanding outing, consider an out-and-back hike of the Horns Pond Trail, which has the easiest grade to the ridge and will reduce the overall trip length to 8.0 miles. Alternatively, you can extend the circuit hike into a two-day trip by camping at one of the tent sites or shelters along the route (see the AMC's *Maine Mountain Guide*, 9th ed., for additional route and campsite information).

A good portion of this hike is above treeline and subject to the full force of the elements. Be sure to plan accordingly and check the weather forecast before departing.

Trip Description

Beautiful Bigelow Preserve encompasses 33,000 acres of pristine wilderness, including the imposing Bigelow Range, which has some of the finest alpine ridge hiking in Maine outside of Katahdin. The range, set dramatically above Flagstaff Lake, is more than 12 miles long, and holds six major peaks. This long circuit hike explores the heart of the preserve with an ascent to beautiful Horns Pond, a ridge traverse along the Appalachian Trail, and climbs to the range's most prominent summits, the twin "cones" of West Peak and Avery Peak.

From the parking area and kiosk, begin walking down the last section of Stratton Brook Road, which ends where Stratton Brook empties into Stratton Brook Pond.

Cross over the brook and continue walking along the fire road that skirts along the pond. At 0.2 mile from the brook, the road forks, with

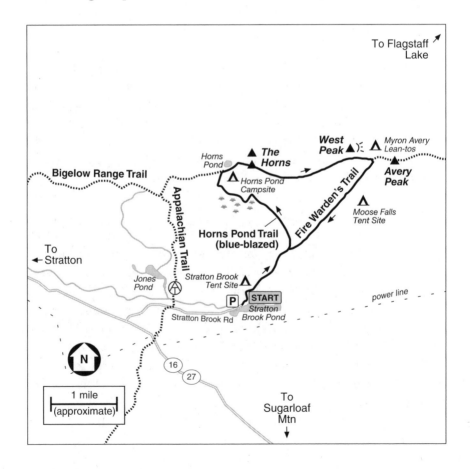

the Fire Warden's Trail (sign) leading left into the woods. The trail runs north for another 0.2 mile, then turns east and crosses level ground for 0.5 mile.

From here, the trail climbs steeply over ledges to a low ridge before settling back to an easy grade. At 1.6 miles from Stratton Brook, the trail reaches the Horns Pond Trail junction. Turn northwest onto the blue-blazed Horns Pond Trail and continue hiking along a moderate grade through an attractive mixed hardwood forest.

The trail passes to the south of a bog depression 3.0 miles into the hike. From here, there are a couple of excellent outlooks with views to South Horn. The trail continues to rise steadily and then becomes steeper before it reaches the junction with the AT at 4.1 miles.

Bear right, and pick up the AT, which reaches the Horns Pond campsite, comprised of lean-tos and tent platforms, in 0.2 mile. A short trail behind the lean-tos leads to Horns Pond, a beautiful alpine tarn. Continuing east, follow the AT as it climbs the summit of South Horn, where there are superb views over the pond.

Descending steeply from South Horn, the trail continues over a series of rises along the crest of the range before making a sharp ascent to the height-of-land atop 4,145-foot West Peak. There are magnificent views

The Bigelow Range rises above Flagstaff Lake, the state's fourth-largest lake.

in all directions from West Peak, from Sugarloaf to the south all the way north to Katahdin.

Descending sharply from West Peak, the trail continues eastward, reaching the Myron Avery Memorial Lean-tos and the northern junction of the Fire Warden's Trail just below Avery Peak. A spring and the old Fire Warden's cabin, now used by the preserve's caretaker, are located nearby.

The Fire Warden's Trail will be your path of descent to complete the circuit. However, if you have enough steam left, consider the 0.4-mile climb to the summit of Avery Peak, which also has excellent views.

The upper portion of the descent on the Fire Warden's Trail is particularly steep, dropping nearly 1,700 feet in elevation over 1.5 miles. After that, the trail flattens out before reaching the Horns Pond Trail junction, from which you departed earlier. From here, continue down the Fire Warden's Trail back to the trailhead and onto the parking area after re-crossing Stratton Brook.

Nature and History Notes

Avery Peak and the Avery Memorial Lean-to were named and dedicated in honor of Myron H. Avery, an avid hiker and one of the principal architects of the Appalachian Trail.

Born in Lubec, Maine, Avery devoted much of his life to realizing the vision of Benton MacKaye, who, in 1921, proposed a series of camps and communities linked by hiking trails along the highest points of the Appalachian mountain range.

Avery founded the Potomac Appalachian Trail Conference, served as chairman of the Appalachian Trail Conference (now known as the Appalachian Trail Conservancy) from 1931 until his death in 1952, and helped organize the Maine Appalachian Trail Club, serving as supervisor of trails from 1935 to 1949 and the club's president from 1949 to 1952.

He tirelessly recruited volunteers for the trail, and scouted, blazed, and built many miles himself. Avery is considered by many to be the Appalachian Trail's first "2,000-miler," having walked the entire length of the trail (though not as a thru-hike) by 1936 to what was then its northern terminus at Sugarloaf Mountain.

TRIP 45
EVANS NOTCH—WILD RIVER LOOP

Aerobic Difficulty: Moderate to difficult
Technical Difficulty: Moderate to difficult
Distance: 10.0 miles round-trip or loop
Estimated Time: 2–4 hours
Location: Hastings–Evans Notch
Maps: USGS Speckled Mountain Quad
      USGS Wild River Quad
      AMC's *Maine Mountain Guide*, 9th ed., map 8
      DeLorme *Maine Atlas*, map 10

Pick your pleasure on this scenic tour along the Wild River, with options for an easy out-and-back cruise, or an adventurous and challenging single-track ride.

Directions
This trip departs from the Hastings Plantation parking area on Wild River Road northwest of Hastings Campground on ME 113 in Evans Notch and 0.1 mile south of the Roost trailhead (Trip 38).

Trail Notes
Caution: The Highwater Trail is a remote, rugged path only suited for experienced riders. Be prepared for obstacles along the path, including blow downs, rocks, roots, and washed-out areas. To complete the loop described below requires fording the Wild River, which may be difficult, dangerous, or impossible during times of high water. As a result, the trail is best ridden in late summer or early fall when the terrain is drier and the water level has dropped.

Be prepared for some vehicle traffic on Wild River Road as it provides access to other trailheads as well as popular U.S. Forest Service Wild River Campground.

Trip Description
This scenic ride along the banks of the Wild River combines two radically different trails. The Highwater Trail is a rough-and-tumble, physically

demanding single-track path, while the serene and gentle Wild River Road courses along easy grades suitable for all ability levels. Depending on your preference, choose one or the other, or combine the two (as described here) for a challenging loop ride.

The loop starts from the Hastings Plantation parking area on Wild River Road. From the kiosk near the parking area, follow the short spur path north to a picturesque suspension bridge that spans the river and leads to the Highwater trailhead.

The trail turns southwest, paralleling the river along its northern bank. From here, it runs for nearly 9 miles, deep into the White Mountain National Forest in New Hampshire before joining the Wild River Trail. For this ride, though, we'll follow the trail for approximately 4.7

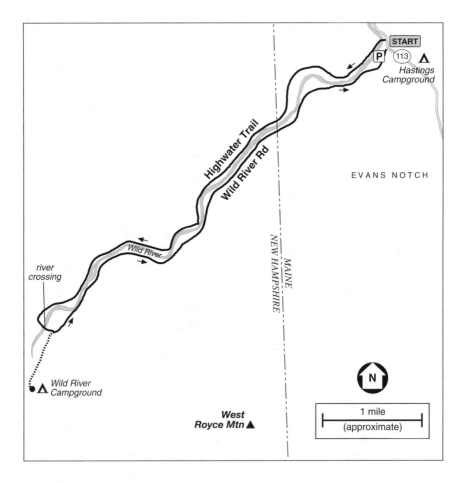

A ride along the Wild River Road is an excellent alternative for less experienced riders.

miles before crossing back over the river and returning on Wild River Road.

Entering the woods, the trail turns southwest and closely parallels the beautiful, boulder-strewn Wild River. The path soon rises north and west to jog around a wide bend in the river. The trail then crosses the first of several feeder streams before sweeping south, returning to the riverbank and entering New Hampshire.

A bit more than 2.0 miles in, you'll reach an old road that was connected to a former bridge crossing. Cross over the road and continue on the Highwater Trail, tracking along the riverbank until you reach the junction of the Shelburne Trail at 5.4 miles.

Here, depending on the water level, you can either drop down to the river and hand-carry your bike across to pick up Wild River Road for the return, or turn around and retrace your path (another option is to continue along the Highwater Trail 2.0 miles farther upstream and cross at the bridge over Moriah Brook).

Across the river, turn right (west) to reach the Wild River Campground in 0.5 mile, or turn east and follow the road as it winds along the southern bank of the river for a pleasant and scenic 5-mile ride back (east) to the Hastings Plantation parking lot.

Nature and History Notes

In 1911, Leon Leonwood Bean returned from an annual hunting trip near the Wild River with cold, wet feet and an innovative idea. He enlisted a local cobbler to stitch leather uppers to a pair of workmen's rubber boots, and the "Maine Hunting Shoe" was born. Unfortunately, 90 of the first 100 boots sold were returned because faulty stitching caused the uppers to separate from the bottoms. Undeterred, L.L. Bean honored his guarantee of satisfaction, refunded the customers' money, and went to work to fix the problem. Since then, the company has grown from a one-man operation to a trusted source of reliable outdoor clothing and equipment with annual sales well in excess of one billion dollars.

More Information

For up-to-date information about conditions on the Highwater Trail, contact the Evans Notch Ranger District of the White Mountain National Forest at 207-824-2134.

TRIP 46
MOUNT BLUE STATE PARK

Aerobic Difficulty: Moderate to difficult
Technical Difficulty: Moderate to difficult
Distance: 9.0-mile loop
Estimated Time: 3 hours
Location: Weld
Maps: USGS Mount Blue Quadrangle
　　　　USGS Weld Quadrangle
　　　　AMC's *Maine Mountain Guide*, 9th ed., map 6
　　　　DeLorme *Maine Atlas*, map 19

Secluded riding on diverse multi-use trails within one of Maine's largest state parks.

Directions

This trip begins from the parking lot of the Mount Blue trailhead at the eastern end of the park's Center Hill Division. From ME 142 in Weld,

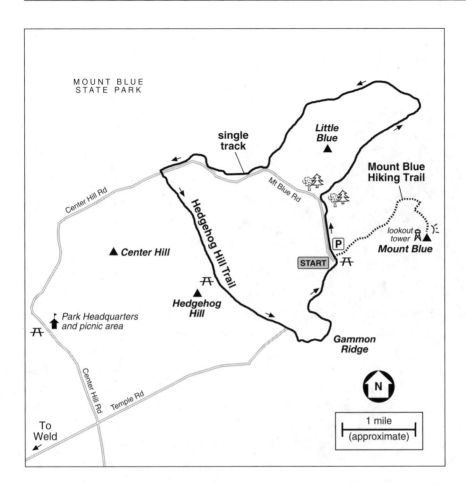

continue straight until you reach Center Hill Road. Turn left, and drive to the height of land where there is an excellent overlook south to Webb Lake. Across the road from the overlook, there is a parking area and trailhead next to park headquarters. Stop and pick up a map at the kiosk here, then continue on Center Hill Road to Mount Blue Road. Turn right onto Mount Blue Road and follow it 4.5 miles to the parking area and trailhead.

Trip Description

With more than 25 miles of multi-use trails to explore, Mount Blue State Park has become a popular destination for mountain bikers. There are two divisions of the park, including the excellent campground and swimming beach along the western shore of Webb Lake, and the vast

Riding along **Mount Blue Road.**

Center Hill section, which lies at the foot of beautiful Mount Blue. This trip wanders from the base of the mountain, combining sections of unpaved Mount Blue Road with jeep, ATV, and single-track trails to form a fun, 9-mile loop.

From the parking area at the Mount Blue trailhead, ride back down Mount Blue Road or pick up the rougher ATV trail that parallels the road. Ride for 0.6 mile until you reach a trail entrance on the right. Follow this trail, which makes a short climb, then levels off and travels beneath a shady canopy of mixed hardwoods.

Just under 2 miles from the parking area, you'll cross a bridge over a small stream and reach a junction. Turn left here and follow the ATV path, which is somewhat rutty and muddy, until it emerges into an open meadow and reaches a T-junction at 3.0 miles (watch for moose here! When I traveled this section, it was covered with fresh tracks).

Turn left at the T-junction, and ride a fun, 0.7-mile descent that leads back to Mount Blue Road. Just before reaching the road, a trail veers right and follows a nice 1-mile section of single-track that parallels the road. Follow this trail, or turn right onto the road and ride the mile to the Hedgehog Hill trailhead on the left.

The Hedgehog Hill Trail makes a short descent, and then travels along a rough section before returning to single-track through the woods. A mile from the road, the trail opens to a grassy section, and then reaches a side trail to a beautiful picnic area atop Hedgehog Hill. This is a great place to get off your bike, take a break, and enjoy the views.

Returning to the trail, continue traveling southeast along a single-track trail that eventually joins an old jeep road then arrives at a clearing and trail junction. The trail to the right leads to the park headquarters and trailhead on Center Hill Road. Continue straight to reach the ATV trail that will lead you back to the Mount Blue trailhead.

The ATV trail crosses Temple Road and Houghton Brook, then turns north and east at the base of Gammon Ridge and ascends to the Mount Blue Shelter and parking area.

Other Options

Combine this loop with a hike up beautiful 3,187-foot Mount Blue, which offers fine views from its conical summit. From the parking area, the trail follows a well-worn footpath for 1.7 miles to the summit ridge and defunct fire tower.

More Information

To reserve a campsite or obtain a map of Mount Blue State Park, contact park headquarters at 207-585-2347.

TRIP 47
CARRABASSETT RIVER RAIL-TRAIL

Aerobic Difficulty: Easy to moderate
Technical Difficulty: Easy to moderate
Distance: 12.0 miles round-trip or 19-mile loop
Estimated Time: 2–4 hours
Location: Carrabassett Valley
Maps: USGS Poplar Mountain
USGS Sugarloaf Mountain
AMC's *Maine Mountain Guide*, 9th ed., map 2
DeLorme *Maine Atlas*, map 29

A beautiful ride along the Carrabassett River on an easygoing rail-trail, with an option for a longer backcountry excursion through the Bigelow Preserve.

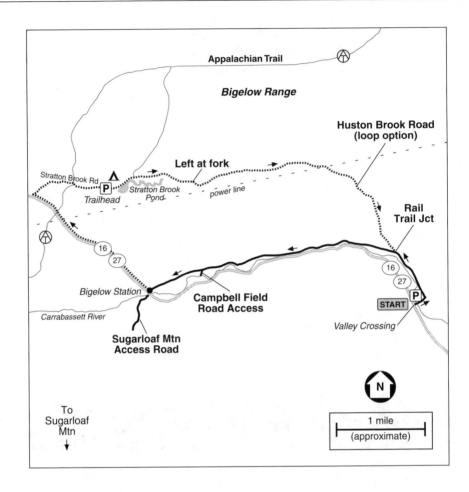

Directions

Carrabassett Valley is located on ME 27/16 just south of Sugarloaf/USA Mountain Resort. From Kingfield, follow ME 27/16 for 8.0 miles and look for a sign on the right for the Carrabassett Town Office at the Valley Crossing junction. Turn right on Carriage Road and cross the bridge over the Carrabassett River. Then, make an immediate left into the town office, fire station, and recreation center complex and parking area.

Trip Description

If there is a prettier, more peaceful place to ride in Maine than the Carrabassett Valley, I have yet to find it. Nestled between Sugarloaf Mountain, Maine's second highest peak, and the prominent Bigelow Range, the valley is especially striking when ablaze in fall colors. This outing travels an

Riding across the Carrabassett River.

easygoing narrow-gauge rail-trail along the beautiful Carrabassett River, with an option to extend the trip into a backcountry excursion through the Bigelow Preserve.

From the town complex parking area, ride back to Carriage Road and turn left. Follow the signs, and turn left again onto Huston Brook Road at 0.1 mile. This gravel road passes several houses and camps before aligning with the south branch of the Carrabassett River.

Just over a mile from the parking area, you'll arrive at the entrance to the rail-trail. The trail veers left, paralleling the river and ME 27/16, while Huston Brook Road continues straight toward the southeastern edge of the Bigelow Preserve. Turn left, and follow the trail as it skirts the riverbank, then jogs away from the water's edge, ascending through beautiful, shady woods.

Half a mile in, the trail drops back to the river and passes a series of beautiful cascades and enticing swimming holes. The path reaches the Campbell Field trailhead 4.0 miles from the trail entrance. A small bridge spans the river here, providing access to a parking area, restroom facilities, and ME 27/16 near the Sugarloaf Outdoor Center.

The trail arrives at its western terminus at Bigelow Station, 1.3 miles past the Campbell Field junction. You can turn around here and ride back, or continue on, and ride the more challenging backcountry loop described below.

To complete the loop, ride through the cluster of buildings at Bigelow Station and turn right onto ME 27/16. Although you'll be riding a 3-mile stretch of pavement here, the route is a scenic byway and provides excellent views to the Bigelow Range. The first mile is a steady climb, then it's downhill for 2.0 miles, across the Appalachian Trail (AT), to Stratton Brook Road. The road is just beyond the sign marking the entrance to the Bigelow Preserve.

Turn right, and follow the dirt road, which passes over the AT 1.0 mile from ME 27/16, and reaches the parking area and kiosk for Bigelow Range hikes (as described in Trip 44) in 1.5 miles. Continue left here, and ride down the unimproved road to Stratton Brook Pond where there are excellent views of Sugarloaf Mountain. Here, you'll almost certainly have to hand-carry your bike across the brook and up the sandy bank on the other side.

Continuing, ride along the path at the edge of the pond. A short distance beyond the brook crossing, the trailhead for the Fire Warden's Trail leaves left. Stay right, and ride for another mile to reach a fork. Stay left at the fork and enjoy a 3-mile stretch of riding through the public reserve land before arriving at its eastern boundary.

Beyond the boundary, you'll pass under power lines and continue down unimproved Huston Brook Road for approximately 2.2 miles to reach the junction where you first started down the rail-trail. From here, continue along Huston Brook Road to Carriage Road, turning right to return to the town complex parking area.

Nature and History Notes

The Carrabassett River Rail-Trail is one of several narrow gauge rail lines in Maine that have been converted for recreational use. The section from Carrabassett to Bigelow was originally laid in 1900 to service a bustling mill at Bigelow Station. In 1927, the section between Bigelow and Huston Brook was removed. In 1983, the first effort was made to improve and maintain the corridor for recreational purposes. In 2001, voters approved a $700,000 upgrade to the trail from Campbell Field to Huston Brook.

Other Options

There are 65 miles of excellent single-track and double-track trails to ride at Sugarloaf/USA's Nordic Center across ME 27/16 from Campbell Field. Access to the trails is free of charge and maps are available at the Sugarloafer Shop located in Village West on the mountain access road. For more information, call 207-237-6718.

TRIP 48
BROWNFIELD BOG

Difficulty: Easy
Distance: Not rated
Estimated Time: 2 hours
Location: East Brownfield
Maps: USGS Brownfield Quad
　　　DeLorme *Maine Atlas*, map 4

A relaxing paddle on a beautiful, quiet bog within the Saco River watershed.

Directions

From Fryeburg, turn south on Route 5/113 and drive to Route 160 in East Brownfield. Turn left (east) onto Route 160 and drive for 1.5 miles to another left onto Lord Hill Road. Immediately after turning onto Lord Hill, turn left onto a dirt road labeled "Bog Access Road." Continue on this road to one of the two launch sites described in the Trip Description.

Trail Notes

Though accessible to most vehicles, the Bog Access Road is minimally maintained and often rough, wet, and muddy.

Because the bog is a designated Wildlife Management Area, paddlers should be aware that hunters frequent the area during open seasons.

Trip Description

Brownfield Bog is a wonderful place to float among island hummocks, wander through weedy channels, or simply drift and ponder the natural

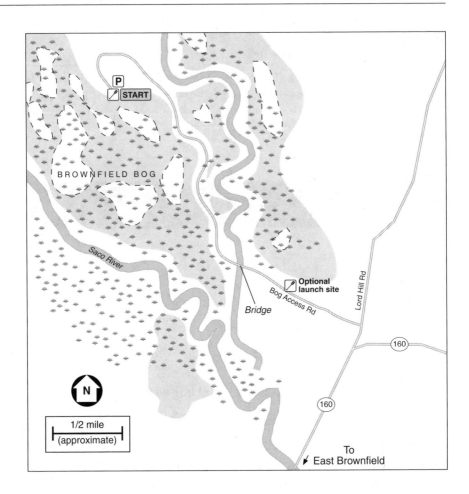

world. The going is often slow, but that's its charm. Just being here is the point. This is a place for relaxation, and a perfect refuge in summer, when battalions of boaters often crowd the Saco River nearby.

The bog is a state-owned Wildlife Management Area encompassing 5,700-acres of wetland habitat, including emergent marshes, shrub wetlands, and, of course, bogs. The best time to paddle here is early morning or dusk, when you're more apt to encounter wildlife including deer, beaver, a wide variety of waterfowl, and the occasional moose.

There are two places to launch your boat and explore the area. A short distance in on the access road, you'll come upon a small shed posted with a list of rules about the area. Park behind the shed, and walk the short spur road to the right that leads to an informal put-in and access to the bog's eastern channel.

Paddling the calm waters of Brownfield Bog.

Better still, continue down the access road, which can be slow going in places, cross over a small wooden bridge, and continue to a fork in the road. The path ahead leads to an open field with access to the water, but it is often wet, rutty, and impassable. Instead, turn left and follow the road through the woods. About a mile in from the fork, the road curls around to the south and emerges into an open area with water access on your left. The best spot to launch is near the end of the road, next to a large, grassy area.

Paddling into the heart of the bog, you'll quickly encounter an abundant variety of plant life. Water lilies flourish here, as well as carnivorous pitcher plants and sundews. The surrounding forest, primarily composed of deciduous species including, birch, aspen, and a variety of oaks, provides an especially beautiful backdrop in fall. Pleasant Mountain rises to the east and the White Mountains to the northwest.

Nature and History Notes

The Northern pitcher plant's large, red-veined leaves curl to form a vase-like, hollow tube with flared lips and downward pointing bristles. Insects, lured by the leaf color, are trapped by the hairs and eventually drown in water held within the tube. As the insects decompose, the plant absorbs its nutrients.

Other Options

Pleasant Pond, just north and east of Brownfield Bog, is another hidden gem near the Saco River. It can only be accessed from the river, and requires a 3-mile out-and-back paddle to do so, but is well worth the effort. For more information about Pleasant Pond, as well as Brownfield Bog, refer to the AMC's guidebook *Quiet Water Maine*.

TRIP 49
UMBAGOG LAKE

Difficulty: Moderate
Distance: 6.0–16.0 miles
Estimated Time: Day trip or extended stay
Location: Magalloway PLT (Maine), Errol and Cambridge (NH)
Maps: USGS Umbagog Lake South
    USGS Umbagog Lake North
    DeLorme *Maine Atlas*, maps 17 and 18
    DeLorme *New Hampshire Atlas*, map 51

Wonderful backcountry paddling on a magnificent lake set within a wild and scenic refuge.

Directions

The southern access for Umbagog Lake is located 10.0 miles north of Grafton Notch on Route 26, just over the New Hampshire border. To access the lake from the Androscoggin River, continue north on Route 26 for 7.0 miles to Errol, New Hampshire. About 100 yards before the Androscoggin River Bridge, look for the Access to Public Water sign at North Mountain Pond Road. Turn right, and follow the road to the parking area and launch site.

Trail Notes

Caution: Like most large lakes, afternoon winds and associated waves are common at Umbagog, which can make paddling, especially in an open canoe, exceedingly difficult and potentially hazardous. Also, be aware that motorized boats are allowed on Umbagog Lake, and there has been

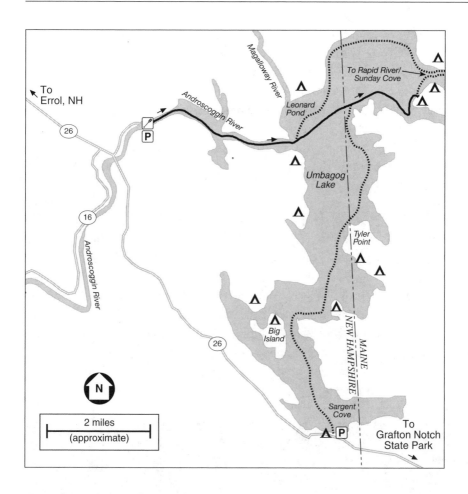

a steady increase in boat traffic in recent years, especially near the southern end of the lake.

Trip Description

Umbagog is a paddler's paradise. Wild, scenic, and accessible, it encompasses a vast and varied shoreline, dozens of islands, interesting rivers, and expansive freshwater marshes. An astonishing concentration of wildlife inhabit the refuge, including moose, bear, osprey, bald eagle, loons, ducks, and, for anglers, several species of fish. For backcountry campers, there are 34 primitive wilderness sites around the lake, (advanced reservation required), accessible only by boat.

You can access the lake from the south at Umbagog Lake State Park, operated by the New Hampshire Division of Parks and Recreation, which includes a campground, boat rentals, and swimming area. But, the more interesting access points are via the Magalloway or Androscoggin Rivers, which flow in and out of the lake respectively, and provide the shortest route to the more remote, northern end of Umbagog. Both rivers are slow moving and relatively easy to navigate against the current, and both are excellent choices if you only have enough time for a day trip.

This trip begins on the Androscoggin and ventures to Leonard Pond, then continues to the Maine side of the lake to explore Sunday Cove and the outlet of the Rapid River. Less than 0.2 mile from the launch, you'll pass an inlet on your right, which provides access to an interesting backwater channel. At 0.8 mile, the river opens, then sweeps right and continues south and east. At 1.5 miles, a channel opens to the left toward Harper's Meadow (the meadow contains an expansive marsh complex that was designated a National Natural Landmark in 1979). Stay along the southern shore and continue upriver. At 1.8 miles, you'll pass an inlet that opens into an area known as Sweet Meadows. This is an excellent place to explore and observe wildlife and provides a welcome alternative if strong winds preclude a paddle out to the lake.

The river joins the outlet to the Magalloway River at Leonard Pond 3.0 miles from the launch. There are several interesting coves, channels,

Water lily at Umbagog Lake.

and inlets to explore here. To the northeast, expansive Leonard Marsh supports an array of nesting waterfowl, as well as northern harriers, ospreys, and elusive American bitterns.

From Leonard Pond, a mile of open water paddling separates you from Umbagog's eastern shore at Pine Point. If the wind is up, take the much longer, but less hazardous, route north along the marsh to reach Sunday Cove and the outlet to the Rapid River. You could easily spend a day exploring this section of the lake. The upper river is a favorite run for whitewater boaters (Class III–IV), and the outlet is a prime spot for fishermen angling for small mouth bass.

Nature and History

Umbagog (pronounced um-BAY-gog) is a Native American word meaning "shallow water." Indeed, while the lake stretches for more than 10 miles north to south, and covers more than 8,500 acres, it has an average depth of only 15 feet. It was established as a National Wildlife Refuge in 1992, conserving the area for future generations.

Regrettably, in recent years, Umbagog Lake has seen a dramatic decline in one of its signature species, the common loon. The lake holds New Hampshire's largest nesting population of loons. Loons are territorial and generally return to the same site year after year. At one time, there were 31 territorial pairs here. But, in 2000, the numbers began to drop, and by 2002, there were only 15 pairs occupying the lake. Although loon pairs rebounded to 18 in 2003 and increased to 20 in 2004 and 2005, the overall reduction in the breeding population remains a concern. With few natural predators, loons are considered an indicator species, and a rapid decline in population points to a potential problem within their ecosystem, here or, perhaps, elsewhere (New England's loons winter over off the coast of Maine and south to Long Island Sound).

The overall decline in the lake's loon population has been the focus of an intensive, ongoing study conducted by the Loon Preservation Committee (LPC) and BioDiversity Research Institute (BRI) in cooperation with th U.S. Fish and Wildlife Service to determine its cause. In 2003, biologists implanted some of Umbagog's loons with transmitters, hoping to track their migratory routes via satellite to determine if the problem stems from their wintering sites.

For more information about loons visit the Loon Preservation Committee website at www.loon.org.

Other Options

For more paddling options on Umbagog Lake, check out the AMC's *Quiet Water Maine* and *Quiet Water New Hampshire and Vermont* guidebooks.

More Information

To reserve a backcountry campsite, contact Umbagog Lake State Park at 603-482-7795, or visit www.nhstateparks.org. For more information about Lake Umbagog National Wildlife Refuge, visit lakeumbagog.fws.gov or call 603-482-3415.

Northern Forest Canoe Trail

The Northern Forest Canoe Trail (NFCT) is a 740-mile water trail established to celebrate the enduring legacy of Northern New England's historic waterways. Completed in 2006, the trail extends from Old Forge, New York, in the Adirondacks to Fort Kent, Maine, along an interconnected system of lakes, ponds, streams, and rivers. The waterway traces historic routes established thousands of years ago by Native Americans, and later followed and depended upon by traders, trappers, and guides. For paddlers today, the trail is both an alluring recreational waterway, and an opportunity to explore the region's diverse natural environment and rich human heritage.

The trail was actually conceived more than twenty years ago, when three friends became interested in paddling and documenting Native American water routes. Eventually they discovered the routes could be strung together through a series of portages into one long passage akin to an Appalachian Trail on water. An important distinction of the NFCT, however, is that it crosses through primarily private and state lands, and more than 40 communities. The NFCT is meant to reflect the region's diverse landscapes from working cities and towns to farms, forests, mountains, and wilderness.

To support access and stewardship, the project was formalized in 2000 with the establishment of Northern Forest Canoe Trails, Inc., a non-profit membership organization based in Waitsfield, Vermont. The organization dedicated itself to "renewing the bonds between communities and their waterways," through a partnership of members, volun-

The Androscoggin River is one of several historic waterways along the NFCT.

teers, private landowners, and local communities. Today, the organization includes a network of more than 100 volunteers living and working in communities along the trail, and works to encourage and promote community events and educational programs about the region.

The trail is divided into 13 sections, each supported by a high-quality map published by NFCT, Inc. The maps provide route and interpretive information including access, portage, and campsite locations, as well as local contacts, permit guidelines, and interesting details about local history, wildlife, and geology. To paddle the entire route takes about 8 weeks and, according to NFCT, Inc., "requires all the skills a canoeist can muster," but the maps also describe the route in ways that enable paddlers to enjoy shorter sections to fit their interests, skills, and schedules. Maine encompasses nearly half of the trail (maps 8 through 13), covering 347 miles of the region's diverse and historic waterways from Umbagog Lake to the St. John River, including the Rangeley Lakes, the Dead River, Flagstaff Lake, the Moose River, Moosehead Lake, the West Branch of the Penobscot River, and the Allagash Wilderness Waterway.

To learn more about the Northern Forest Canoe Trail contact NFCT, Inc., at 802-496-2285 or visit www.NorthernForestCanoeTrail.org.

TRIP 50
KENNEBAGO RIVER—RANGELEY LAKES REGION

Difficulty: Easy
Distance: 7.0 miles round-trip
Estimated Time: 3–4 hours
Location: Oquossoc—Rangeley Lakes Region
Maps: USGS Oquossoc Quadrangle
　　　　USGS Kennebago Quadrangle
　　　　DeLorme *Maine Atlas*, map 28

A quietwater paddle on a serpentine river in the heart of moose country.

Directions

From Rangeley, drive 6.5 miles west on Route 4 (also Route 16 here) to a junction with Route 16 in Oquossoc. A small kiosk at the junction has information about the region and restroom facilities. Turn right (north) on 16 and drive 1.3 miles. The Kennebago River Road leaves to the right here (there is access to the river 2.0 miles up the road). A bridge passes over the Kennebago River 0.2 mile farther on Route 16. Limited parking is available just before the bridge, on the west side of the road.

Trail Notes

Though gated, the Kennebago River Road is open for public access. Sign in at the gatehouse, which is manned from 7:00 A.M.–6:00 P.M.

The small parking area next to the bridge on Route 16 fills up fast in summer. Arriving early in the morning will not only enhance your prospects for parking, but for wildlife sighting as well.

Trip Description

The Rangeley Lakes Region is one of the oldest resort destinations in Maine. Yet, despite its popularity, it has retained much of the relaxed north woods charm that first lured sports enthusiasts here more than 150 years ago. If you're drawn to the sweet smell of balsams, the plaintive cry of loons, or the thrill of sighting a bull moose on a remote stretch of water, Rangeley will charm you too.

The Kennebago River flows into the heart of the region and is among more than 100 lakes, ponds, and rivers within the watershed. This trip explores a serpentine stretch of the river known for its excellent fishing and abundant wildlife, particularly moose. When I paddled here, early on a July morning, I encountered two bull moose jostling for territorial rights less than a half-mile in.

There are several ways to access the Kennebago. You can put in beneath the bridge on the west side of Route 16 and paddle upriver as far as you want before turning around. Or, spot a vehicle at the bridge and travel 2.0 miles in on Kennebago River Road to an informal put-in known locally as "Steep Bank Pool." With advanced notice, you can also arrange for a shuttle (and boat rentals) with the folks at nearby Grant's Kennebago Camps or Cupsuptic Campground to design a trip from any

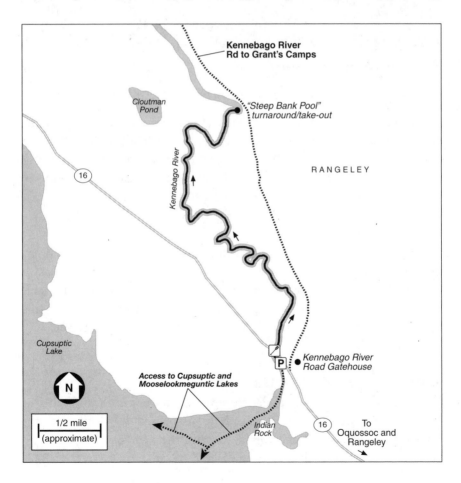

A moose encounter on the Kennebago River.

number of spots along the river.

Paddling upriver from Route 16, the Kennebago soon turns to the northwest. About a half-mile in, you'll reach a fork in the river. Stay left unless, like me, you enjoy exploring false inlets and hidden coves. It was at a cove near here that I encountered a large bull moose lazily feeding on aquatic plants. To my surprise (and delight), a second bull moose came crashing through the woods soon after, though he was quickly dispatched by the rightful proprietor.

For the next mile, the river continues to cut through the boreal forest in serpentine bends and wide oxbows, then turns north and passes an outlet from Cloutman Pond. The river then sweeps around a wide bend to the southeast before turning north and east toward Kennebago River Road. At 3.5 miles, the river approaches the take-out/turnaround at "Steep Bank Pool."

Nature and History Notes

Native Americans had established hunting and fishing camps in this region long before so-called "flatlanders" discovered it. Remnants of the trail they traveled to reach the lakes from the south still exist today. Anglers from New York and Rhode Island began arriving in the 1840s when news spread about the huge native brook trout locals were pulling from a spot where the Kennebago River flows into the lakes, known locally as "Indian Rock." Sporting camps, public houses, and hotels sprung up soon after. Rangeley became even more widely known when *Harper's* magazine published a fifteen-page article about the region in 1877. By 1900, there were 200 fishing guides servicing anglers here. Today, the region is enjoyed for a broad spectrum of outdoors activities, including hiking, biking, paddling, and winter sports, but enthusiastic anglers still flock here, enticed by the prospect of landing a world class trout.

Other Options

You can also combine this trip with a paddle out to Mooselookmeguntic Lake and Cupsuptic Lake from the put-in at Route 16. The Kennebago drains into the lakes at a point known as Indian Rock, less than a half-mile from the bridge. For a shorter, but equally enjoyable out-and-back paddle, put in on the Cupsuptic River at the boat launch, 4.0 miles north of the Kennebago River Bridge. You can paddle in about a mile and a half before the river becomes impassable at Little Falls.

Also Nearby

Bald Mountain, in nearby Oquossoc, is an excellent hike (2.2 miles round-trip) for families or anyone who wants to get a bird's eye view of the entire lakes region. There are picnic tables and an observation tower on the summit.

More Information

For more information about the Rangeley Lakes Region, visit www.rangeleymaine.com. For shuttles, lodging, or camping information call Grant's Kennebago Camps at 800-633-4815, or Cupsuptic Family Campground at 207-864-5249.

5

Greater Moosehead Lake & 100-Mile Wilderness

Including Baxter State Park

THIS REGION ENCOMPASSES THE HEART AND SOUL of the Maine Woods, an incomparable expanse of forests, lakes, rivers, and mountains that, in places, seem as wild today as when Thoreau traveled here in search of wilderness more than a century ago. From Moosehead Lake, the largest lake contained within a single state east of the Mississippi River, to mile-high Mount Katahdin, this region is truly an explorer's paradise. The famed 100-Mile Wilderness, the most remote stretch of the Appalachian Trail, cuts across the landscape from Monson to the height of land on Katahdin's Baxter Peak. The region also features the AMC's Katahdin Iron Works property, the core of the organization's Maine Woods Initiative, and the site of the Little Lyford Pond Camps. Highlighted trips include an excursion to Moosehead's Mount Kineo Peninsula (Trip 52), a rim hike above spectacular Gulf Hagas (Trip 53), and a traverse of the Knife Edge, the most alluring ridge hike in New England (Trip 55).

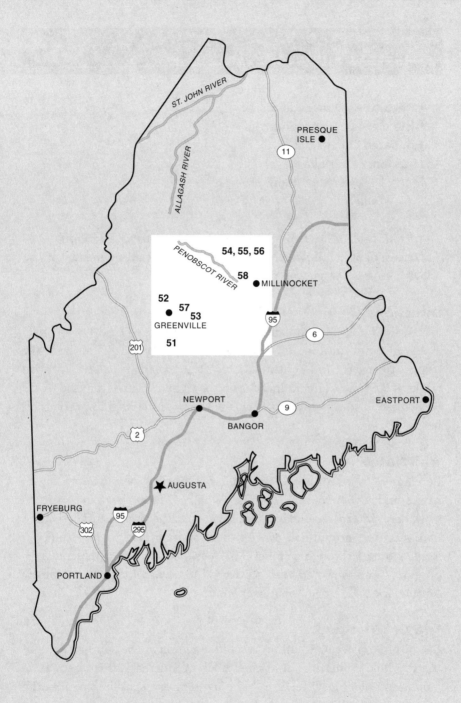

TRIP 51
BORESTONE MOUNTAIN SANCTUARY

Difficulty: Easy to moderate
Distance: 4.0 miles round-trip
Estimated Time: 3 hours
Location: Elliotsville Plantation
Maps: USGS Barren Mountain West
  DeLorme *Maine Atlas*, map 41

**An enjoyable hike through old growth forest to an Audubon
Nature Center followed by a steep scramble to an open summit
with impressive views.**

Directions
From ME 6/15 in Monson, drive north for 0.5 mile to Elliottsville Road.
Turn right and continue for 7.8 miles to Big Wilson Stream. Cross the
bridge, turn left, and continue across the Canadian Pacific Railroad
tracks at 8.5 miles. The trailhead is on the right, 0.1 mile from the tracks
on Bodfish Road. There are parking spots across the road from the trailhead.

Trail Notes
Borestone Mountain is a Maine Audubon Society sanctuary that wel-
comes hikers year-round. There is a small fee to support the society's
work here. Interpretive maps are provided at the trailhead. The staffed
nature center, located half way up the mountain next to Sunrise Pond,
is open June 1 through October 31. The sanctuary also conducts youth
programs and weekend retreats for adults, with lodging at historic
Adirondack-style lodges on Sunset Pond.

Trip Description
Beautiful Borestone Mountain is a hidden jewel at the southern end of
the 100-Mile Wilderness. A Maine Audubon Sanctuary, this serene little
mountain (1,947 feet) features old growth forest, sparkling ponds, and
expansive views from its craggy summit peaks. Half way up the trail,

there is a staffed interpretative center with historical artifacts, and wildlife and nature exhibits. This is a perfect hike for families or anyone interested in learning about the natural wonders of Maine's northern forest.

There are two ways to reach the nature center at Sunrise Pond. You
can follow the jeep road, or pick up a newly cut trail that leaves the road
just beyond the gate and follows a wooded path, returning to the road just
south of the pond. This trip takes the jeep road on the ascent and returns
via the shorter nature trail. Whichever way you choose to go, be sure to
pick up the interesting interpretive map provided at the trailhead.

From the gate, begin walking up the jeep road, past the entrance (left)
to the new nature trail. The road passes beneath a hardwood forest and
soon reaches an old sugarhouse. From here, the road begins to rise and

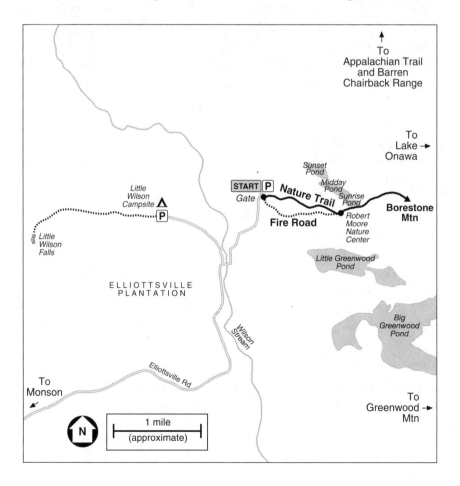

Sunrise Pond, Borestone Mountain Sanctuary.

climb steadily through a series of switchbacks. At 0.6 mile, a side trail leads right to Little Greenwood Overlook. From the ledges here, there are good views south to Little Greenwood Pond and Greenwood Mountain.

Farther up the road, the forest turns to predominantly spruce, fir, and white pine. At 1.2 miles, the road meets the outlet of the new nature trail, then passes a side road that leads to the private residence of the sanctuary's manager. At 1.3 miles, the road reaches the Robert T. Moore Nature Center on Sunrise Pond. This is a wonderful place to stop and study the exhibits and learn about the area's natural history. There are also restroom facilities nearby and places to sit and enjoy the pond.

Beautiful Sunrise Pond, one of three ponds here, sits beneath the mountain's conical peaks. The other ponds include Midday Pond and Sunset Pond. All three are fed by springs and were named according to the time of day the sun shines on them. Though there are no fish here, the ponds are teeming with other life. Sitting in quiet solitude at Sunrise Pond late one afternoon, I was treated to an amazing frog chorus that disrupted the quietude but was equally enchanting.

From the Nature Center, the trail to the summit curves around the pond, crosses over an outlet, and begins a steep 0.5-mile scramble over rocky outcrops to the open western peak. The path continues, descending slightly into a saddle and then rising to the true summit on the eastern peak. To assist visitors, Maine Audubon Society, with assistance from the Maine Conservation Corps, has placed handholds and safety rails on steep, exposed sections of the trail.

The unobstructed views from the summit are magnificent. The Appalachian Trail runs north along a string of mountains known as the Barren-Chairback Range, impressive Lake Onawa sits to the east, and Midday and Sunset Ponds sparkle below. To the south, there are excellent views to Big Greenwood Pond. This is an outstanding summit to visit during fall foliage season.

To descend, carefully retrace your steps to the West Peak and then down the steep-sided mountaintop. Back at the Nature Center, you can continue the descent down the road, or pick up the new nature trail. This woods path is shorter and cuts through a beautiful section of the mountainside.

Nature and History Notes

In the early 1900s, Robert T. Moore operated a successful fox farm on what is now Borestone Mountain Sanctuary. In 1958, he bequeathed the majority of his holdings, including the fabulous Adirondack-style lodges on Sunset Pond, to the National Audubon Society. In 2000, the sanctuary was transferred to Maine Audubon.

Borestone's forest is more than a century old. The spectacular trees here are a haven for wildlife, including pileated woodpeckers, raccoons, and owls. For birders, some of Maine's most sought after species spend summers here, including Blackburnian, Cape May, and bay-breasted warblers.

Other Options

Combine this hike with a side trip to spectacular Little Wilson Falls, a 57-foot waterfall located east of Borestone Mountain in a deep slate canyon (see map). Camping is available at the Maine Forest Service's Little Wilson Campsite. The hike from the campsite to the falls is 1.6 miles.

More Information

Visit Maine Audubon's website at www.audubon.org to learn more about Borestone Mountain, nature programs, and summer retreats.

TRIP 52
MOUNT KINEO

Difficulty: Moderate
Distance: 4.0 miles round-trip
Estimated Time: 3 hours
Location: Moosehead Lake near Rockwood
Maps: USGS Mount Kineo Quad
    DeLorme *Maine Atlas*, map 41

A paddle and hiking adventure to a precipitous peninsula overlooking the state's largest lake.

Directions
From Greenville, drive 20.0 miles north and west on ME 6/15 to Rockwood. Turn right off ME 6/15 on the only road leading to Rockwood Village, just before a sharp left bend. This road will bring you into the village and down to the Rockwood Boat Landing.

Trail Notes
The only approach to Mount Kineo is from the water. You can paddle across from Rockwood, or be ferried over on the Kineo Boat Launch, which departs daily, on the hour, from 8 A.M. to 5 P.M. in summer from the Rockwood Boat Landing. Boat rentals are available at Northwoods Outfitters on Main Street in Greenville (207-695-3288).

Caution: The Indian Trail is steep in places and runs along the exposed cliffs of the mountain. Hikers with children, or those preferring an easier ascent route, can also reach the summit via the Bridle Trail, which is longer and without views, but has moderate grades.

Trip Description
At 34 miles long, and 117 miles square, Moosehead is Maine's largest lake and the largest body of water within one state east of the Mississippi River. The region is often referred to as the "Gateway to the Great North Woods," and is, indeed, one of northern Maine's most spectacular settings. Outside of chartering a floatplane, there is perhaps no better way to take in this vast, expansive country than from atop the precipitous

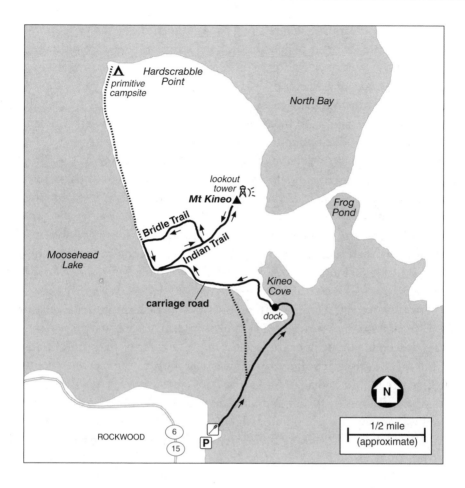

cliffs of magnificent Mount Kineo.

True to any worthy outdoor experience, simply getting to Kineo can be a challenge in itself. The mountain rises dramatically from the middle of Moosehead Lake at the western tip of a peninsula jutting from the eastern shore. The only way to reach it is by water.

Fortunately, there are a couple of ways to do this. The more adventuresome can paddle across the lake from the small village of Rockwood, which lies a mile south of Kineo's southern shore. Alternatively, you can be ferried over on the Kineo Boat Launch, which departs from the Rockwood Boat Landing daily and on the hour from 8 A.M. to 5 P.M. during summer. Paddlers should check the weather before departing, as Moosehead, like any large lake, is subject to afternoon wind and waves, making the short crossing potentially difficult. If you choose to paddle across, you can land anywhere along the southern shore and pick up the trail along the shore, or paddle into Kineo Cove and depart from there.

From the boat dock at Kineo Cove, follow the gravel carriage road to a Maine Bureau of Parks and Lands bulletin board, where you will pick up the footpath that leads west along the southern shoreline, beneath Kineo's towering cliffs. At 0.8 mile from the dock, you'll reach the Indian Trail and Bridle Trail Junction. The Indian Trail leaves sharply to the right and climbs straight uphill. Follow this trail to the top of the cliffs where there are good views to the southeast. The trail continues across open cliffs and woods and rejoins the Bridle Trail, which enters from the left at 1.2 miles.

From here, the trail continues northeast, drops into a small wooded depression, then rises again, reaching the 1,806-foot summit in 0.4 mile. The summit of Mount Kineo is wooded; however, there is a restored lookout tower here, which offers excellent, 360-degree views.

To descend, retrace your path for 0.4 mile to reach the junction where the Bridle Trail diverges right. The trail drops into the woods, turns west, and descends gradually to the lakeshore. At this junction, a trail leaves right and travels north along Kineo's western shore to Hardscrabble Point where the Maine Bureau of Parks and Lands has established a primitive campsite. To return to the southern shore or Kineo Cove, turn left here and walk along the shore path, which passes the Indian Trail Junction in 0.3 mile. Continue along the shore, retracing the initial path of your ascent.

Nature and History Notes

Mount Kineo's spectacular 800-foot cliffs have drawn people for centuries. The name is an Indian word, thought to mean "high bluff." According to the Moosehead Historical Society, more than 3,000 years ago, Native Americans were traveling here from great distances to gather the mountain's flint-like rock to make stone tools, arrowheads, and other implements. In fact, Kineo flint is so unusual scientists have been able to track it across much of the eastern United States and Canada to Indian tribes that include Norridgewocks, Abenakis, Delawars, Mohawks, and Iroquois.

Henry David Thoreau made two journeys to Mount Kineo, by steamer in September 1853, and again in July 1857, when he and a Native American guide traversed the lake in a birch-bark canoe. Writing about Kineo's

The only way to reach Mount Kineo is by water. You can paddle across, or take the Kineo Boat Launch (shown here), which departs from the Rockwood Boat Landing on the hour during summer.

sheer east face in his book *The Maine Woods*, he mused: "The celebrated precipice is so high and perpendicular that you can jump from the top, many hundred feet, into the water which makes up behind the point. A man on board told us that an anchor had been sunk ninety fathoms at its base before reaching bottom! Probably it will be discovered erelong that some Indian maiden jumped off it for love once, for true love never could have found a path more to its mind." While there's no record of a broken-hearted maiden leaping from the mountain's cliff top, the cove below the east face is, in fact, the deepest part of the lake. However, at a depth of 250 feet, the anchor would have only sunk about 42 fathoms.

By the time of Thoreau's second arrival, the first in a series of large hotels on Kineo had already been built. Demand from summer visitors was so great that, by 1911 the Kineo House could accommodate over 500 guests and was considered one of the finest hotels in the country. However, with the advent of the automobile, the number of visitors to Kineo began to dwindle. By 1933, the Maine Central Railroad had eliminated its Kineo branch. In 1938, the hotel was sold and later, during demolition, it caught fire and burned to the ground.

In 1990, the Land for Maine's Future Program provided funding for Mount Kineo's acquisition from a private owner. The purchase was negotiated with help from the Nature Conservancy and the Maine Department of Conservation. The Maine Bureau of Parks and Lands now manages Kineo, including the primitive campsite at Hardscrabble Point, and four hiking trails.

More Information

For more information about outdoor opportunities in the Moosehead Lake Region, stop in at Northwoods Outfitters on Main Street in Greenville (207-695-3288), or visit their website at www.mainoutfitter.com.

Preserving the Maine Woods

In most people's minds, the Maine Woods (or North Woods) conjures up thoughts of huge tracts of relatively undeveloped forestland in western and northern Maine. However, in the late 1980s, paper companies and timber investment companies started selling lands throughout the region, some to development companies. Since then, timberland has changed hands at an alarming rate, and the marketing of these parcels usually touts development potential. Between 1998 and 2003, 5.5 million acres of Maine timberland—more than a quarter of the state's land area—changed hands.

However, the cooperation among environmentalists and sports enthusiasts, politicians from opposite poles, and diverse organizations with widely differing priorities gives us hope. Already, the Appalachian Mountain Club, the Nature Conservancy, a host of other conservation organizations, the state of Maine, outdoor clubs, and local communities have worked together to protect key swaths of land. By 2002, outright land purchases and conservation easements permanently protected 1.05 million acres of Maine Woods.

More recently, the AMC has increased its commitment to the Maine Woods. It started in December 2003, when it embarked on the largest conservation effort in its 127-year history: the Maine Woods Initiative. The Initiative seeks to address the ecological and economic needs of the Maine Woods region by supporting local forest products jobs

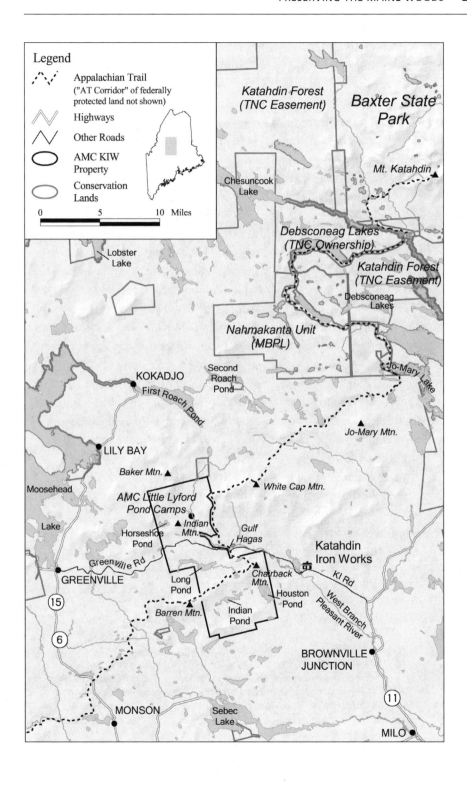

Legend

- Appalachian Trail ("AT Corridor" of federally protected land not shown)
- Highways
- Other Roads
- AMC KIW Property
- Conservation Lands

0   5   10   Miles

Katahdin Forest (TNC Easement)

Baxter State Park

Chesuncook Lake

Mt. Katahdin

Debsconeag Lakes (TNC Ownership)

Katahdin Forest (TNC Easement)

Debsconeag Lakes

Nahmakanta Unit (MBPL)

Lobster Lake

KOKADJO

First Roach Pond

Second Roach Pond

Jo-Mary Lake

Jo-Mary Mtn.

LILY BAY

Baker Mtn.

Moosehead

White Cap Mtn.

AMC Little Lyford Pond Camps

Lake

Horseshoe Pond

Indian Mtn.

Gulf Hagas

Katahdin Iron Works

Greenville Rd

KI Rd

GREENVILLE

Long Pond

Chairback Mtn.

Houston Pond

West Branch Pleasant River

15

Barren Mtn.

Indian Pond

6

BROWNVILLE JUNCTION

11

MONSON

Sebec Lake

MILO

and traditional recreation, creating new multi-day backcountry experiences for visitors, and attracting new nature-based tourism to the region. The region of the Maine Woods identified for this project is the "100-Mile Wilderness," a roadless corridor stretching from Monson to Katahdin that contains a segment of the Appalachian Trail as well as Gulf Hagas, a magnificent gorge known as the "Grand Canyon of Maine," a National Natural Landmark. The AMC's investment will make paddling, hiking, skiing, and snowshoeing available to visitors, while reducing overuse on some portions of the Appalachian Trail.

In the initiative's first phase, AMC purchased from International Paper a 37,000-acre tract known as the Katahdin Iron Works Tract. The AMC will draw on its long history in Maine and New Hampshire in developing new trails and a range of accommodations that are scaled appropriately for the natural resources of the area. At the time of this publication, the AMC is developing a management plan to determine which portions of the property will be managed for natural resource protection, recreation, certified sustainable forestry, and multiple use. The AMC purchase ensures that these 37,000 acres—rich with opportunities for paddling, hiking, cross-country skiing, and snowshoeing—will be protected and remain open to the public for recreation use. For more information about the Maine Woods Initiative, go to www. outdoors.org/mwi.

Trips 53 and 57 are set within the 100-Mile Wilderness on the Katahdin Iron Works Tract, and the sidebar "An Outdoor Traveler's Getaway to Little Lyford Pond Camps" on page 243 describes the myriad hiking, biking, and paddling excursion you may take here, using the AMC's idyllic Little Lyford Pond Camps as base camp.

100-Mile Wilderness Map Credits: Cartography by Cathy Poppenweimer. Conservation land data provided by the Maine Office of GIS and the AMC. Data on lakes, rivers, and highways provided by the U.S. Geological Survey. Appalachian Trail information developed by the Appalachian Trail Conservancy.

TRIP 53
GULF HAGAS

Difficulty: Moderate to difficult
Distance: 8.0-mile loop
Estimated Time: 6 hours
Location: Bowdoin College Grant East, northwest of Brownville
 Junction
Maps: USGS Barren Mountain East
 USGS Hay Mountain
 AMC's *Maine Mountain Guide*, 9th ed., map 3
 DeLorme *Maine Atlas*, map 42

An exceptional rim hike along Maine's "Grand Canyon" with
side trips to its numerous waterfalls, cascades, chutes, and
pools.

Directions

To reach the eastern trailhead, drive north on ME 11 and turn west onto
the Katahdin Iron Works Road, 4.0 miles north of Brownville Junction.
Follow this road for 6.8 miles to the Iron Works gatehouse. Register with
the caretaker and pay the access fee. Beyond the gate, the road crosses
the West Branch of the Pleasant River. At the fork, stay right. In 3.4
miles from the gatehouse, the road reaches a second fork. Stay left here
and continue down the gravel road, crossing the river a second time. The
road reaches the Gulf Hagas/Appalachian Trail parking area 6.8 miles
from the gatehouse.

Guests staying at the AMC's Little Lyford Pond Camps (LLPC) can
reach Gulf Hagas from the west by a path that leaves directly from the
camps (see **Other Options**, below). To reach LLPC from Greenville,
turn right on Pleasant Street, just after Northwoods Outfitters on Main
Street. Follow this road toward the airport, and past Autumn Brooke
Farm. Continue down the road, following the LLPC signs, to the North
Maine Woods gate (fee), approximately 12 miles from Greenville. Beyond
the gate, continue following the LLPC signs for approximately 5 miles to
reach the camps.

Trail Notes

Though there is relatively little elevation gain (700 feet) along the length of this trail, the rim is largely uneven, rocky, and rugged, and can be particularly slippery when wet. Some of the side trails to the falls and pools are quite steep. Use caution, and allow plenty of extra time when traveling here. Since 1995, the Maine Appalachian Trail Club (MATC) has placed a full-time "ridgerunner" at Gulf Hagas during the high season to help manage safety concerns and the potential for environmental damage posed by the number of hikers passing through the area. Ridgerunners also document site usage and serve to educate hikers about the region. The "Gulf Hagas Area" map, published by MATC, is available at the gatehouse, and has excellent descriptions of both the trails and natural features of the region.

Trip Description

Deep within the 100-Mile Wilderness, the West Branch of the Pleasant River cuts through a spectacular gorge, known as Gulf Hagas. For more than 2 miles, the river tumbles and churns through the slate canyon forming an attractive series of waterfalls, pools, and chutes. The Gulf is so extraordinary, the National Park Service pronounced it a Registered Natural Landmark in 1968 for its "exceptional value in illustrating the natural history of the United States." This trip travels the rim of the canyon, which offers outstanding views from atop its sheer cliffs and access to many of the Gulf's scenic wonders.

From the parking area, follow the blue-blazed access trail, which soon joins with the white-blazed Appalachian Trail (AT) at the southern bank of the river. Here, you'll have to ford the river, which is about 100 feet wide and, usually, no more than knee-deep in summer, but there are numerous submerged, slippery rocks, so cross with care. During spring, the river is often impassable. It's a good idea to bring along an extra pair of shoes or sandals to keep your boots dry for the remainder of the hike.

Across the river, the trail continues along the AT, reaching Pleasant River Road 0.1 mile from the riverbank. The path to the Gulf continues left, following the AT and soon passes beneath the Hermitage, a stand of old-growth white pines, which were purchased by the National Parks Service in 2002 and added to the Appalachian National Scenic Trail Corridor. A side path (left) leads to a small clearing where you can view the trees, some of which are well over 100 feet tall. Beyond the Hermitage, the trail

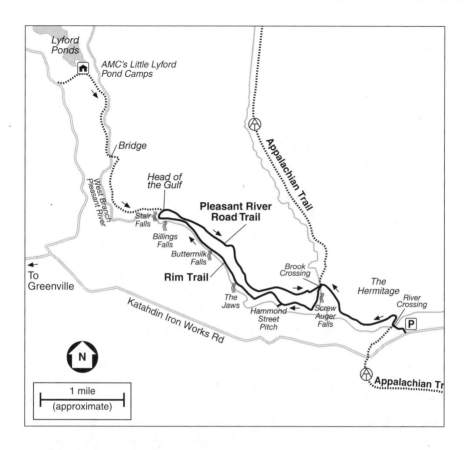

continues north and west, arriving at Gulf Hagas Brook in 1.3 miles.

Just before the brook, the relocated AT turns sharp right, while the Pleasant River Road Trail follows blue blazes across the brook to a junction with the Rim Trail. From here, the Pleasant River Road Trail continues straight (toward the Head of the Gulf), which is the path we'll follow on the return. For now, cross the brook and follow the Rim Trail, which diverges left and drops toward the canyon. The Rim Trail soon arrives at a spur path leading to spectacular Screw Auger Falls. The path is steep, but the falls are not to be missed. Over the next 0.2 mile, more spur paths lead to a series of beautiful cascades and pools below the falls.

The Rim Trail continues west and next reaches a side spur to Hammond Street Pitch, 0.7 mile from the brook. The overlook here rises nearly 100 feet above the gorge. At 0.9 miles, a connecter path (right) leads to the Pleasant River Road Trail. At 1.2 miles, another series of side paths begins, which access views of the Jaws, where the river is squeezed through a narrow channel between ledge outcrops that jut from the canyon walls. At 1.8 miles, the trail reaches a spur to a pool below frothy Buttermilk Falls. Here, again, a path diverges right, leading in 0.3 mile to the Pleasant River Road Trail.

The trail continues along the edge of the river and, at 2.8 miles, passes a ledge above Billings Falls, which drops into a large pool. A short side trail to Stair Falls is reached soon after. At 2.9 miles, the path reaches a short side trail leading to the Head of the Gulf. Here the river cascades around a rocky island, which provides a great spot to enjoy a break before the return trip.

From the Head of the Gulf, the trail diverges away from the river and turns north and east to reach the Pleasant River Road Trail. A trail to the left here, marked with LLPC signs, continues along the West Branch of the Pleasant River, leading to the AMC's Little Lyford Pond Camps in 2.2 miles (see **Other Options**, below). To return to the AT parking area, continue along the Pleasant River Road Trail, which skirts back along the side of a mountain above the gorge, and reaches the Rim Trail junction 2.0 miles from the Head of the Gulf. From here, retrace your path across Gulf Hagas Brook, picking up the white-blazed AT and then the blue-blazed access trail after recrossing the West Branch of the Pleasant River.

Ascending a side trail from Screw Auger Falls, Gulf Hagas.

Nature and History Notes

Today, the region encompassing Gulf Hagas is best known as the 100-Mile Wilderness, the most remote stretch of the entire Appalachian Trail. Yet, during the nineteenth century, the area was a thriving community that included hundreds of homes, a hotel, and a railroad. The settlement developed around a thriving iron industry known as the Katahdin Iron Works, which operated from 1843 to 1890. Iron ore was mined from nearby Ore Mountain and brought to the Iron Works where it was super heated in a blast furnace to separate the iron from other minerals in the ore. To heat the furnace, the Iron Works produced charcoal using 16 brick kilns that each burned 50 cords of wood at a time. The blast furnace produced pig iron ingots, each weighing about 80 pounds. At the height of production during the 1880s, the Iron Works produced 18 to 20 tons of pig iron per day. At the same time, the region also became known as a summer resort destination, touted for its curative, mineral-rich springs, outdoor sporting activities, and beautiful scenery.

However, by 1890, the Iron Works had succumbed to outside competition, improved technologies in the production of iron, and the advent of the steel industry. Katahdin Iron Works became a State Historic Site in 1965. Remnants of the blast furnace, a charcoal kiln, and storyboards describing this fascinating aspect of Maine's history are located next to the gatehouse entrance east of Gulf Hagas.

Other Options

From the AMC's Little Lyford Pond Camps, Gulf Hagas can be reached via a 2.2-mile path that runs south along the West Branch of the Pleasant River. The trail follows closely to the riverbank before reaching a dirt road at 1.0 mile. Turn left onto the road and cross a bridge over the river. Just beyond the bridge, the trail leaves the road and diverges right, into the woods. Continuing south, the trail parallels the river, passes Lloyd Pond, then turns east and reaches a trail junction at 2.0 miles. Turn right here to reach the Head of the Gulf and the Rim Trail in 0.2 mile. In winter, this is an excellent pathway to reach the Gulf on cross-country skis. Snowshoes are recommended for exploring the rim from there.

More Information

For more information about the AMC's Little Lyford Pond Camps, visit www.outdoors.org.

TRIP 54
SOUTH TURNER MOUNTAIN/SANDY STREAM POND

Difficulty: Moderate
Distance: 5.5 miles
Estimated Time: 4 hours
Location: Baxter State Park
Maps: USGS Mount Katahdin
　　　　AMC's *Maine Mountain Guide*, 9th ed., map 1
　　　　DeLorme *Maine Atlas*, maps 50 and 51

**A great introductory hike to Baxter State Park combined with
a visit to a beautiful pond frequented by moose.**

Directions
To reach the southern entrance to Baxter State Park, take I-95 north to
Exit 244. Turn west onto Route 157 and drive to Millinocket. From Millinocket, follow the signs for Baxter State Park, which lead in 18.0 miles
to the Togue Pond Gatehouse (fee). Just beyond the gatehouse, stay right
at the fork and drive 8.1 miles to the Roaring Brook Campground and
day-use parking area.

Trail Notes
Please note that Roaring Brook is one of the most popular trailheads in
the park. When the parking lot is full (an almost daily occurrence in August), no more visitors are allowed in. Arrive early, or plan your trip with
alternatives in mind.

Trip Description
This trip is an excellent introduction to the spectacular hiking opportunities within Baxter State Park. The height-of-land atop South Turner
Mountain provides some of the best views in the park, and a near perfect
panorama of the entire east face of the Katahdin massif. The route described here combines a hike to South Turner's craggy summit with a side
loop around Sandy Stream Pond on the return. The pond is an outstanding place to sight moose and other wildlife, especially at dawn and dusk.

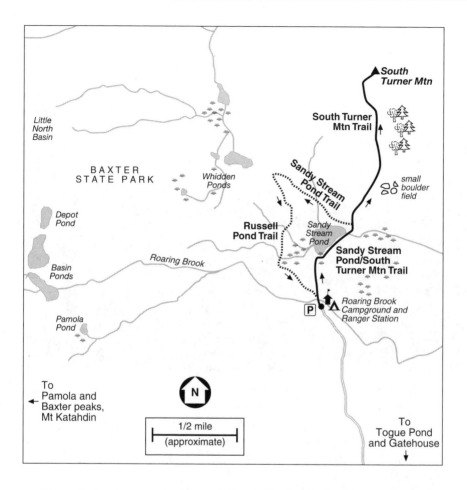

The trip begins on the Russell Pond Trail, which departs from the ranger station at Roaring Brook Campground. Sign in at the hiker's register before departing. Follow the Russell Pond Trail due north to the crossing over Roaring Brook. At 0.2 mile, stay right and pick up the Sandy Stream Pond/South Turner Mountain Trail. The path crosses over level terrain and approaches the southern shore of the pond at 0.3 mile. At 0.4 mile, the trail veers right, crosses an outlet brook, and continues around the pond's southeastern shoreline. Along this section, there are side paths leading to the water's edge, which provide excellent opportunities to look for moose on your way in. Please note that this is a Wildlife Area Only Zone; visitors are asked to stay on designated trails and keep a respectful distance from any wildlife that may be in the area.

A view of South Turner Mountain from Keep Ridge.

At 0.7 mile, the trail forks with the South Turner Mountain Trail leading right and the Sandy Stream Pond Trail continuing to the left. Stay right and follow the South Turner Mountain Trail across a small boulder field at 0.9 mile. At 1.1 miles, the trail rises steeply through mixed hardwoods, then reaches a side trail to a spring at 1.5 miles. The trail continues its ascent of the mountain's southwestern slide, emerging onto open ledge at 1.8 miles. Follow the cairns and blue-paint blazes over the ledges to reach the summit at 2.0 miles from Roaring Brook Campground.

From the summit of South Turner Mountain, there are fine views of the Russell Pond area to the northwest and magnificent views westward over the Whidden Ponds, Basin Ponds, Little North, South and Great basins of Katahdin. On a clear day, this peak provides a spectacular, panoramic vantage point to enjoy the full expanse of the Katahdin massif.

To descend, retrace your route to the Sandy Stream Pond Trail junction (1.3 miles). From here, you can continue to retrace your route back to Roaring Brook Campground for a 4-mile out-and-back trip, or turn right and follow the Sandy Stream Pond Trail. The pond trail skirts the northeast shore of the pond, then continues northwest to a junction with the Russell Pond Trail. Turn left (south) onto the Russell Pond Trail to complete a 1.5-mile loop around the pond and back to Roaring Brook Campground. When you reach the ranger station, be sure to sign out at the hiker's register.

Nature and History Notes

The moose (*Alces alces*) is Maine's state animal (adopted in 1979) and the largest member of the deer family in the world. There are four subspecies of moose recognized in North America. The eastern or Taiga moose is the subspecies found in Maine. The largest bulls may stand more than 7 feet at the shoulder and weigh up to 1,400 pounds. A mature bull's antler spread can exceed 5 feet. Both cows and bulls have "dewlaps," or "bells," which are skin flaps that dangle from the throat region. To date, researchers have not discovered a purpose for this unusual feature.

Moose subsist on "browse," the leaves and twigs of woody plants, including willow, maple, birch, and mountain ash. Balsam fir is an important source of food in winter. In summer, moose frequent ponds, lakes, river, and streams to forage on sodium-rich aquatic plants.

Moose were plentiful in New England during colonial days, and an important food source for early settlers. However, by the early 1900s, the moose population in Maine had plummeted to an estimated 2,000 animals. The decline was primarily attributed to unrestricted hunting. The state prohibited moose hunting in 1935, and the population gradually recovered. By 1980, the state was able to institute a limited annual moose hunt. Today, there are an estimated 29,000 moose in Maine, inhabiting virtually every region of the state.

More Information

For a complete description of hiking opportunities within Baxter State Park, consult the AMC's *Maine Mountain Guide*, 9th ed. For information about rules and regulations, camping options, or to make reservations, contact the Baxter State Park Reservation Clerk at 207-723-5140 or visit the park's website at www.baxterstateparkauthority.com

"Forever Wild": Baxter State Park

Baxter State Park is the crown jewel of Maine's state parks and a gleaming testament to one man's persistence, vision, and generosity. Percival Baxter, Maine's governor from 1921 to 1925, first visited the area on a fishing trip with his father in 1903. Although there is no extant record of that journey, Baxter was obviously inspired by it. For years after, he tried to convince the state legislature to buy Katahdin, the state's highest peak, and the land surrounding it. In a 1921 speech to the legislature, he argued, "Maine is famous for its twenty-five hundred miles of seacoast, with its countless islands; for its myriad lakes and ponds; and for its forests and rivers. But Mount Katahdin Park will be the state's crowning glory, a worthy memorial to commemorate the end of the first and the beginning of the second century of Maine's statehood. This park will prove a blessing to those who follow us, and they will see that we built for them more wisely than our forefathers did for us."

Despite his eloquence and persistence, the legislature was not persuaded. So, in 1930, Baxter simply bought nearly 6,000 acres using his own funds, and then gifted it to the state, an act of determination and generosity that he would repeat throughout his lifetime. By 1933, the Maine legislature had officially designated the area "Baxter State Park."

Over the next 30 years, through a combination of his personal resources and fundraising, Baxter continued to acquire land, which he would then bestow to the state. The last parcel, acquired in 1962, brought his total gift to the people of Maine to more than 200,000 acres. The gifts came with one overarching stipulation, that the area ". . . shall forever be used for public park and recreational purposes, shall be forever left in the natural wild state, shall forever be kept as a sanctuary for wild beasts and birds, that no road or ways for motor vehicles shall hereafter ever be constructed thereon or therein."

Simply put, Baxter wanted the park to be "used to the fullest extent, but in the right unspoiled manner."

Percival Baxter's final gift to the park was a trust fund of nearly 7 million dollars, which he left to ensure the park would be maintained and kept forever wild. Following his death on June 12, 1969, his ashes were scattered throughout the park. His lifelong dream, encapsulated from a 1941 speech, is inscribed on a plaque placed on a boulder by Katahdin Stream. It reads, "Man is born to die. His works are short-lived. Buildings crumble, monuments decay, and wealth vanishes, but Katahdin in all its glory forever shall remain the mountain of the people of Maine."

Today, Baxter State Park encompasses 46 mountain peaks and ridges, 18 of which rise above 3,000 feet. Mount Katahdin, a spectacular massif, rises nearly a mile to a height of 5,267 feet. In addition, there are numerous lakes, ponds, and streams that support an abundance of wildlife. There are more than 200 miles of trails within the park, as well as a primitive tote road, which winds south to north for 41 miles. The park has ten campgrounds (open seasonally May 15 to October 15), some of which are "hike-in only" facilities. To protect the park's resources, there are strict limits for both camping and day-use. There is no electricity, running water, or paved roads.

For more information about Baxter State Park, or to inquire about camping reservations, call 207-723-5140, or visit the park's website at www.baxterstateparkauthority.com.

Enjoying the tranquility at Daicey Pond, Baxter State Park.

TRIP 55
KATAHDIN—THE KNIFE EDGE LOOP

Difficulty: Difficult
Distance: 10.0-mile loop
Estimated Time: 10 hours
Location: Baxter State Park
Maps: USGS Mount Katahdin
   AMC's *Maine Mountain Guide*, 9th ed., map 1
   DeLorme *Maine Atlas*, map 50 and 51

A demanding loop hike across Maine's most famous mountain, including a traverse of the renowned Knife Edge ridge.

Directions
To reach the southern entrance to Baxter State Park, take I-95 north to Exit 244. Turn west onto Route 157 and drive to Millinocket. From Millinocket, follow the signs for Baxter State Park, which lead in 18.0 miles to the Togue Pond Gatehouse (fee). Just beyond the gatehouse, stay right at the fork and drive 8.1 miles to the Roaring Brook Campground and day-use parking area.

Trail Notes
Caution: This is unquestionably the most difficult hike in this book, and arguably the most challenging dayhike in New England. In addition to the physical demands posed by its overall length and elevation gain (3,700 feet), much of the route is well above treeline and severely exposed to the full force of weather. The 1.1-mile section known as the Knife Edge can be particularly unnerving, with its sheer drops on either side of a narrow, difficult passage. Do not attempt this climb if you are afraid of heights, or if there is the slightest indication of inclement weather approaching. Even in fair weather conditions, you are well advised to pack appropriate gear, including foul-weather clothing, a headlamp, and ample food and water.

Trip Description
The Katahdin massif encompasses four peaks, a broad, sloping plateau, and a spectacular, serrated ridge that in places is little more than 2 feet

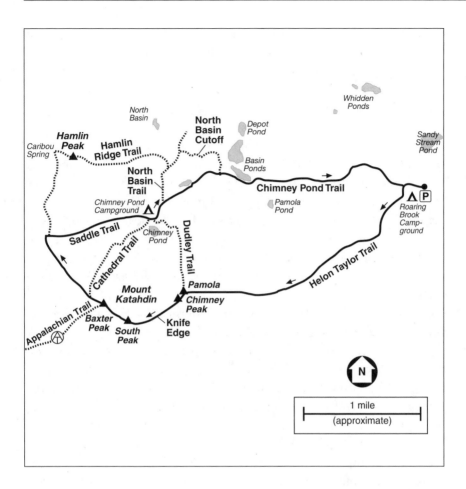

wide. It is Maine's highest mountain, rising dramatically above the surrounding landscape to a height of 5,267 feet, and the northern terminus of the Appalachian Trail (AT). For many thru-hikers, Katahdin is the culmination of a six-month, 2,000-mile pilgrimage. For day-hikers, it is arguably New England's most alluring and challenging peak.

There are four major approach routes to Katahdin's height of land on Baxter Peak, including the southwestern ascent via the Hunt Trail along the AT. The more popular routes approach the mountain's striking glacial cirque from the northeast. From east to west, they include, the Helon Taylor Trail, which ascends rocky, exposed Keep Ridge to Pamola Peak; the steep, boulder-strewn Dudley Trail, which also ascends to Pamola Peak and departs from Chimney Pond Campground; the impressive Cathedral Trail, with its three rocky spires; and the Saddle Trail, which is often referred to as the "easiest" route to the summit, though a more apt description might be, "the least difficult." The Hamlin Ridge Trail also bears mentioning here. Though it is a longer route, this beautiful trail ascends to Hamlin Peak along exposed Hamlin Ridge, providing magnificent views (and access) to Katahdin's principal peaks.

A popular route taken by day-hikers forms a nearly 10-mile loop, which departs from Roaring Brook Campground along the Chimney Pond Trail (3.3 miles), ascends from Chimney Pond Campground to the Tableland via the Saddle Trail (0.9 mile), traverses the Tableland to Baxter Peak (1.3 miles), crosses the Knife Edge to Pamola Peak (1.1 miles), and descends Keep Ridge via the Helon Taylor Trail (3.2 miles). This loop is also frequently done in the reverse (as described below) and has the benefit of completing the most difficult sections while you're fresh, as well as providing an opportunity to cool off in the beautiful Basin Ponds near the end of the route.

Beyond the scenic attributes (which all of these trails have), the route you choose should largely depend upon the physical condition of your party, condition of the trail (given time of year, etc.), and weather conditions. Another important factor to consider is the descent route. Generally, neither Dudley nor Cathedral is recommended for the descent (though, either trail can be done if necessary). Trail conditions and pertinent route and weather information can be obtained at both the Roaring Brook and Chimney Pond Campground's Ranger Stations. Finally, you can substantially reduce the overall route length by securing a bunk or campsite at Chimney Pond and broadening the trip to 2–3 days. However, unless you book well in advance you may find securing a spot at Chimney Pond nearly as difficult as the intended climb!

Before departing, sign the register located at the Ranger's quarters at Roaring Brook Campground. There is an interesting scale model of the mountain here. Follow the Chimney Pond Trail, which tracks along the east side of Roaring Brook and reaches the junction with the Helon Taylor Trail in 0.1 mile. The trail follows the old Leavitt Trail and was renamed for a former superintendent of the park.

Turn left onto the Helon Taylor Trail, which climbs through the forest to an outlook and then levels off. At 1.0 mile, the trail climbs steeply, then drops to Bear Brook. From Bear Brook, the trail ascends through a stand of balsam and spruce trees, climbs along a boulder field and emerges onto Keep Ridge. The trail now continues along the open ridge,

In places, Katahdin's precipitous Knife Edge is little more than 2 feet wide.

providing excellent views (in fair weather) of Pamola, Chimney Peak, and the Knife Edge.

The trail continues its ascent along the exposed ridge surmounting rocks and boulders, and reaches the Pamola summit (4,902 feet) in 3.2 miles near a junction with the Dudley Trail. The views here take in the entire ridge across to Hamlin Peak and down to South Basin and Chimney Pond. This is a good place to assess weather conditions and turn back, if necessary.

The crux of the route begins here, as you traverse the infamous Knife Edge, the most difficult and spectacular ridge hike in the East. For 1.1 miles, the route crosses over a jumbled heap of granite boulders along a narrow, extremely exposed arête that drops precipitously on either side. From Pamola Peak, follow cairns and blue-paint blazes southwest toward the abrupt, steep cleft between Pamola and Chimney Peak. This section can be unnerving, but patience and careful consideration will reveal good handholds and foot placements. After descending into the saddle, follow the blue blazes and carefully scramble up the other side to reach Chimney Peak.

From here, the route traverses a narrow path, which at times is little more than 2 feet wide. Follow the blazes across a section of the trail known as the Sawteeth, then ascend steeply to South Peak. From South Peak, continue along the ridge and climb to the height of land on Baxter Peak (5,267 feet). In fair weather, the views from Baxter Peak are simply exceptional, taking in the entire ridge and continuing northward across the park's many peaks and valleys. To the south, the views stretch across a vast expanse of ponds, lakes, and distant mountains.

A few steps west of the large cairn on Baxter Peak is the weathered sign that marks the northern terminus of the Appalachian Trail. One can only imagine the thoughts and emotions of thru-hikers who have managed to reach this site after walking an estimated five million steps from Springer Mountain, Georgia.

The descent from Baxter Peak follows the Saddle Trail across a broad, open plateau known as the Tableland. The gradual descent along the initial part of this path is a welcome relief from the climbing, scrambling, and traversing achieved thus far.

The Saddle Trail passes the Cathedral, Baxter Peak Cutoff, and Cathedral Cutoff trails and descends to an abrupt right turn, reached in 1.0 mile from Baxter Peak. From here, the trail drops from the Tableland down Saddle Slide, a steep, 0.2-mile section of loose dirt and boulders. Use caution here so as not to displace any rocks onto hikers who may be below you. The trail continues to descend over boulders and through scrub and stunted birch trees, crosses a brook, then moderates along a rocky, well-worn path that reaches Chimney Pond Campground 2.2 miles from Baxter Peak. From the edge of the pond, the mountain now rises more than 2,000 feet above you.

The final leg of the loop descends along the moderate Chimney Pond Trail, which arrives at Roaring Brook Campground in 3.3 miles. The trails to North Basin and Hamlin Ridge leave left 0.3 mile from Chimney Pond. At 0.6 mile, the trail follows the side of a depression known as Dry Pond. In 1.0 mile, the trail reaches the North Basin Cutoff, which leaves left. Continuing the descent, the Chimney Pond Trail crosses over a wide bridge and skirts around the east end of Basin Ponds over uneven, rocky ground. At 1.3 miles, a short side path leads left to the water. Here you can cool off with a refreshing swim, or sit by the shore and enjoy the excellent views back to Katahdin.

From Basin Ponds, the trail follows the Roaring Brook Trail along rocky terrain and soon reaches a large boulder marking the halfway point. From here, the trail continues through stands of birch and other hardwoods and crosses the outlet brook of Pamola Pond at 2.3 miles. At 2.6 miles, the trail reaches the southern bank of Roaring Brook, which, except for a short section, it then follows to the Helon Taylor trailhead and then on to Roaring Brook Campground. When you reach the campground, be sure to sign out at the register before departing.

Nature and History Notes

The first recorded ascent of Katahdin was in 1804. Charles Turner, Jr., led a survey party of eleven to the summit via a route from the southwest. When Henry David Thoreau climbed the mountain in 1846, he also made his approach from the south side. His account of the ascent, recorded in *The Maine Woods*, vividly describes the terrain: "The mountain seemed a vast aggregation of loose rocks, as if some time it had rained rocks, and they lay as they fell on the mountain sides, nowhere fairly at rest, but leaned on each other, all rocking-stones, with cavities between, but scarcely any soil or smoother shelf. They were the raw materials of a planet dropped from an unseen quarry. . . ."

Thoreau turned back before reaching the summit proper, probably due to inclement weather, but perhaps also to a slight apprehension: "The tops of mountains are among the unfinished parts of the globe, whither it is a slight insult to the gods to climb and pry into their secrets, and try their effect on our humanity. Only daring and insolent men, perchance, go there. Simple races, as savages, do not climb mountains, their tops are sacred and mysterious tracts never visited by them. Pomola is always angry with those who climb to the summit of Ktaadn."

More Information

For a thorough description of Katahdin and the many other peaks in Baxter State Park, consult the AMC's *Maine Mountain Guide*, 9th ed. Readers interested in the natural and cultural history of Mount Katahdin should refer to *Katahdin: An Historic Journey* by John Neff, to be released by AMC Books in 2006.

TRIP 56
BAXTER STATE PARK PERIMETER ROAD

Aerobic Difficulty: Moderate to difficult
Technical Difficulty: Easy to moderate
Distance: 41 miles
Estimated Time: Day- or multi-day trips
Location: Baxter State Park
Maps: USGS Mount Katahdin
 AMC's *Maine Mountain Guide*, 9th ed., map 1
 DeLorme *Maine Atlas*, maps 50 and 51

Exploring the pristine wilderness of Maine's flagship state park on two wheels.

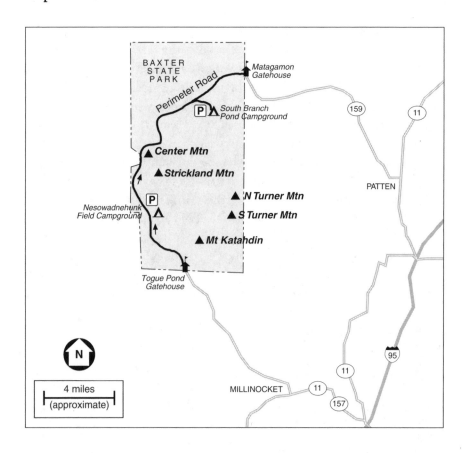

Directions

To reach the southern entrance to Baxter State Park, take I-95 north to Exit 244. Turn west onto Route 157 and drive to Millinocket. From Millinocket, follow the signs for Baxter State Park, which lead in 18.0 miles to the Togue Pond Gatehouse (fee). The northern entrance at Matagamon Lake is reached by driving on I-95 to Exit 264. Turn north on ME 11 and drive to the intersection of ME 159 in Patten. Turn left and follow ME 159 for 24.0 miles to the Matagamon Gatehouse (fee).

Trail Notes

Caution: The Perimeter Road may be subject to heavy traffic during the peak travel seasons, particularly in the southern region of the park, and especially during weekends and holidays. That said, early fall is probably the best time to visit, as the road is generally drier, and bugs (mosquitoes, no-see-ums, black flies) are less abundant.

Be aware that there are no services for bicyclers within the park. Riders should be prepared for mechanical mishaps, and be sure to carry ample food and water, as well as clothing appropriate to a wilderness environment. For a complete list of rules and regulations, visit Baxter State Park's official website at www.baxterstateparkauthority.com.

Trip Description

Exploring Baxter State Park on two wheels is an interesting way to enjoy this pristine wilderness setting. Although bicyclers traveling within the park are restricted to maintained roads, the Perimeter Road (also known as the Park Tote Road) winds through excellent scenery, providing many opportunities to observe Baxter's natural wonders. To honor the provisions of the trust created by Percival Baxter, the park's founder, the Perimeter Road is unpaved and relatively unimproved. It is composed of dirt and gravel and best suited to mountain bikers. The road extends for 41 miles, climbing and descending across several long, challenging grades, from the Togue Pond Gatehouse at the southern end of the park, to the northern gatehouse at Matagamon Lake.

The best way to see the park from the seat of your bike is to plan a multi-day tour, which allows for a series of point-to-point trips from campground to campground (advance reservations are strongly advised). This will also allow you to arrange extra time for hiking excursions to some of the park's 46 mountains. However, a multi-day tour within Baxter

A view to Katahdin from a side path on the Baxter Perimeter Road.

requires that you carry all of your provisions with you, so advanced preparation and experience with bicycle camping is recommended.

Alternatively, you can establish a base camp at one of Baxter's ten campgrounds and ride a series of day trips. Access roads to and from both the Daicey Pond and Kidney Pond cabin sites are open to bikers, affording an excellent base to explore the park's spectacular southern region. Better yet, head north to South Branch Pond Campground where there is less traffic and equally alluring scenery. The ponds lie in a spectacular valley between South Branch Mountain and Traveler Mountain. Campground facilities include lean-tos, a bunkhouse, tent sites, and rental canoes.

For point-to-point trips, start from Nesowadnehunk Field, which lies at the park's western boundary, 16.8 miles north of the Togue Pond Gatehouse. From there, you can embark on a 17-mile sojourn of Baxter's more remote northern territory. Although there are limited views along this section of the road, there is also less vehicle traffic, making for a much more peaceful ride than through the park's southern region. The route skirts the southeastern tip of Nesowadnehunk Lake, then crosses the western flanks of Strickland Mountain and Morse Mountain (the two highest points along the Perimeter Road) before turning northeast and following the North Branch of Trout Brook. At 10.5 miles, the road reaches the Burnt Mountain Picnic Area. From there, it's 6.5 miles to Trout Brook Crossing. The South Branch Pond Campground Access Road departs from the crossing to the campground, adding another 2.3 miles to the trip.

Turning south from Nesowadnehunk Field, the Perimeter Road parallels Nesowadnehunk Stream to Foster Field. At 1.5 miles, the road passes Ledge Falls, then the Slide Dam Picnic Area at 3.2 miles. From there, the road cuts between Doubletop Mountain and Mount OJI. There are excellent views of both mountains from Foster Field at 6.5 miles. From Foster Field, the access roads to Kidney Pond and Daicey Pond depart south. Both ponds are reached in 1.5 miles, and both are well worth the extra effort required to reach them. Beyond Foster Field, the Perimeter Road turns southeast, providing occasional views of Katahdin, then skirts Tracy Pond, and reaches Katahdin Stream Campground at 9.1 miles, and Abol Campground at 11.1 miles. From Abol Campground, the Perimeter Road descends to Abol Pond, and then reaches the Togue Pond Gatehouse at 16.8 miles.

More Information

For information about camping options or to make reservations, contact the Baxter State Park Reservation Clerk at 207-723-5140 or visit the park's website at www.baxterstateparkauthority.com.

TRIP 57
LONG POND

Difficulty: Easy
Distance: Limited only by 623-acre pond and 75-acre flowage
Estimated Time: Unlimited
Location: Bowdoin College Grant—east of Greenville
Maps: USGS Hay Mountain Quad
　　　USGS Barren Mountain East
　　　AMC's *Maine Mountain Guide*, 9th ed., map 3
　　　Maine Atlas, map 41

The lake's east–west axis, islands, and narrow width provide not only wind protection but also a lengthy shoreline to explore.

Directions
From Greenville, where Routes 6 and 15 turn left, go north on Main Street/Lily Bay Road for 100 yards, and turn right onto Pleasant Street/East Road. Go straight for 12.4 miles to the Hedgehog Checkpoint (fee). Continue for 1.8 miles, and turn right onto Greenville–KI Road. Go 1.1 miles, and turn right onto Long Pond Road (look for Long Pond Campsite sign on left). Go 2.2 miles to the bridge over Trout Brook, and then go another 100 yards, turn left, and go 0.2 mile to the campsite. At time of publication, access was being moved but will remain public.

Trail Notes
From early May through mid-October, there is a gate fee for the use of the KI Jo-Mary Multiple Use Forest. Visitors to the AMC's Little Lyford Pond Camps are eligible for a reduced gate fee of $10 per adult (up to age 70) per visit. However, this must be purchased with your reservation and a printed confirmation must be presented to the gate attendant. Otherwise, the regular gate fees will apply.

Trip Description
Long Pond, which lies within a 37,000-acre parcel now owned and managed by the Appalachian Mountain Club, provides a wonderful place to paddle, especially when winds from the north or south turn the region's

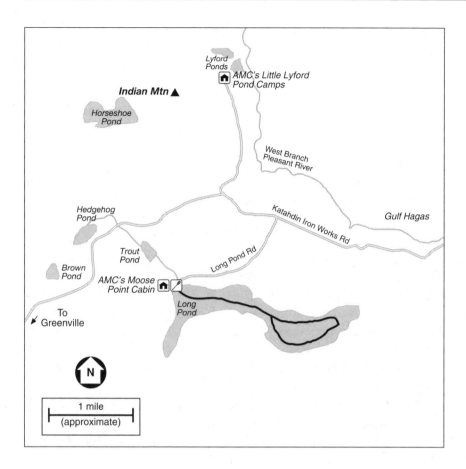

Indian Mtn ▲

Lyford Ponds

AMC's Little Lyford Pond Camps

Horseshoe Pond

West Branch Pleasant River

Hedgehog Pond

Katahdin Iron Works Rd

Gulf Hagas

Trout Pond

Brown Pond

Long Pond Rd

AMC's Moose Point Cabin

To Greenville

Long Pond

N

1 mile
(approximate)

larger lakes into a foaming froth. The lake's east–west axis, islands, and narrow width provide not only wind protection but also a lengthy shoreline to explore. For a map of the greater area, see page 217.

Deciduous trees have repopulated logged areas on the hillsides. Look for large stands of conifers on steeper slopes and on the spectacular distant mountains that you can see from many vantage points around the pond. Portage around the right side of an old dam at the outlet to explore a small flowage of about 75 acres. Look here for deer and moose that often frequent this area. You may also see beaver and otter. Besides the area at the outlet, two more marshy areas occur on the pond's east side.

The several camps along the shore—including rustic log cabins that date to the 1800s—do not mar the wild feel of Long Pond. The pond is also known for its great spring fishing.

One such cabin is the AMC's Moose Point Cabin, a remote, primitive camp that is operated on a self-service bases from mid-May to October and mid-December to March. Here you can enjoy the spectacular view of White Cap Mountain while getting active outdoors with snowshoeing, cross-country skiing, paddling, swimming, and fishing from the cabin door. For availability and reservations, call 603-466-2727 or go to www. outdoors.org/lodging.

Nature and History Notes

The AMC's Katahdin Iron Works Tract, which abuts much of Long Pond, is part of its Maine Woods Initiative. See "The Maine Woods" on page 216. The property serves as an important link in a protected greenbelt the AMC envisions from Monson northeast to Baxter State Park. The Katahdin Iron Works (KIW) property includes the headwaters of the West Branch of the Pleasant River, an important natural resource that supports a native brook trout fishery and flows through Gulf Hagas, a National Natural Landmark around which you can hike (see Trip 53). Several remote ponds valued for paddling and fly-fishing are part of the property. The parcel buffers 17 miles of the protected Appalachian Trail corridor and Gulf Hagas area, offering additional wildlife and watershed protection.

The AMC is also creating a 10,000-acre ecological reserve to permanently protect the West Branch watershed, and special management zones that will protect other riparian areas and unique natural areas such as Caribou Bog.

Other Options

The Hermitage and Gulf Hagas are both accessible from the Appalachian Trail where it crosses the Greenville–KI Road, about a half-mile east of the turnoff onto Long Pond Road (see Trip 53). More opportunities for outdoor recreation from the AMC's nearby Little Lyford Pond Camps include hiking, mountain biking, backcountry and cross-country skiing, snowshoeing, and fly-fishing (see "An Outdoor Traveler's Getaway to Little Lyford Pond Camps" on page 243).

More Information

For other paddling opportunities nearby, check out the AMC's *Quiet Water Maine*. For other hiking opportunities, consult the AMC's *Maine*

Mountain Guide, 9th ed. For lodging information or to make reservations for Little Lyford Pond Camp or Moose Point Cabin, contact the AMC at 603-466-2727 or visit the AMC's website at www.outdoors.org.

An Outdoor Traveler's Getaway to Little Lyford Pond Camps

AMC's Little Lyford Pond Camps (LLPC) provides an excellent backcountry base to explore the peaceful ponds and wild mountains of Maine's Great North Woods. Situated within the famed 100-Mile Wilderness, LLPC includes a main lodge, bunkhouse, and seven rustic cabins, each with a wood stove. Breakfast and dinner are served family style at the lodge, and trail lunches are available. There is also Moose Point Cabin, a self-service cabin located nearby on the southern shore of Long Pond (see Trip 57).

Recreation opportunities abound in the 100-Mile Wilderness, and when at LLPC, they are waiting just outside your door. Hiking trails connect to Gulf Hagas (Trip 53) and the Appalachian Trail, and the AMC has recently built hiking trails on nearby Indian Mountain (with views

An early morning paddle on the AMC's Little Lyford Pond.

of Katahdin) and has plans for increasing the hiking opportunities in the area. In winter, access to the camp is by cross-country skis, and the opportunities for further skiing and snowshoeing are as unlimited as the woods and trails surrounding the camp.

The two Little Lyford Ponds are on the camp property (encircled by loop trails for hiking or skiing access) and there is a boathouse with canoes and kayaks, a dock and a swimming platform. Loon and moose frequent the Little Lyford Ponds, so though the Ponds feel extremely remote, you won't be alone. Canoes are available for exploring other nearby ponds, including Indian Pond, Horseshoe Pond, and Long Pond, and instruction for fly-fishing is available. A drive over logging roads will take you to the historic Katahdin Iron Works site, or the towns of Greenville and Brownville.

Directions and Logistics

To reach the AMC's Little Lyford Pond Camps from Greenville, turn right on Pleasant Street, just after Northwoods Outfitters on Main Street. Follow this road toward the airport, and past Autumn Brooke Farm. Continue down the road, following the LLPC signs, to the North Maine Woods gate (fee), approximately 12 miles from Greenville. Beyond the gate, continue following the LLPC signs for approximately 5.0 miles to the reach the camps.

To reach Long Pond directly from Greenville, turn right on the Greenville–Katahdin Iron Works (KI) Road, 1.8 miles past the gate/ checkpoint. Continue east for 1.1 miles, and turn right onto Long Pond Road (look for the Long Pond Campsite sign on the left). Follow this road for 2.2 miles to the bridge over Trout Brook, then go another 100 yards, turn left, and go 0.2 mile to the campsite.

From early May through mid-October, there is a gate fee for the use of the KI Jo-Mary Multiple Use Forest. Visitors to the AMC's Little Lyford Pond Camps are eligible for a reduced gate fee of $10 per adult (up to age 70) per visit. However, this must be purchased with your reservation and a printed confirmation must be presented to the gate attendant.

TRIP 58
DEBSCONEAG LAKES WILDERNESS

Difficulty: Moderate
Distance: 6–18 miles round-trip
Estimated Time: 5 hours to multi-day
Location: T2 R10 WELS—northwest of Millinocket
Maps: USGS Abol Pond
        USGS Rainbow Lake East
        DeLorme *Maine Atlas*, map 50

A paddle through a chain of lakes in a pristine wilderness watershed at the foot of Mount Katahdin.

Directions

Take I-95 north to Exit 244. Turn west onto Route 157 and drive to Milli-nocket. From Millinocket, follow the signs for Baxter State Park. In Spen-cer Cove (Millinocket Lake on the right and Ambajejus Lake on the left), cross over (left) to the Golden Road, which parallels the Baxter State Park access road. Follow the Golden Road for 2.9 miles to an unimproved ac-cess road, which leaves left to reach Omaha Beach on Debsconeag Dead-water (sign). Follow the access road for 2.9 miles to a fork. Stay left at the fork to reach the put-in at Omaha Beach. Turning right at the fork leads over rough road to campsites at Little Omaha Beach.

Trail Notes

Caution: Depending on the season, the access road to Omaha Beach (and Little Omaha Beach) at Debsconeag Deadwater can be very rough in spots and may be impassable for vehicles without sufficient clearance.

Campsites on the Debsconeag Lakes are first come, first served. How-ever, except for sites on Debsconeag Deadwater at Omaha Beach and Little Omaha Beach, fire permits are required. To obtain a fire permit, contact the Central Region Headquarters of the Maine Forest Service at 207-827-1800.

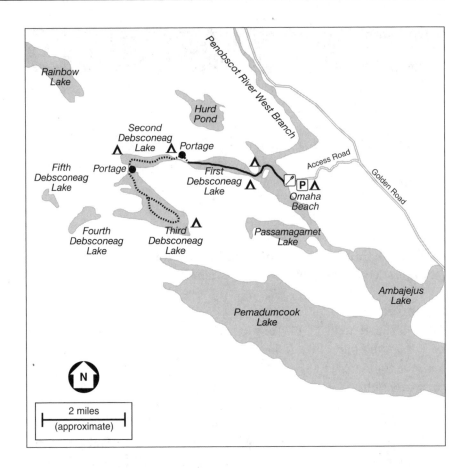

Trip Description

The Debsconeag chain of lakes lay at the foot of Mount Katahdin amid a pristine wilderness watershed containing the highest concentration of remote ponds in New England. To Native Americans, Debsconeag means "carrying place," an apt description given the network of portage paths they established long ago to connect these beautiful, secluded waterways. This trip ventures across these ancient routes and into the heart of the Northern Forest from Debsconeag Deadwater to Third Debsconeag Lake.

The trip begins from beautiful Omaha Beach, which fringes the eastern shore of Debsconeag Deadwater. Omaha's broad, sandy beach is a great spot to swim, picnic, or to establish a base camp for exploration (three sites available). Little Omaha Beach lies a half-mile to the northwest of Omaha in a more secluded cove with two campsites. Paddling north and west from Omaha, you'll pass Little Omaha, and soon reach

Debsconeag Deadwater from the sandy shore of Little Omaha Beach.

the main outlet of the West Branch of the Penobscot River. Across the outlet, a large island fronts the channel to First Debsconeag Lake. Paddle around the island's northern tip, then south between smaller islands to reach the channel (you can also access the channel via a narrow passage between the deadwater's western shore and the southern tip of the island, but the current is stronger).

Once inside the channel, follow the half-mile passage into First Debsconeag Lake. There are excellent campsites on either side of the channel. Like its sister lakes, First Debsconeag is fringed by a mature Acadian forest, much of which has not been harvested for more than 70 years. The paddle from the channel to the western end of First Debsconeag is approximately 1.5 miles.

To continue on to Second Debsconeag Lake, pick up the 0.75-mile-long portage trail that runs parallel to the creek connecting the two lakes. Compared to First Debsconeag, Second Debsconeag is much shallower, with a maximum depth of just 28 feet. Watch for submerged boulders when paddling near the shoreline. A primitive campsite is located on the northwestern shore, a little more than a mile's paddle beyond the portage trail.

At just over a thousand acres, Third Lake is the largest of the Debsconeags (all told, there are five lakes, three ponds, and one deadwater). It can be reached from Second Debsconeag by a portage trail just east of the inlet brook on the southern shore. The footpath is steeper than the portage from First Lake, but only about 0.3 mile long. Third Debsconeag runs in a northwest to southeast orientation, and is nearly 3.0 miles long. The short paddle to Minister Cove around the bend and to the south of the portage trail is a good place to explore and watch for wildlife. A narrow arm at the southwestern corner of Third Lake leads to the portage trail to Fourth Debsconeag. At the southeastern corner of the lake, there is a campsite near a mile-long portage trail leading to Pemadumcook Lake.

Nature and History Notes

The Debsconeag Lakes are within an ecological region known as the Acadian forest. Acadian forests represent a mixture of forest types between the transition zone of the boreal spruce-fir forest to the north, and the broadleaf deciduous forest to the south, coupled with the varying influences of a maritime climate. The region is distinguished by a distribution of red spruce, jack pine, balsam fir, maple, birch, and a smattering of hemlocks, and is home to abundant wildlife including moose, deer, bear, bald eagle, and beaver. The lakes are prized for their native fish including brook trout, lake trout, and salmon.

In 2002, The Nature Conservancy (TNC) entered into an historic agreement with Great Northern Paper to acquire 41,000 acres within the region for preservation. The Debsconeags Wilderness Reserve encompasses the chain of lakes as well as a 15-mile section of the Appalachian Trail within the 100-Mile Wilderness. The arrangement between the Great Northern Paper and TNC also included a conservation easement over an additional 200,000 acres of adjacent land. The agreement was a huge victory for the host of organizations involved in the Katahdin Forest Project, an initiative to protect Maine's North Woods from development while ensuring public access, traditional recreational use, and sustainable forestry. The easement bound together the Debsconeags Wilderness, the State's Nahmakanta Reserve, Baxter State Park, the Allagash Wilderness Waterway, and other tracts, creating nearly 500,000 acres of contiguous conservation land.

More Information

For more information about the Debsconeag Lakes and a host of other paddling opportunities nearby, check out the AMC's *Quiet Water Maine*.

Appendix A:
Northern Maine Hiking, Biking & Paddling

NORTHERN MAINE IS SOMETIMES REFERRED TO as the state's "big sky country." More often, this vast region is simply called "the County." Indeed, at nearly 6,700 square miles, Aroostook County encompasses more land than Connecticut and Rhode Island combined, and is the largest county east of the Mississippi River. Here you'll find miles of rolling fields and low-lying mountain peaks, huge tracts of remote woodlands, and more than 2,000 lakes, ponds, rivers, and streams, including the fabled Allagash Wilderness Waterway. For adventurous explorers, the region provides abundant opportunities to discover another Maine, one dominated by remote wilderness, agrarian roots, and a rich Acadian cultural heritage.

Hiking

Topographically, Northern Maine is composed of widely scattered mountains amid gently rolling terrain. The western two-thirds of the County is comprised of remote wilderness largely owned by lumber and paper companies, which manage public access for recreation, and Maine Public Reserve Lands. The eastern portion is dominated by wide-open spaces and farmland that produce potatoes and other crops. At 2,260 feet, trailless Peaked Mountain is the highest point of land. Recommended hikes include Quaggy Jo Mountain, located in Aroostook State Park, Hedgehog Mountain, and remote Deboullie Mountain, which can be combined with a paddling excursion to Deboullie and Togue Ponds (see below).

- South of Presque Isle, 1,213-foot Quaggy Jo Mountain overlooks Echo Lake and is comprised of two peaks (the mountain's name is derived from the Indian name *Qua Qua Jo*, which translates to "twin peaked"). Both summits are reachable via short trails that provide fine views of the surrounding countryside. Established in 1939, 800-acre Aroostook State Park was Maine's first state park, and is a great spot for hiking, fishing, camping, boating, and picnicking.

- 1,594-foot Hedgehog Mountain is located south of Winterville, just off Route 11. There is a camping area and picnic site next to the parking lot. A 0.6-mile trail leads from the picnic site to the mountain's summit. The views from atop Hedgehog take in the Fish River and Lake St. Froid to the west, and Portage Lake to the south.

- Secluded Deboullie Mountain rises amid a 22,000-acre tract of Public Reserve Land that encompasses rugged mountains, forested ridges, and scenic ponds. At 1,981 feet, Deboullie is the highest mountain within the region. The 2.5-mile trail to the mountain's summit skirts the northern edge of Deboullie Pond, crosses an intermittent rockslide (*Deboullie* is a French word for "rock slide"), and then rises steeply to a defunct fire tower on the summit that provides panoramic views across the region.

For detailed descriptions of these mountains and other hiking opportunities within Northern Maine, consult the AMC's *Maine Mountain Guide*, 9th ed. For information about access and camping within Aroostook State Park and Maine Public Reserve Land, visit www.maine.gov/doc/parks/.

Biking

Aroostook County offers the most extensive system of off-road biking trails in Maine. A multi-use network of rail-trails provide 600 miles of unimpeded riding amid quaint communities, rolling farmlands, thick forests, scenic rivers, and diverse wetland habitats. In addition, the Nordic Heritage Center in Presque Isle, considered one of the world's finest Nordic ski facilities, has also developed 21 miles of superb single-track trails, all of which are free to riders.

- The Aroostook Valley Rail Trail links more than 70 miles of gently rolling trails connecting the towns of Caribou, Woodland, New Sweden, Washburn, Perham, Stockholm, and Van Buren. The trail combines the old pathways used by the Aroostook Valley Railroad and the Bangor and Aroostook Railroad. Trailheads are accessible from several points including Washburn, Caribou, Stockholm, and Van Buren.

- The Houlton to Phair Junction Rail Trail is 40 miles long and extends from Houlton through the towns of Monticello, Bridgewater, Mars Hill, and loops through the southern edge of Presque Isle.

- Along the northern border with Canada, the Saint John Valley Heritage Trail connects the communities of Fort Kent, Saint John, and Saint Francis. The trail is over 16 miles long, and parallels the southern bank of the Saint John River through scenic forest-covered terrain. The trail links with the regional multi-use trail networks and a spur of the Trans Canadian Trail System. It is also part of a National Park Service sponsored effort to interpret the French-speaking Acadian Culture of Northern Maine.

- The Nordic Heritage Center (NHC) features professionally designed mountain-bike trails including "Easy," "More Difficult," and "Most Difficult" loops. A section of the trail system is lighted for night riding, and the loops connect to the regional rail-trails. The center also features a terrain park and skills-development area with teeter-totters, ramps, rails, and dirt jumps. Riding is free of charge, and camping is available. For more information, visit the Nordic Heritage Ski Club website at www.nordicheritagecenter.org.

For additional information about rail-trails in Northern Maine (and other rides throughout the state), visit the Explore Maine website at www.exploremaine.org/bike, or the Rails-to-Trails Conservancy website at www.railtrails.org, or contact these local shops:

Aroostook Bicycle and Sport
36 Chapman Rd.
Presque Isle, ME 04769
207-764-0206

The Ski Shop
31 Main St.
Van Buren, ME 04785
207-868-2737

Paddling

With its abundance of water, Northern Maine is a compelling destination for intrepid paddlers. Here you'll find endless opportunities to explore wild and remote lakes, tranquil ponds, and celebrated rivers including the beautiful Saint John River, and the famed Allagash Wilderness Waterway (for additional information about these rivers, see Appendix B). Recommended trips include the Mattawamkeag River and Mattawamkeag Lake, the wilderness ponds within the Deboullie Reserve Land, and Allagash Lake, considered one of the most beautiful lakes in all of Maine. For a complete description of these and other paddling options within the region, consult the AMC's *Quiet Water Maine*, 2nd ed., and *AMC River Guide: Maine*, 3rd ed.

- The scenic Mattawamkeag River flows east into Upper Mattawamkeag Lake, along an established canoe trail north of Island Falls. The wild, wooded shoreline along the river is a thriving habitat for wildlife, including deer, beaver, osprey, and bald eagle. Upper Mattawamkeag is connected to Mattawamkeag Lake via a mile-long passage known as the Thoroughfare. Mattawamkeag is largely undeveloped, and the state has set aside more than 3,000 acres of the lake's southern shoreline to protect habitat for wildlife, sustain access for recreation, and to preserve the scenic views, which extend all the way to Mount Katahdin. An additional 190 acres on Big Island (which includes a significant stand of old growth forest), and Long Point have also been preserved. Primitive campsites are available near Sand Cove, east of Big Island, and at the southern end of the lake.

- The Deboullie Public Reserve Land includes a cluster of deep, beautiful, and decidedly remote ponds nestled among the rugged mountains mentioned previously. The ponds include Deboullie, Gardner, and Pushineer, which have threatened blueback trout (a char found in only ten bodies of water in Maine), and Togue Pond, which is stocked with salmon, and more frequented by anglers. Among the ponds here, Gardner is the most remote and wild. Gardner is reached via a short portage trail near a primitive campsite at the western tip of Deboullie.

- Allagash Lake, northwest of the Allagash Wilderness Waterway at Chamberlain Lake, is among the most difficult lakes to reach in Maine, but well worth the effort. Many consider this deep, clear lake to be the state's most beautiful body of water. It is the only lake in Maine where motors of any kind (including electric) are prohibited. Paddlers looking for a wild, remote experience will appreciate Allagash's tranquil setting. Access is via portage and paddle from either nearby Johnson Pond, or from the Allagash Lake Ranger Station, which requires a 1-mile carry.

Appendix B:
Maine's Whitewater Rivers & Wilderness Waterways

AN OUTDOORS GUIDE TO MAINE would not be complete without including the state's fabulous whitewater rivers and legendary wilderness waterways. No other state in New England offers paddlers such exciting and diverse opportunities to explore the thrill of pulsating, wave-bound rapids, or the tranquility and allure of a pristine wilderness excursion. Whether you're a novice paddler interested in exploring the water routes established long ago by Native Americans in birchbark canoes, an experienced backwoods traveler drawn to wild, remote rivers, or a modern kayaker who enjoys the rush of playing on crashing waves in a 6-foot cocoon of molded plastic, Maine's celebrated waterways have something for everyone.

Whitewater

The Rapid, the Penobscot, the Kennebec, the Dead . . . these names alone are enough to quicken the pulse of experienced whitewater boaters drawn to standing waves, huge drops, and boiling eddies. Yet, Maine also has an array of quickwater rivers for less experienced boaters to enjoy. From the gentle tug of a Class I rapid to the fury and chaos of a Class V descent, here are a few recommended trips:

- The Ossipee River flows east for 17.5 miles from Lake Ossipee in New Hampshire, across the Maine border, and into the Saco River near Cornish. It has dependable flow in spring, and is best run below the second dam in Kezar Falls. The nearly 7-mile section from Kezar Falls to the Saco River is very scenic, with quickwater or Class I–II rapids the entire way.

- The Saco is one of New England's most popular rivers. In fact, some would say it is too popular. During summer, rafts of boaters pile up along the Saco's beautiful, sandy banks, especially between Conway (New Hampshire) and Fryeburg. Yet, the Saco is a great river to run in early spring when melting snow quickens its pace. Farther south, near East Limington, the Saco provides a great spot for experienced paddlers to improve their whitewater skills at a 0.5-mile section of Class II+ (up to Class IV in high water) rapids known as Limington Rips.

- The Rapid River is both difficult and remote, two characteristics that provide dedicated boaters exactly the enticement they're drawn to. This beautiful river flows from Lower Richardson Lake to Umbagog Lake (Trip 49) along a series of heart-stopping Class III–IV rapids. A worthy journey for experienced boaters.

- In Maine, no other place draws as many whitewater enthusiasts as the Forks. Here, the mighty Kennebec joins the Dead to form a perfect spot for river running. On a busy weekend when there are dam releases on both rivers, the area can see hundreds of rafters, kayakers, and canoeists enjoying the thrill of rapids, holes and drops like "Big Mama," "Three Sisters," and "Magic Falls." Below Harris Station (dam), the Kennebec River flows through a beautiful, wild gorge that creates exceptional Class III, IV, and V whitewater. Meanwhile, the Dead River provides one of the best stretches of whitewater in the state. For 15 miles, from Flagstaff Lake to the upper Kennebec River, the gradient averages 29 feet per mile, creating a near continuous section of incredible Class II–III rapids.

- The renowned Penobscot River offers boaters everything from wilderness trips (see below) to challenging rapids. Whitewater paddlers are mostly drawn to the Penobscot's West Branch below Ripogenus Dam, where Class III–IV rapids churn through beautiful Ripogenus Gorge. From there, the river continues for another 22.0 miles through a series of drops, rapids, and falls to Debsconeag Deadwater.

- The Mattawamkeag River is a large tributary of the Penobscot River that runs from Island Falls (east of Baxter State Park) south and west to Mattawamkeag. The mostly wild section from Kingman to Mattawamkeag is particularly interesting, with Class I–III rapids. This is a good trip to combine with a visit to Mattawamkeag Wilderness Park, which abuts the river, and includes hiking trails and a campground in a very scenic, less-visited setting.

For more information about these and other rivers in Maine, refer to *AMC River Guide: Maine* and the AMC's *Classic Northeastern Whitewater Guide*. Additional information is available through the American Whitewater Association website at www.americanwhitewater.org/rivers/state/ME. To learn whitewater skills, or join a group outing, contact the AMC's Maine Chapter, or the Maine Outdoor Adventure Club (see Appendix E, "Conservation and Recreation Organizations," for address information). For information about guided trips and commercial rafting operations, visit the Maine Office of Tourism website at www.visitmaine.com (click on "things to do"—outdoor recreation), or Raft Maine, an association of professional whitewater rafting outfitters at www.raftmaine.com.

Wilderness Waterways

There is perhaps no better way to discover the essence of the Maine woods than by traveling its historic and fabled waterways. The allure of remote waters amid spectacular landscapes and abundant wildlife, coupled with the warmth of a campfire and nights spent under a star-filled sky, combine to excite the imagination and rouse a sense of adventure. The trips outlined here require effort and planning, but are among the best in the nation, and will surely leave you with lasting memories of the Pine Tree State.

- For good reason, the 34-mile Moose River Bow trip is one of Maine's most popular canoe trips. It can be completed in three to four days at any time of the year and requires little in the way of whitewater skills. Because it forms a loop, there is no shuttle required. Add to that accessibility, magnificent scenery, and abundant wildlife, and you'll appreciate its popularity. The trip begins south of Jackman from beautiful Attean Pond, home to nearly 60 islands, and then journeys to Holeb Pond via a portage trail. From there, the trip follows Holeb Stream to the Moose River, which circles back to connect with Attean Pond. The river meanders for nearly 24 miles, and completely encloses Number 5 Bog, a National Natural Landmark. Along the way, there are many opportunities to view wildlife, including moose, loon, bald eagle, and beaver. For a complete description of this fabulous trip, including portage trails and camping opportunities, consult the AMC's *Quiet Water Maine*, 2nd ed.

- The backwoods journey from the outlet stream of Lobster Lake down the upper West Branch of the Penobscot River to Chesuncook Lake (Maine's third-largest lake) traces a similar route paddled in 1853 and again in 1857 by Henry David Thoreau, trips he later described in *The Maine Woods*. While much has changed since Thoreau's time, this trip still provides an exceptional journey through Maine's North Woods. This is an excellent trip for inexperienced paddlers as there are no rapids (only a few stretches of quickwater), and no portages. There are more than a dozen campsites within the 20-mile section between Lobster Stream and Chesuncook Lake. For more information about this trip, including paddling opportunities on both Lobster Lake and Chesuncook Lake, consult the AMC's *Quiet Water Maine*, 2nd ed.

- The wild, pristine upper Saint John River runs along the remote northwest corner of Maine, and is the longest stretch of free-flowing river in eastern America. This exceptional waterway flows for 130 miles without passing a single settlement. It grows from a gentle stream at the outlet of Baker Lake to a powerful Class II–III river that will challenge and reward experienced canoeists. It is only accessible during a short window of spring runoff between mid-May and the first week of June, and can be run in six to seven days depending upon your departure point. For less experienced paddlers, a guide is strongly recommended. In 1998, the Nature Conservancy purchased 185,000 acres along 40 miles of the upper Saint John from International Paper for 35 million dollars. Since that time, a series of separate transactions and land consolidations have extended the Conservancy's protection along the river to nearly 80 miles and increased total ownership to 188,000 acres, ensuring the preservation of this beautiful watershed for future generations.

- The Allagash Wilderness Waterway is undoubtedly the East's best known, and most celebrated canoe route. Established in 1966, the route follows a 92-mile corridor of lakes, ponds, rivers, and streams through the heart of the Maine Woods. The Waterway was further protected in 1970 when it was named the first state-administered component of the National Wild and Scenic River System. One of the most popular trips along the Waterway comprises a seven- to ten-day journey from Telos Landing near the northwest corner of Baxter State Park to Allagash Village. The trip crosses vast expanses of open water on Chamberlain Lake and Eagle Lake, as well as Class II–III rapids and portages on the Allagash River. Depending on water levels, the trip is runnable from May through early October, but early spring and fall (with sufficient rainfall) is best. For more information about the Waterway including a natural history guide of the region, visit the Maine Bureau of Parks and Lands website at www.state.me.us/doc/parks. Additional information regarding access, fees, rules and regulations, camping, outfitters, and guide services is available by contacting North Maine Woods, the organization that manages public access to the region (207-435-6213, or www.northmainewoods.org).

Appendix C:
Outfitters & Guide Services

THERE ARE AN ARRAY OF OUTSTANDING outfitters and guide services located throughout Maine. This listing is intended as a service to readers. It is not intended to be comprehensive, or an endorsement of any of the businesses/services listed.

For a complete listing of guide services and other resources, contact the following:

The Maine Association Sea Kayaking Guides and Instructors
www.maineseakayakingguides.com

Maine Professional Guides Association
P.O. Box 336
Augusta, ME 04332
www.maineguides.org

Outfitters by region:

Southern Region

Allspeed Bicycle & Ski
1041 Washington Ave.
Portland, ME 04103
207-878-8741
www.allspeed.com

Cycle Mania
59 Federal St.
Portland, ME 04101
207-774-2933
www.cyclemania1.com

Eastern Mountain Sports
87 Marginal Way
Portland, ME 04101
207-541-1919
www.ems.com

Excursions Coastal Maine Outfitting Co.
U.S. Route 1
Cape Neddick, ME 03902
207-363-0181
www.excursionsinmaine.com

Gorham Bike and Ski
1440 Congress St.
Portland, ME 04102
207-773-1700
www.gorhambike.com

Harbor Adventures
P.O. Box 345
York Harbor, ME 03911
207-363-8466
www.harboradventures.com

H2Outfitters
Orr's Island, ME 04066
207-833-5257
www.h2outfitters.com

Kittery Trading Post
U.S. Route 1
Kittery, ME 03904
888-KTP-MAINE
www.kitterytradingpost.com

LL Bean/LL Bean Outdoor Discovery School
Freeport, ME 04033
800-441-5713 (Online)
877-552-3268 (Flagship Store)
www.llbean.com

Maine Island Kayak Company
70 Luther St.
Peaks Island, ME 04108
800-796-2373 or
207-766-2373
www.maineislandkayak.com

Midcoast Region

Breakwater Kayak Co.
Next to the Public Landing
Rockland, ME 04841
877-559-8800
www.breakwaterkayak.com

Ducktrap Kayak
2175 Atlantic Hwy. (U.S. Route 1)
Lincolnville Beach, ME 4849
207-236-8608

Frozen Paddler
271 Old Bath Rd.
Wiscasset, ME 04578
207-882-9066
www.frozenpaddler.com

H2Outfitters
Orr's Island, ME 04066
207-833-5257
www.h2outfitters.com

Hurricane Island Outward Bound School
75 Mechanic St.
Rockland, ME 04841
866-746-9771
www.hurricaneisland.org

Kennebec Tidewater
On the waterfront
Route 24
Richmond, ME 04357
207-737-2112 or
877-895-2112
www.kennebectidewater.com

LL Bean/LL Bean Outdoor Discovery School
Freeport, ME 04032
800-441-5713 (Online)
877-552-3268 (Flagship Store)
www.llbean.com

Maine Island Kayak Company
70 Luther St.
Peaks Island, ME 04108
800-796-2373 or
207-766-2373
www.maineislandkayak.com

Maine Kayak (multiple locations)
P.O. Box 674
Unity, ME 04988
866-624-6352
www.mainekayak.com

Maine Sport Outfitters
Route 1
Rockport, ME 04856
Retail Store: 888-236-8797
Adventures: 800-722-0826
www.mainesport.com

Schooner Landing
Main St.
Damariscotta, ME 04543
207-563-5732
www.seaspiritadventures.com

Sea Spirit Adventures
1440 State Route 32
Round Pond, ME 04564
207-529-4732

Seaspray Kayaking
412 State Rd.
Brunswick, ME 04011
888-349-7772
www.seaspraykayaking.com

Tidal Transit Kayak Company
18 Granary Way
Boothbay Harbor, ME 04538
207-663-7140
www.kayakboothbay.com

Water Walker Custom Kayak Tours
152 Lincolnville Ave.
Belfast, ME 04915
207-338-6424
www.touringkayaks.com

Downeast Region

Acadia Bike/Coastal Kayaking Tours
48 Cottage St.
Bar Harbor, ME 04609
207-288-9605
www.acadiafun.com

Acadia Mountain Guides
198 Main St. (summer only)
Bar Harbor, ME
207-866-7562
www.acadiamountainguides.com

Aquaterra Adventures
One West St.
Bar Harbor, ME 04609
877-386-4124 or
207-288-0007
www.aquaterra-adventures.com

Cadillac Mountain Sports
32 High St.
Ellsworth, ME 04605
207-667-7819

26 Cottage St.
Bar Harbor, ME 04609
207-288-4532
www.cadillacmountainsports.com

Castine Kayak Adventures
Sea St.
Castine, ME 04421
207-326-9045
www.castinekayak.com

Maine State Sea Kayak Guide Service
254 Main St.
Southwest Harbor, ME 04679
207-244-9500
www.mainestatekayak.com

SeaMyst Guide Service (formerly MooseLook Guide Service)
150 Corea Rd.
Prospect Harbor, ME 04669
207-963-7223
www.mooselookguideservice.com

National Park Sea Kayak Tours
39 Cottage St.
Bar Harbor, ME 04609
800-347-0940
www.acadiakayak.com

Old Quarry Ocean Adventures
130 Settlement Rd.
Stonington, Maine 04681
207-367-8977
www.oldquarry.com

Sunrise Canoe and Kayak
RR 1, Box 344A
Machias, ME 04654
207-255-3375 or
877-980-2300
www.sunrisecanoeandkayak.com

Western Lakes and Mountains

Aardvark Outfitters
108 Fairbanks Rd.
Farmington, ME 04938
207-778-3330
www.aardvarkoutfitters.com

Alpine Shop of Rangeley
2623 Main St.
Rangeley, ME 04970
207-864-3698
www.alpineshoprangeley.com

Ecopelagicon
7 Pond St.
Rangeley, ME 04970
207-864-2771
www.ecopelagicon.com

Mountain Woman Guide Service
Rangeley, ME 04970
207-562-4971
www.mountainwomanguideservice.com

Northern Lights Hearth & Sports
639 Wilton Rd.
Farmington, ME 04938
207-778-6566

Rivers Edge Sports
38 Carry Rd. (Route 4)
Oquossoc, ME 04964
207-264-5582
www.riversedgesports.com

Saco River Canoe and Kayak
1009 Main St.
Fryeburg, ME 04037
888-772-6573 or 207-935-2369
www.sacorivercanoe.com

Seasonal Cycles
2593 Main St.
Rangeley, ME 04970
207-864-2100

True North Adventure Ware
162 Main St.
Bethel, Maine 04217
207-824-2201

Greater Moosehead Lake and 100-Mile Wilderness

Bangor Ski Rack
24 Longview Dr.
Bangor, ME 04401
207-945-6474 or
800-698-6474
www.skiracksports.com

Epic Sports
Six Central St.
Bangor, Maine 04401
800-466-2296 or
207-941-5670
www.epicsportsofmaine.com

Indian Hill Trading Post
Route 15
Greenville, ME 04441
800-675-4487
www.indianhill.com

Nicatou Outfitters
Route 157
Medway, ME 04460
866-746-3253 or 207-746-3253
www.mainecampingtrips.com

Northwoods Outfitters
Main St.
Greenville, ME 04441
207-695-3288
www.maineoutfitter.com

Appendix D: Lodging

Resources For Camping, Lodging, and Outdoor Recreation

Appalachian Mountain Club
Reservations 609-466-2727
www.outdoors.org/lodging

The AMC runs a variety of outdoor destinations in Maine, including:

- *Little Lyford Pond Camps (LLPC)*. Traditional sporting camp in the heart of the 100-Mile Wilderness (see "An Outdoor Traveler's Getaway to Little Lyford Pond Camps," page 243) or www.outdoors.org/lodging/lyford.
- *Moose Point Cabin*. A self-service cabin on Long Pond (see Trip 57), not far from LLPC. See www.outdoors.org/lodging/lyford.
- *Echo Lake Camp*. Remote and rustic with tent platforms with beds, dining, and rec hall, in the midst of Acadia National Park on Mt. Desert Island. See www.outdoors.org/lodging/camps.
- *Knubble Bay Camp*. Self-service cabin sleeps fifteen. Located on Georgetown Island, with views of the Knubble Bay, a great place for kayaking. See www.outdoors.org/lodging/camps.
- *Beal Island Campground*. For campers who want to explore Knubble Bay but prefer to bring their own tent and a cookstove. See www.outdoors.org/lodging/camps.

- *Swan's Falls Campground.* Tent sites, fireplaces, and more, in a pine forest along the Saco River with access to wonderful canoeing and the White Mountains. See www.outdoors.org/lodging/camps.

The Maine Atlas and Gazetteer
DeLorme Publishing
Yarmouth, ME 04096
207-846-7000
www.delorme.com

Maine Bureau of Parks and Lands
22 State House Station
18 Elkins Lane
Augusta, ME 04333
207-287-3821
www.state.me.us/doc/parks

Maine Campground Owners Association
10 Falcon Rd., Suite 1
Lewiston, Maine 04240
207-782-5874
www.campmaine.com

Maine Camping Online—Resource and links for over 150 campgrounds in Maine
www.mainecamping.com

Maine Innkeepers Association
304 U.S. Route 1
Freeport, ME 04032
207-865-6100
www.maineinns.com

Maine Lodging and Resort Guide—Unofficial Maine State Lodging Directory
www.visitmaine.net

Maine Office of Tourism
59 State House Station
Augusta, ME 04333-0059
888-624-6345
www.visitmaine.com

Maine Outdoors—Online site for a variety of outdoor recreation
information
www.maineoutdoors.com

White Mountain National Forest—Evans Notch
18 Mayville Rd.
Bethel, ME 04217
207-824-2134
www.fs.fed.us/r9/forests/white_mountain/

Helpful Books

Hot Showers! Maine Coast Lodgings for Kayakers and Sailors, 2nd ed.
By Lee Bumsted
Distributed by Audenreed Press
www.biddle-audenreed.com

Appendix E: Conservation & Recreation Organizations

Appalachian Mountain Club (AMC)
5 Joy St.
Boston, MA 02108
617-523-0636
www.outdoors.org

AMC Maine Chapter
795 Lawrence Rd.
Pownal, ME 04069
207-415-6702
home.gwi.net/amcmaine/main.htm

Baxter State Park Authority
64 Balsam Dr.
Millinocket, ME 04462
207-723-5140
www.baxterstateparkauthority.com

Bicycle Coalition of Maine
P.O. Box 5275
Augusta, ME 04332
207-623-4511
www.bikemaine.org

Chewonki Foundation
485 Chewonki Neck Rd.
Wiscasset, ME 04578
207- 882-7323
www.chewonki.org

Forest Society of Maine
115 Franklin St., 3rd Floor
Bangor, ME 04401
207-945-9200
www.fsmaine.org

Island Institute
P.O. Box 648
386 Main St.
Rockland, ME 04841
800-339-9209
www.islandinstitute.org

Maine Appalachian Trail Club (MATC)
P.O. Box 283
Augusta, ME 04332-0283
www.matc.org

Maine Audubon Society
20 Gilsland Farm Rd.
Falmouth, ME 04105
207-781-2330
www.maineaudubon.org

Maine Bureau of Parks and Lands
22 State House Station
18 Elkins Ln.
Augusta, ME 04333
207-287-3821
www.state.me.us/doc/parks

Maine Coast Heritage Trust/Maine Land Trust Network
Bowdoin Mill
One Main St.
Topsham, ME 04086
207-729-7366
www.mcht.org
www.mltn.org

Maine Department of Inland Fisheries and Wildlife
284 State St.
41 State House Station
Augusta, ME 04333
207-287-8000
www.state.me.us/ifw

Maine Island Trail Association (MITA)
58 Fore St., Bldg. 30, 3rd Fl.
Portland, ME 04101
207-761-8225
www.mita.org

Maine Outdoor Adventure Club (MOAC)
P.O. Box 11251
Portland, ME 04104
207-775-MOAC
www.moac.org
    Portland Monthly Meeting: 7 P.M. first Wednesday of each month,
    Unitarian Universalist Church, Allen Ave.
    Bangor Monthly Meeting: 7 P.M. on the Tuesday before the first
    Wednesday of the month, Epic Sports, 6 Central St.

National Park Service (Acadia)
P.O. Box 177
Bar Harbor, ME 04609
207-288-3338
www.acadia.net/anp/

The Nature Conservancy—Maine Chapter
14 Maine St., Suite 401
Brunswick, ME 04011
207-729-5182
www.nature.org

New England Mountain Bike Association (NEMBA)
Maine Chapter:
    207-892-9228; www.maine-nemba.org
Mount Agamenticus Chapter:
    P.O. Box 40, Cape Neddick, ME 03902
    207-332-5497; www.mtanemba.org

Northern Forest Canoe Trail
P.O. Box 565
Waitsfield, VT 05673
802-496-2285
www.NorthernForestCanoeTrail.org

Portland Trails
305 Commercial St.
Portland, ME 04101
207-775-2411
www.trails.org

Rails-to-Trails Conservancy
1100 17th St., 10th Fl., NW
Washington, D.C. 20036
202-331-9696
www.railtrails.org

Southern Maine Sea Kayaking Network (SMSKN)
P.O. Box 4794
Portland, ME 04112
www.smskn.org

U.S. Fish and Wildlife Service—Maine Offices
www.fws.gov/northeast/me.htm

Appendix F: Recommended Reading

Alden, Peter and Cassie, Brian. *National Audubon Society Field Guide to New England*. Knopf, 1998.

Appalachian Mountain Club. *AMC River Guide: Maine*. 3rd ed. AMC Books, 2002.

Appalachian Mountain Club. *Maine Mountain Guide*. 9th ed. AMC Books, 2005.

Bumsted, Lee. *Hot Showers! Maine Coast Lodgings for Kayakers and Sailors*. 2nd ed. Audenreed Press/Biddle Publishing Co., 2000.

Chunn, Cloe. *50 Hikes in the Maine Mountains*. 3rd ed. Backcountry Guides/The Countryman Press, 50 Hikes Series, 2002.

Ferguson, Gary. *National Geographic Guide to America's Outdoors: New England*. National Geographic, 2000.

Gibbs, David and Hale, Sarah L. *Mountain Bike! Maine: A Guide to the Classic Trails*. Menasha Ridge Press, 1998.

Gibson, John. *50 Hikes in Coastal and Southern Maine*. 3rd ed. Backcountry Guides/The Countryman Press, 50 Hikes Series, 2001.

Gorman, Stephen. *Northeastern Wilds: Journeys of Discovery in the Northern Forest*. AMC Books, 2003.

Hayes, John and Wilson, Alex. *Quiet Water Maine: Canoe and Kayak Guide*. 2nd ed. AMC Books, 2005.

Johnson, Shelley and Smith, Vaughan. *Guide to Sea Kayaking in Maine: The Best Day Trips and Tours from Casco Bay to Machias*. The Globe Pequot Press, 2001.

Marchand, Peter J. *North Woods: An Inside Look at the Nature of Forests in the Northeast*. AMC Books, 1994.

Mascott, Cynthia. *The Official Rails-to-Trails Conservancy Guidebook: Connecticut, Rhode Island, Massachusetts, Vermont, New Hampshire, Maine*. The Globe Pequot Press, 2000.

Miller, Dorcas S. *Kayaking the Maine Coast: A Paddler's Guide to Day Trips from Kittery to Cobscook*. Backcountry Guides, 2000.

Monkman, Jerry and Marcy. *Discover Acadia National Park: AMC Guide to the Best Hiking, Biking, and Paddling*. 2nd ed. AMC Books, 2005.

Neff, John. *Katahdin, an Historic Journey: Legends, Explorations, and Preservation of Maine's Highest Peak*. With Illustrations by Michael McCurdy. AMC Books, 2006.

Older, Julia and Sherman, Steve. *Nature Walks along the Seacoast: Massachusetts, New Hampshire, Maine*. AMC Books, 2003.

Parsons, Greg and Watson, Kate B. *New England Waterfalls: A Guide to More Than 200 Cascades and Waterfalls*. The Countryman Press, 2003.

Thoreau, Henry D. *The Maine Woods*. Princeton University Press, 2004.

Venn, Tamsin. *Sea Kayaking Along the New England Coast*. 2nd ed. AMC Books, 2004.

Index

About the Author

TY WIVELL is an avid outdoorsman who has been exploring the wilds of New England for the past fifteen years. He studied journalism at California State University, Northridge, and photography at the New Hampshire Institute of Arts and Sciences. Today, he works as a freelance writer, photographer, and manufacturers representative in the outdoor industry from his home in Greenland, New Hampshire. This is his first book for AMC Books.

The Appalachian Mountain Club

Founded in 1876, the AMC is the nation's oldest outdoor recreation and conservation organization. The AMC promotes the protection, enjoyment, and wise use of the mountains, rivers, and trails of the Northeast outdoors.

People

We are nearly 90,000 members in 12 chapters, 20,000 volunteers, and over 450 full time and seasonal staff. Our chapters reach from Maine to Washington, D.C.

Outdoor Adventure and Fun

We offer more than 8,000 trips each year, from local chapter activities to major excursions worldwide, for every ability level and outdoor interest— from hiking and climbing to paddling, snowshoeing, and skiing.

Great Places to Stay

We host more than 135,000 guest nights each year at our AMC Lodges, Huts, Camps, Shelters, and Camp- grounds. Each AMC Destination is a model for environmental education and stewardship.

Opportunities for Learning

We teach people the skills to be safe outdoors and to care for the natural world around us through programs for children, teens, and adults, as well as outdoor leadership training.

Caring for Trails

We maintain more than 1,400 miles of trails throughout the Northeast, including nearly 350 miles of the Appalachian Trail in five states.

Protecting Wild Places

We advocate for land and riverway conservation, monitor air quality, and work to protect alpine and forest ecosystems throughout the Northern Forest and Highlands regions.

Engaging the Public

We seek to educate and inform our own members and an additional 1.5 million people annually through AMC Books, our website, our White Mountain visitor centers, and AMC Destinations.

Join Us!

Members support our mission while enjoying great AMC programs, our award-winning AMC Outdoors magazine, and special discounts. Visit www.outdoors.org or call 617-523- 0636 for more information.

THE APPALACHIAN MOUNTAIN CLUB
Recreation • Education • Conservation
www.outdoors.org

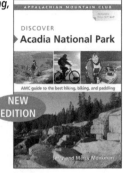

AMC Book Updates

AMC BOOKS STRIVES to keep our guidebooks as up-to-date as possible to help you plan safe and enjoyable adventures. If after publishing a book we learn that trails are relocated or route or contact information has changed, we will post the updated information online. Before you hit the trail, check for updates at www.outdoors.org/publications/books/updates.

While hiking or paddling, if you notice discrepancies with the trail description or map, or if you find any other errors in the book, please let us know by submitting them to amcbookupdates@outdoors.org or in writing to Books Editor, c/o AMC, 5 Joy Street, Boston, MA 02108. We will verify all submissions and post key updates each month.

AMC Books is dedicated to being a recognized leader in outdoor publishing. Thank you for your participation.

AMC BOOKS & MAPS

EXPLORE THE POSSIBILITIES